'I can highly recommend this comprehensive an
aspects of the child psychotherapist's work, b
settings. Deirdre Dowling's approach to child psycnoanaiytic psycnotnerapy
has been influenced by her training and interest in the British Independent
tradition in psychotherapy, as well as ideas from any school that helps
illuminate a way forward – very much a Winnicottian approach. She looks
in detail at the therapeutic process, such as creating a therapeutic setting,
making assessments, engaging with parents and working in a team. She also
faces the challenges of the work, such as when despair, doubt and anger
have to be faced. And she looks at child therapy in a variety of settings. All
of this is illustrated with clear and vivid clinical examples. Her book will
appeal to professionals and families seeking help.'

– **Roger Kennedy**, Training Analyst at the British
Psychoanalytical Society, Consultant Child Psychiatrist and
Chair of The Child and Family Practice

'This is a book that honours the creative, imaginative and ultimately
therapeutic process of children's play. Beyond that, Deirdre Dowling provides an honest, informative and comprehensive overview of the process of
child psychotherapy and all that this means. Dowling's knowledge and
experience shine throughout, the book's narrative enriched by poignant
accounts of her practice. That said, she is also unafraid to name the self-
doubt, the questioning and sometimes profound personal and professional
challenges that accompany working with deeply troubled children.'

– **David Le Vay**, Play Therapist/Dramatherapist,
Senior Lecturer MA Play Therapy, University of Roehampton, London,
and Clinical Partner with the Bridge Therapy Centre

'This is a remarkable book, describing the process of child and adolescent
psychotherapy in clear and vivid detail, and is compelling to read. At a time
when manuals on various kinds of therapy are required, this book is
essential, enriched with compassion, patience and humour. The subtitle
Playing with Ideas shows Deirdre Dowling's own way of making a creative
space with patients, but play is not trivial, it includes dealing with 'the
complexity of the body and mind, and our natural resistance to exploring
painful issues and facing change'; the painful feelings of both therapist and
patient and how these are managed are described. The book is rich in
examples of the history of child and adolescent psychotherapy, in vignettes
from stories and films illustrating emotions, and in moving case examples
from patients. Deirdre Dowling is honest and generous in describing her
own emotions in working with distressed children and young people. This

book should be read by anyone who wants to work as a therapist with such children – it is realistic about the effort, but inspiring about its effect. Teachers, social workers and doctors will also feel they understand better the children and young people in their care.'

– **Dilys Daws**, Hon. Consultant Child Psychotherapist,
Tavistock Clinic, Adviser to the Association for Infant
Mental Health-UK, Author of *Through the Night: Helping
Parents and Sleepless Infants* (1993) and
*Finding Your Way with Your Baby: Emotions of
Parents and Babies* with Alexandra de Rementeria (2015)

An Independent Practitioner's Introduction to Child and Adolescent Psychotherapy

An Independent Practitioner's Introduction to Child and Adolescent Psychotherapy: Playing with Ideas is a comprehensive guide to child and adolescent psychotherapy, taking the practitioner from the initial meeting through the therapeutic process with young people of different ages, to the ending of psychotherapy. It includes approaches to working with parents and the family, introduces theoretical ideas simply and provides references for further learning.

Part of the popular Independent Psychoanalytic Approaches series, this book is written from an Independent perspective, but it is also an account of Deirdre Dowling's approach, developed from her considerable experience of working in the NHS and now as a private practitioner.

An Independent Practitioner's Introduction to Child and Adolescent Psychotherapy will be an indispensable guide for child psychotherapists (especially trainees), colleagues working in child and family mental health settings, play therapists, counsellors and support staff in schools and child care professionals working therapeutically in residential and community settings.

Deirdre Dowling was Head Child and Adolescent Psychotherapist at the Cassel Hospital, West London Mental Health Trust. She trained at the British Association of Psychotherapists, qualifying first as a child and adolescent psychotherapist in 1991, then as an adult psychotherapist in 2006. She worked at the British Psychotherapy Foundation for five years as Curriculum Lead of the Independent Child and Adolescent Psychotherapy Training and is also a teacher and supervisor.

Independent Psychoanalytic Approaches with Children and Adolescents series

Series Editor: Ann Horne and Monica Lanyado

An Independent Practitioner's Introduction to Child and Adolescent Psychotherapy

Playing with Ideas

Deirdre Dowling

Routledge
Taylor & Francis Group

LONDON AND NEW YORK

First published 2019
by Routledge
2 Park Square, Milton Park, Abingdon, Oxon OX14 4RN

and by Routledge
52 Vanderbilt Avenue, New York, NY 10017

Routledge is an imprint of the Taylor & Francis Group, an informa business

British Library Cataloguing-in-Publication Data
A catalogue record for this book is available from the British
Library

Library of Congress Cataloging-in-Publication Data
Names: Dowling, Deirdre, author.
Title: An independent practitioner's introduction to child and
adolescent psychotherapy: playing with ideas/Deirdre Dowling.
Description: Abingdon, Oxon; New York, NY: Routledge, 2019. |
Series: Independent psychoanalytic approaches with children and
adolescents | Includes bibliographical references and index.
Identifiers: LCCN 2018053253 (print) | LCCN 2018054197
(ebook) | ISBN 9781315146812 (e-Book) | ISBN 9781138506244
(hbk.: alk. paper) | ISBN 9781138506275 (pbk.: alk. paper) |
ISBN 9781315146812 (ebk.)
Subjects: | MESH: Psychotherapy—methods | Child | Adolescent
Classification: LCC RJ504 (ebook) | LCC RJ504 (print) | NLM WS
350.2 | DDC 618.92/8914—dc23
LC record available at https://lccn.loc.gov/2018053253

ISBN: 978-1-138-50624-4 (hbk)
ISBN: 978-1-138-50627-5 (pbk)
ISBN: 978-1-315-14681-2 (ebk)

Typeset in Times New Roman
by Swales & Willis, Exeter, Devon, UK

Dedicated to the next generation, Caitlin and Mike

Contents

    the value of supervision   112

10 Working towards an ending   121

PART 3
Therapeutic work with children and parents in crisis   131

11 Behind closed doors: therapeutic work with children and
    adolescents living with mentally ill and vulnerable parents   133

12 Therapeutic work with children whose parents have
    separated or divorced   150

PART 4
Taking child psychotherapy outside the
psychotherapy room   161

13 New pathways: applying psychotherapy to other settings   163

    Final thoughts: playing with ideas   180

    Index   181

Acknowledgements

Many people have helped me write this book, but I would like to particularly thank Ann Horne and Monica Lanyado, the editors of the series. Without their support and encouragement, this book would not have been completed. They have been patient, knowledgeable and always open to new ideas. I have also valued the feedback from those who have read my book, chapter by chapter, particularly Harry, my husband, my brother David Bean and my colleague, Caroline Freud Penney. Also my thanks to my creative writing teacher, Ruth Brandt, whose classes taught me to aim to bring every sentence alive. I have been very fortunate in working with such good colleagues over the years, as a social worker, a child psychotherapist on the Family Service at the Cassel Hospital, West London, at the Lantern Family Service, and on the Independent Child and Adolescent Psychoanalytic Psychotherapy training at the British Psychotherapy Foundation. In each setting, I have learnt such different skills and perspectives and I wanted to give a flavour of this diversity in the final chapter where I explore therapeutic work in different settings. The contributions from the child psychotherapists there give this book a broader view than I could have achieved alone. The many children and families I have treated and those I have supervised and taught in the UK and overseas have all contributed to the ideas discussed here and stimulated me to keep looking for ways to improve my skills. Finally, thanks to my husband Harry, who did the cooking and kept the home going for many months while I was writing this book, as well as encouraging me every step of the way.

Foreword

Ann Horne and Monica Lanyado[1]

It is with very great pleasure that we contribute this Foreword to Deirdre Dowling's new book *An Independent Practitioner's Introduction to Child and Adolescent Psychotherapy*. Deirdre's has been a wise voice in psychoanalytic child psychotherapy for many years now. It is this wisdom – the sense of being in conversation with an intelligent practitioner who has thought at considerable depth about the process of becoming and being a child psychotherapist – that strikes the reader so convincingly from the first chapter onwards. This is not a book that proselytises a particular theoretical position; it is one that, rooted in psychoanalytic reflection, offers a range of ways of thinking and observing, of engaging with children, adolescents and their families and carers, of coping with pain and seeming failure, and of rediscovering and celebrating the child's innate capacity for emotional growth and development.

Beginning with the setting in both psychoanalytic and physical terms, Deirdre provides for the reader a sense of what a psychoanalytic view can offer and how this might add much to the picture one gains of the child patient. The choice she has made to introduce specific psychoanalytic concepts, clearly explained as to their meaning and function, is one the reader will find useful: this is a brief but essential list which offers an excellent starting point (and a point for refreshment for those of us who might imagine that we know these things). Hers is an inclusive approach and one appreciative of other and complementary ways of working, emphasising the value – as well as the occasional strains! – of multi-professional work. Bringing a wealth of experience from her considerable social work experience as well as from her role as a psychotherapist involved in training within and beyond her own profession, Deirdre is aware of the exposure of those who work with children in distress and is insightful and firm about the place of supervision, consultation and space for reflection.

The individual children and young people whose stories illuminate the chapters keep us aware that this is not dry theory to be applied to every referred patient; these are individuals whose struggle and whose humanity engross us and – especially in Chapter 11 where the vulnerability of parents is such a factor in their lives – move us most deeply. We join with the children in the search for understanding and for a more creative and positive way of functioning for them in the future.

Although its author describes this book as a personal account of the context, task, knowledge, journey and survival skills of a very Independent child psychotherapist, we find it to be just the book we had hoped to see when she brought us her original outline for *An Independent Practitioner's Introduction to Child and Adolescent Psychotherapy*. Indeed, it exceeds our hopes. Readers who already work with young people and encounter their emotional hardships will find in this book much to expand their understanding and much to support them in their task. For those who might be considering making a move into this work, Deirdre Dowling offers an exceptional guide to the training and task of the child psychotherapist today. More importantly, she does this without ignoring the difficulties and pressures, she offers alternative ways of thinking and – best of all – provides wise counsel. We recommend this book most highly.

Note

1 Series Editors – Independent Psychoanalytic Approaches with Children and Adolescents.

Preface

This book grew from my involvement in training and supervising child psychoanalytic psychotherapists in the UK and in teaching psychotherapeutic approaches to work with children overseas. It is a personal account drawing on a wide range of ideas that I find helpful as a child psychotherapist. It is also very much within the Independent child psychotherapy tradition following Winnicott who encouraged psychotherapists to take a playful creative approach within a carefully thought-through psychotherapeutic structure.

My aim has been to make child and adolescent psychoanalytic psychotherapy accessible to many. Those who are thinking of becoming child psychotherapists, those just starting the training, or child care workers, like myself in the past, who are struggling to understand how to help troubled children without a formal psychotherapy training. It may also be of use to commissioners and policy makers considering what psychoanalytic psychotherapy offers to vulnerable children and their families to help break the transmission of trauma and distress across generations.

Like many child psychotherapists, my journey to this approach was circuitous. My fascination for stories and character led to my degree in English/American literature and then a postgraduate training in social work. I specialised in working with children and families, and then managed a team responsible for looked-after children. I became disillusioned with how many foster and adoptive placements broke down because the children we placed were too troubled by their past to make real relationships with their new substitute families. I realised I did not have the skills or experience to understand these children's behaviour and unhappiness. An unexpected encounter at that time, about 45 years ago, gave me an insight into psychotherapy as a treatment that might help these children. I was anxious about a decision to remove a small child from her depressed and neglectful private foster parent into care, as I feared the impact this would have on the child, who had no other family. I was told about the Anna Freud Clinic and contacted them for advice. They invited me to a Wednesday consultation meeting where I nervously presented the case. Anna Freud was there, elderly but quite fierce in my eyes, and she told me in her summary of the discussion, that if we removed the child from foster care to be placed with another family, the child would need intensive psychotherapeutic help to recover. We followed her advice, and I regularly met with the social worker there for consultation on my work with her, while the child received intensive psychotherapy from a trainee, three times a week. I saw the young girl slowly grow in confidence and self-esteem from this specialised form of help. This led to my decision to begin the four years' training in child psychoanalytic psychotherapy in the Independent tradition with the British Psychotherapy Foundation (then the British Association of Psychotherapists). I began to offer treatment to those same traumatised children I had worked with as a social worker, but in a child and adolescent community mental health team. On qualifying, I moved to the Family Service of the Cassel Hospital, a psychotherapeutic inpatient service for families in severe distress in west London where I worked for many years until the service closed.

Fortunately, I was then offered the opportunity to take on the Clinical Lead role in the Independent Child and Adolescent Psychoanalytic Psychotherapy training where I had studied many years earlier, and I also developed my private practice where my work is focused now.

These experiences have shaped my approach to child psychotherapy with its emphasis on seeing the therapeutic work with the child in the context of the family, and the importance of working with the parents. The book begins more simply in Part 1 and Part 2 with a description of the why and how of child psychoanalytic psychotherapy, the key concepts and therapeutic techniques. It becomes more complex in the second half of the book as I move on to consider specialist work, which offers the reader and the more experienced child psychotherapist the opportunity to build on the ideas initially outlined in the book.

Introduction

Psychotherapy can be surprising, complex and challenging. Winnicott (1968) saw play as the creative space where each of us 'plays with ideas' in our imaginative world, and he considered this an essential aspect of psychotherapy. In child psychotherapy, we create that space in our therapeutic relationship with children, play, stories and conversation being their natural medium for thinking aloud. In psychoanalytic psychotherapy, we offer a therapeutic relationship in which trust can develop, and this frees the young person's creativity to solve problems. The therapist encourages the child or adolescent to lead the play and conversation about difficulties that have arisen. Within the clear therapeutic structure of the regular 50-minute session, ideas and feelings about problems emerge, often in an unexpected way. The child psychotherapist has to be open and receptive to any cues, spoken or non-verbal, that might lead to a growing understanding of the young person's underlying emotional difficulties. Sarah, who I introduce below, found an imaginative way to tell me about how she was feeling using the play materials in the therapy room.

> Sarah, a young girl, nine years old, was referred for psychotherapy because she was so often unhappy and angry at home and at school. Her early life had been troubled by family crises and many moves of home. Her mother, recognising that these early stresses had affected her daughter's emotional development, wanted help for her now. I had been puzzled how to reach this young girl in our weekly sessions as she seemed so uninterested in the play materials or conversation until, one week, she found a way to 'talk' to me. She walked in to the therapy room and purposively went to her box of play materials, getting out string, paper, felt tip pens, sticky tape and scissors. She created a washing line across the room and then she drew drawing pictures of storm clouds, lightning and rain on squares of paper which she hung from the line. When it was finished, she turned to me triumphantly and said: 'Here's my weather map'. I said I thought her pictures were about how she felt inside, that it had been a difficult week since I saw her last, with storms, unhappiness, and maybe some fights. She nodded, and we went on to think together about what had been so

distressing at home. Feeling understood in this way made it easier for Sarah to begin talking to me about herself in future sessions, although periodically, she would put up a new weather line, letting me know when it was hard for her to put her thoughts into words.

Finding a way to talk about what feels important to the child is a key part of establishing any new therapeutic relationship. It can sometimes take many weeks.

When child or adolescent patients begin psychotherapy, their inner turmoil is often hidden, and we only see the symptoms; the angry, destructive or withdrawn behaviour caused by their distress. We often discover that, beneath the surface, the young person is very self-critical, knowing that this behaviour is alienating those who are close. Helping a child or adolescent begin to be in touch in a more compassionate way with these internal conflicts becomes the focus of therapy. With a greater self-understanding, it is more possible for young people to accept themselves and allow some care and concern, first from the psychotherapist and then from others. Much work is needed to achieve this open and trusting exchange of ideas between patient and psychotherapist. (In this book, I use the word patient, which derives from the Latin word *patiens*, 'one who suffers', rather than 'client', as it is closer to the meaning in therapy.) Recovery is often a slow process and hard to achieve, because of the complexity of the developing body and mind, and our natural resistance to exploring painful issues and facing change.

Initially the child psychotherapist faces the challenge of creating a therapeutic alliance, developing an understanding of the problems distressing the patient and then working together with the young person to face these one by one. In this book, I will explore how this can be achieved, looking at individual psychotherapy in different settings and then how these ideas have been applied elsewhere. I will introduce theoretical ideas I have found helpful in my own work and when teaching others, hoping this will encourage the reader to look further.

In **Part 1** I map out the territory of child psychotherapy. This begins by describing the therapeutic process and then follows the child psychotherapist from setting up a therapy room, through to meeting the child and the parents and formulating an assessment. I continue next to look in more detail at children's emotional development and how we shape our therapeutic work to their level of understanding. I also consider brief therapies and engaging parents in ongoing work. Most child psychotherapists work as part of a team, so I then take some time to consider the dynamics of team life and the importance of a reflective space, before concluding with a chapter on a therapeutic approach to endings, a crucial aspect of the work.

In **Part 2** I consider the more challenging aspects of child psychotherapy when we can lose a sense of direction, or make mistakes, and how supervision can help us make sense of these difficulties. In **Part 3** I consider, in more detail, the impact on young people facing particular distressing events in the family, like parental mental illness or divorce, and what we can learn from research to guide us. **Part 4** is focused on child psychotherapy as it has developed and adapted to specialist settings.

I would like to add that all the clinical vignettes are imaginary, created out of a fusion of many children and families I have seen, to protect their confidentiality.

This book can only be an introduction to the work of the child and adolescent psychoanalytic psychotherapist which I hope will be of interest to those, working therapeutically with children and teenagers, who may be interested in developing their skills. The training of a child psychoanalytic psychotherapist in England takes four years and includes one's own psychoanalysis four times a week, theoretical teaching and clinical practice under supervision. However, the ideas and techniques I introduce are relevant to many therapists and those working with troubled children and can begin a learning process which I have found continually rewarding over the years. Each new young person I meet or hear about in supervision brings a new challenge to my understanding and sometimes new insight into how to do this difficult but crucial work. From my perspective, the aim of child psychotherapy is to remove the obstacles that prevent children and young people from developing emotionally, so that they have the skills to tackle life's challenges in their own individual way. Once children or teenagers are more secure in their family relationships and friendships, when they can study or work and are developing interests in the outside world, it's likely our work is done. They are ready to work towards ending psychotherapy.

Reference

Winnicott, D.W. (1968) Communication between infant and mother and mother and infant, compared and contrasted. In L. Caldwell & H. Taylor Robinson (eds) *The Collected Works of D.W. Winnicott*, vol. 8, pp. 227–238. New York and London: Oxford University Press, 2016.

Part I

Mapping the territory

Chapter 1

The therapeutic process

In the Introduction, I mentioned Winnicott's (1968) idea that psychotherapy should offer a creative space where the patient and therapist can play with ideas. He believed that to achieve understanding and emotional change requires us to trust the unconscious process in the child's creative play or the adolescent's conversation to reveal core problems concerning the sense of self. This can only occur within a reliable therapeutic relationship, where the patient feels safe.

So how do we establish that creative space in our therapeutic work? Often, as child psychotherapists, we don't have willing patients in the room. Young people are there because their parents or carers are worried about them. So, creating and maintaining a therapeutic alliance can be difficult. I am aware of a noticeable difference in sessions when a young person has joined me in the search to understand what is wrong, rather than dodging and diving to avoid emotional contact and painful realities.

In this chapter, I will look at five aspects of the therapeutic process that help create a framework for the treatment. They are: creating a safe space for therapy, understanding children's play and communication, understanding our defences and making interpretations, working with our feelings, and 'working through', the process of change. Of course, these different aspects of therapy are interconnected, like the different-coloured threads that create a pattern in a piece of weaving. But it is helpful to look at each thread individually to see, in practice, how it contributes to the whole.

Creating a safe space for therapy

We create a safe setting in psychotherapy by our ability to listen deeply and observe closely, as we try to understand the underlying themes in a child's play or a young person's conversation with us. Many children have not experienced such careful attention before and they respond with relief that there is someone available to hear their worries. They may also feel anxious, and resistant to being in this dependent position, particularly if the adults in their lives so far have not been trustworthy.

Being thought about deeply is a necessary precursor to being able to think about and understand one's own moods and feelings. In his chapter 'The theory of thinking' (1962a) W.R. Bion describes how children learn to understand their own feelings by having them heard and reflected back in a manageable form by the parent caring for them. Bion calls this 'containment' (1962b). Winnicott (1945) uses the term 'holding' in a similar way, but he stresses the importance of parents' practical care given to their children in a loving way, to develop this sense of inner security. We have all seen an infant or toddler wailing with frustration after falling down or losing a toy, who can only be soothed by a loving and firm parent who comforts and tries to understand what is wrong.

Bion suggests also that the baby or infant who is not comforted in this way, but is left alone to cope with overwhelming feelings, experiences a sense of terror he calls 'nameless dread' (Bion 1962a: 183). A mother, feeling alone and distressed, may be unable to comfort the child because she feels frightened by the intensity of these feelings in her baby. Perhaps this is because the baby's crying triggers her own memories of being distraught as a small child. She may withdraw, or react angrily, especially if she has no one to support her in these difficult moments. An infant can survive some distressing times if, at others, the mother and father offer comfort and love. We only have to be good enough parents (Winnicott 1953). But the infant or child who is left alone too often with unmanageable feelings will never learn to calm down and may become irritable or withdrawn. These are the children we so often see later in psychotherapy: loners, full of anxiety, or subject to outbursts of aggression that alienate those around, who might otherwise try to help.

So, by our close attention in therapy, and our ability to be in touch with the child's feelings, we offer an emotionally holding experience. This can help the child begin to understand what is wrong. Sometimes, with very emotionally deprived children, it is as if we are starting at the very beginning, naming the feelings for the first time.

Many years ago, when I was a social worker, I was asked to see Tom, a West Indian boy about 10 years old, who was very withdrawn at school. He had been brought up by his depressed lonely father who worked long hours to keep him. They had only recently settled in this country. When I saw Tom for regular weekly meetings, he would watch my face with close attention, reminding me of a small infant studying his mother's face, trying to work out the feelings he saw there. He would sometimes ask me if I was happy or sad, as if he did not know how to read my expressions or behaviour, nor his own. I would tell him what I thought he was feeling at that time, and how that made me feel, and this led to conversations about his life and his loneliness. I was not a trained child psychotherapist then, but I recall how Tom became more animated and how he looked forward to our conversation on my weekly visits. He gradually gained the confidence to reach out and be comforted by others around him, like the teachers in the special school he attended.

It was as if this lad knew that he was missing a thoughtful person who could help him understand himself and he sought this out in me. I have met this longing for an understanding adult often in the more deprived and troubled children I have seen. Although they may be resentful and suspicious of psychotherapy, they may also be looking for a sense of connection and understanding, and this need has survived intact, despite their fury and disappointment with adults about their early deprivation or trauma.

Understanding children's play and communication

What is truer than truth? The story.
                    Jewish proverb

Playing and telling stories is the natural way for children to think about themselves and their world. When we provide young people with play and drawing materials in therapy, we are letting them know that we see their imaginative world as an important source of ideas, a way of exploring their concerns. In fact, it is not until young people start to express themselves spontaneously and imaginatively, and we begin to link this with how we think they feel and see life, that children really understand how therapy works.

The purpose of play and encouraging young people to tell stories is to discover their inner world, by this I mean their view of themselves and their life experiences. When the therapist is more directive, suggesting topics for the play session or asking a series of questions, children reveal only what is on the top of their minds or what they think the therapist wants to hear, rather than the underlying emotional tensions and conflicts that have troubled them. So, when a young person spontaneously begins to tell a story, maybe by setting up a scene with two armies fighting, I encourage the storyteller to elaborate. Who is involved? What led to the battle? What has made them angry? Usually this tale develops, sometimes in a way unexpected to both the child and me, as fears and fantasies rise to the surface of the child's mind and become themes in the narrative. As the Jewish proverb suggests, these stories have their own truth as the young people are talking about themselves, but the feelings are held at a safe distance in the story, so they do not feel exposed. At first, I just listen and show interest, but gradually I may begin to empathise with the challenges facing the characters. I might talk about how the characters may feel, and why I think the events happened, and at some level the young people recognise this story is about themselves too.

Over the weeks, these stories develop in the sessions, and themes emerge which represent aspects of the child's feelings about himself. The beauty of a child's play and stories is that they resonate on many levels as they are rich in metaphor and symbolism like poetry and myth. However, children may resist this idea in practice. Peter Wilson suggests why in his paper about latency children (6–10-year-olds) entitled 'Latency and certainty'. He writes that, despite the fascinating play of children at this age, they often deny it has any meaning beyond the concrete facts, to the frustration of the therapist:

> The latency child presents the psychotherapist with a peculiar doubled-edged challenge: to overcome seemingly unmoving, even obtuse resistance, and to unravel and understand rich and imaginative fantasy material. There is, in a sense, no ambiguity.
>
> (Wilson 1989: 59)

No ambiguity because, he suggests, ambiguity is not easily tolerated at this age. Children insist on knowing and on being certain, to defend themselves from having to face complex feelings at an age when their confidence can feel precarious because of the many new skills they are trying to learn. One of the interesting questions is whether the process of a child playing through such a fantasy is itself curative, as the process of imaginative play brings about internal change, or whether the play needs to be put into words and consciously linked to the child's own experience by the psychotherapist to be understood and internalised. I am not sure.

One of the challenges of psychotherapy is managing the anxiety that arises when a child begins to explore a painful or worrying issue that has been shut away, as it was too upsetting to face. Children naturally break off and direct their attention elsewhere when feelings become too intense, and we allow this to happen so that they can face their anxieties at a pace they can manage. Alternatively, the child may become quite disruptive and I will discuss how to manage this later in this chapter. As children become more resilient, we may draw attention to this defensive avoidance, to encourage them to face issues they may have been too fragile to consider before. But this is a matter of careful judgement by the therapist.

Children's stories have elements of fantasy, magic and reality interwoven, and the symbolism of their play allows us to explore the meaning of their play in more depth. Like the young girl I described in the opening chapter, who hung pictures of stormy weather on a line to describe the emotional turbulence of her life. Children's fairy tales are alive with this imagery, as in the Grimm brothers' story of Snow White where the poisoned apple that the witch gives the princess is a symbol of her envy and hatred of this beautiful young princess. A similar image was used by a young girl in her play with me. She made me a 'nice' cake out of plasticine but when I broke it open

I saw that inside was a worm, an unpleasant surprise. It was a powerful way of communicating her fear from past experience that beneath the surface of our 'nice' relationship there lurked feelings of hatred.

As psychotherapists, we allow our imaginations to range freely as we sit and observe children's play or listen to teenagers talk about their lives. It is an interactive process and we have to be aware which aspects of our own experience we are bringing to the relationship and what belongs to the patient. Cultural differences can be crucial here in defining how we experience particular symbols and words, partly because of the diverse meanings they carry in different societies but also because the reality of the children's living environment can be so different. A Malaysian therapist once told me that his fear of spiders and the snakes came from growing up in the tropics where they can threaten life, and they had a very different meaning for him than for children raised in England where they can represent something scary, but in reality quite harmless. Allowing children to tell us what their story characters and symbols mean to them, and testing out our associations carefully, ensures we enter their imaginary world and feel it as they do.

Freud suggested that our dreams are another fertile avenue for exploring our inner world, the royal road to the unconscious (1900). In my experience, children's dreams are often less disguised than adults' and easier to understand, although they may take some unravelling before children become open to our suggestions about their meaning. As in psychotherapeutic work with adults, it is important never to take a dream on its own, out of the context of the child's recent therapeutic work. A little girl may tell you there is a monster in her dream who threatens to eat her up, or a scary cat who will scratch her face, but these images of hunger, fear and anger need to be understood as part of the child's history and ongoing clinical material. Talking to children about their dreams allows them to become part of the child's conscious mind, and often defuses the terror of nightmares as this dream material becomes part of the child's ordinary understanding of life.

Playing does not come easily to all children. For some, their imaginative world is terrifying, and they feel safer in the structured world of games and conversation. Others are too withdrawn or 'lost', as Anne Alvarez describes them, appearing to have no interest in us or the world, because they no longer expect to be comforted by this experience. This can occur when children have been so deprived as infants or have become locked away in an autistic-like state. Alvarez (1992) describes how we have to reclaim these children by offering ourselves as live company. We invite them to play or talk with us, and when they do briefly come out of their shells, we amplify these moments with lively encouragement. Our aim is to gradually restore these young people's belief that people, and the world, have something to offer them. In her book, *Live Company*, Alvarez describes beautifully the patient, determined approach needed for therapy with very deprived or autistic children.

Once the therapeutic alliance has been established, the critical issue of what to interpret and when becomes important. I will explore this in the next section.

Understanding the defences and making interpretations

A challenging aspect of psychotherapy is to know what to say and when, how to put our thoughts and observations into words for our young patients so that they make sense to them. We have to be sensitive to a child's emotional capacity to hear what we want to say before we speak. If the child is too upset, bewildered or suspicious, then our words will have no meaning or, worse, will be interpreted negatively. Of course, talking is only part of the therapeutic response. How well we are able to listen, and provide a calm and thoughtful presence, is just as important. Helping children put their feelings and thoughts into words makes it possible for them to begin to understand themselves, to think things through. Then they can communicate their feelings of anger and distress to others, and there is no longer such a need for them to act them out in their behaviour.

This skill of responding to a child and making interpretations at the right time and in the right words is one that develops with time. I am using the word interpretation in its broadest sense as it is defined in the Oxford dictionary: the action of explaining the meaning of something.

There is a more particular use of the word in psychoanalytic thinking where the definition of an interpretation is more focused on making latent meaning evident:

> Interpretation is the process of putting into words – making conscious and known to the patient – fantasies, aspects of relationships, anxieties, conflicts and defences, and insights into the way the patient's mind works which previously could not be known because they were unacceptable and thus had remained repressed in the unconscious mind.
>
> (Lanyado & Horne 1999: 168)

Before I discuss this further, I would like to consider more simply why and how we speak in the session. Imagine watching a child play. You might show interest by briefly reflecting on what you see, or you might ask a few opening questions to help the child or the adolescent tell you more and develop the story. What and how questions are often more useful than why at this early stage, as they encourage children to describe in detail what is happening and build up their narrative.

Anthony, a withdrawn teenager, was referred for psychotherapy because of his anxiety and lack of confidence. He tells me in his session that he had spent the afternoon trying to write a song. I encourage him to tell me more about his song. At the same time, I am alert to his mood, how anxious he is talking to me. Anthony offers to play the song to me on his phone. I listen. The lyrics relate to his life, how confused and alone he often feels. I do not say anything at first as I do not want to stop the flow or for Anthony to feel I am intruding, but when I feel the timing is right, I suggest that the song tells us about him too. He nods and says no more, but that moment of connection between us has been important and I can return to these themes later or in a future session.

This is where psychotherapy is more of an art than a science. There are no clear rules to approaching this type of conversation. But there are guidelines that can help us recognise what level of intervention children can use at a given time.

First it is important to understand how defences work, as we need to approach these self-protective strategies in children with respect when making an interpretation, so as not to expose them to too much anxiety. Anna Freud was a psychoanalyst who worked with children as well as adults. She developed the idea of defences originally outlined by her father, Sigmund Freud, as a way of thinking about how we emotionally protect ourselves from being overwhelmed by anxiety and painful feelings. These defences are unconscious strategies by the ego (the psychological self) to avoid facing conflict and anxiety within ourselves or in our interpersonal relationships. Each of us has developed a characteristic defensive style that has been necessary as we grow up, but defences can become rigid, and interfere with our emotional development. Alternatively, some young people do not have enough of a protective shell and are easily overwhelmed by feelings of anger or anxiety, which can make them feel as if they are falling apart inside. These children need help to develop appropriate defences through the experience of a relationship where these feelings are held and understood.

Anna Freud described these defences in her book *The Ego and the Mechanisms of Defence* (1966 [1936]). Since then, the concept of defences has been developed by many but the central idea of protecting the self from painful realities remains. Below I will introduce those defences we observe and most often meet in our work with children. One you may recognise is *denial* when painful feelings, like anxiety or dependency, are denied or avoided. Another is *splitting*, a very typical defence of children under five and teenagers, if they are under stress. Then the world is seen in stark terms of good and bad: 'I'm good and you are bad' or vice versa. It occurs originally because the infant cannot manage conflicting feelings of love and hate towards the loved parent, so the unacceptable angry feelings are split off to protect the good ones. As we grow mature, we develop the capacity to bring together our love and hatred for those closest to us, the love moderating the hate so we can achieve a more balanced view of them as whole people.

Projection is a defence that contributes to splitting. Here, unacceptable feelings that belong to the self are attributed to someone else. The therapist will be told she is stupid or angry when the child wants to be rid of this persecuting feeling. Projective identification was a concept introduced by Melanie Klein (1946) to describe a type of projection in which unacceptable infantile parts of the self, in fantasy, are split off into the mother or therapist, as a powerful communication or as an intrusion to control the other. A baby's cry can have this quality when it is urgent and it almost compels the mother to act to meet the infant's need in that moment. Although this is a complicated idea, it helps explain those moments in therapy when it feels like the child's distress has got inside the therapist and made thinking difficult. *Reversal* is a defence used when unacceptable feelings are turned into their opposite. The young person says 'I'm fine, I'll manage' to cover up the hidden anxiety that things can't be managed at all. *Somatisation* is another unconscious defence, very typical of younger children, where their emotional pain is held in the body as a physical symptom, like a stomach-ache, which holds the hidden feelings that cannot be thought about or expressed in words. In Chapter 13, I will talk further about the therapeutic work done by child psychotherapists in hospitals with somatic complaints in children.

Another important defence to recognise is *identification with the aggressor* where a young person, who was hurt and powerless as a victim of abuse, takes on the role of the abuser towards another victim, as a way of triumphing over these fears. When working with defences like these, the child psychotherapist has to find a way of recognising the young person's anxiety without challenging the defence directly, as this will only increase the child's resistance. A young girl may arrive in the session and insist she is fine, although I know she has been isolating herself because she is miserable. I listen to her conversation and wait until a comment of hers makes this unhappiness easier to address, maybe later in the session. Or I make a more general observation that 'life can be miserable sometimes'. In this way the emotion is acknowledged but kept at a distance, and not felt so personally.

A similar respect for defences is discussed by Anne Alvarez in her book *Live Company*. She suggests that developing a defensive structure may be an achievement for vulnerable children, helping them protect themselves from being overwhelmed by painful feelings. She advises us we have to support these defences so as not to undermine their attempts to manage themselves and their relationships. This is a helpful idea when thinking about *omnipotence*, a defence in which the child asserts power or control as a defence against a feeling of powerlessness. A young boy boasts that he is so strong that he could fight anyone in the playground. Rather than disillusion him with the painful reality that he is too small to do so, a more gentle and ego supportive response would be to suggest that he's looking forward to the day when he has the strength to take on those boys who want to fight him.

Displacement is a defence where ideas or feelings are detached from their source and attributed elsewhere. Children naturally displace their feelings into their stories where their characters reflect their own experiences but at a safe distance from themselves. As therapists, this allows us to talk about difficult feelings at a safe distance. Puppets can be valuable tools in work with children, as children can imaginatively attribute their feelings to them. A Mickey Mouse puppet is allowed to be naughty or rude to the therapist, when the child feels too inhibited to do so. The puppet might also appear to be a more sympathetic listener than I am, and an unhappy child will sometimes talk to a loved puppet held in my hand although he has refused to tell me directly what is wrong.

Another defence is *manic excitement*. Children often escape into manic activity or excited behaviour to avoid the unhappy feelings that would come to mind if they allowed themselves to stop and think. This is one of the dynamics underlying children's risky behaviour in sessions or the way they flit restlessly from one activity to another. This excited behaviour must be carefully managed in therapy to avoid children's play getting out of hand when they become 'manic' to avoid the sadness or despair that may be troubling them underneath.

Finally, there is the development of a *false self* as a defensive measure. D. W. Winnicott (1960) first used this term to describe how an infant may form a split-off false self to adapt to a mother who responds to the baby in terms of her own needs, due to her depression or emotional problems, rather than reflecting the baby's actual moods. This is in contrast to the mother who responds sensitively to the infant's spontaneous gestures. Her empathic response gives the baby a feeling of being alive, allowing a true self to develop out of spontaneously lived experience. The child who develops a protective false self may appear to be calm and confident, but this can cover up feelings of vulnerability and deprivation or emptiness that have no safe place to be expressed at this time. The false self serves a useful function in protecting the true self until this recovery is possible.

Winnicott suggests that when a young person is feeling more secure, held in a more loving and stable relationship, these underlying feelings of neediness can emerge. Young people caring for a parent who is physically or mentally ill, can developed a false self, a competent persona which may hide their need for nurturing as they grow up. In psychotherapy, once a young person feels held in a reliable therapeutic relationship, there is an opportunity to share these more vulnerable feelings and unmet needs and for the true sense of self to begin to emerge.

Thinking more about interpretations

A child's mode of defences, the emotional level of functioning and the quality of the child's relationship with his therapist are all aspects that need to be considered when thinking about interpretations.

In her more recent book *The Thinking Heart* (2012), Anne Alvarez discusses three levels of interpretation suited to the child's emotional development and state of mind. She stresses the importance of the tone of our voice and our choice of words as much as the content.

In the first level of interpretation, the child psychotherapist describes why something is happening and attributes meaning. 'You are upset because you are late and you feel it's my fault.' For children who are in a more troubled, persecuted state of mind, this may be too complex a thought. What they need is the therapist to recognise and understand the quality of their experience, what is happening: 'You are so upset'. This is the second level of interpretation, where the focus is on description of what is happening. She points out, though, that if the child is feeling too disturbed, locating the experience in the child in this way could feel like an accusation or it might flood the child with too much feeling. Then it can be helpful to make it a more general comment like 'It's so upsetting to be late'.

Finally, she considers a third level of interpretation needed by the very withdrawn, deprived or disengaged child who does not expect to find anything helpful in the therapist, or in life itself. Then, she suggests, it's important for the therapist to give a more active, intensifying response, sometimes in a heightened voice. The purpose is to give meaning where it has not been seen before, as a way of reclaiming the child to life. A withdrawn child who might enjoy a moment of play in the session, and sees that the therapist is really interested and interesting, might momentarily come alive with a sense of pleasure and excitement. It is this experience which needs to be amplified and intensified by the therapist, as an important moment of engagement with life. I remember this happening with Mary, an autistic teenager whom I saw for therapy for several years.

> Not knowing what else to do, in a rather dull session when Mary was rather uninterested and pre-occupied, I suggested we make a portrait of her using plasticine. I began with her help to make a simple figure whose clothes and hair colour matched hers. She was excited and pleased when she saw it completed.
>
> I said, with a delighted tone in my voice too: 'You really like it when we both make a model together, and it looks like you!'
>
> This led us to make a sequence of models, one each week which she shaped according to how she was feeling about herself. It was an important 'conversation' between us that she could lead, very different from the passive disengagement she had shown in the early therapy sessions.

Anne Alvarez calls this type of therapy 'reclamation', and it does feel like parts of the child's self are being reclaimed, little by little. She also suggests this therapeutic process is 'working towards' rather than working through, emphasising the need for the therapist to connect emotionally with the more withdrawn and disturbed patient before 'working through' is possible, as described in the final part of this chapter.

Working with our feelings in the transference and counter transference

> The process of therapy is an interplay of two minds, of the patient's transference and the therapist's counter-transference. ... [This] process requires a continuing capacity to monitor oneself ... and to seek room in the therapeutic session for observing this interaction.
>
> (Horne 2006: 28)

Observing one's feelings and understanding them as a response to a young person's state of mind is one of the key skills of a psychoanalytic psychotherapist that becomes refined over time. This skill allows the therapist to feel the quality of the relationship the young patient brings to therapy and to see how it subtly changes as the therapeutic work progresses. As we grow up, we internalise a pattern of relationships from our early experience of parents and siblings, and this shapes our expectations of others, particularly those who are in parental roles and our view of ourselves. These early and current relationships are transferred to the therapeutic relationship, where the feelings, anxieties and hopes evoked by these important family relationships can be recognised and understood by the psychotherapist. This is the transference relationship.

My emotional response as a psychotherapist to the transference relationship is called the countertransference, as I pick up the verbal and non-verbal cues in the young person's response to me in the session. I remember vividly my first meetings with Mary, the autistic teenager I mentioned earlier. She had little speech, but she communicated her loneliness and confusion in the way she carried herself, edging into the room sideways, with her hands protecting her face, looking furtively at me. I could feel myself responding with a bewildered sympathy, not knowing how to reach her, feeling out of my depth. Looking back, after many years of work with this young woman, I think that in the countertransference I was recognising that she felt out of her depth in this bewildering world. She wanted to be with people, but she so quickly felt overwhelmed in their presence that it was a frightening experience too.

I was touched to see this experience described eloquently in a documentary, *Life, Animated* (2016). In the film, we see Owen Suskind, a young adult, telling an audience about growing up with autism. Owen talks about how he wanted to be with people but he did not know how to reach them. He describes how he and his family struggled to communicate until they found a way, after he had used the words of a Disney character, Mickey Mouse, to tell his parents about himself. The simplicity of Disney's cartoon characters' speech and their vitality had made them accessible to Owen in a way that was less challenging than ordinary relationships with family and friends, and he could use the cartoon characters' language to express himself.

Working with autistic children and toddlers teaches us to be very in touch with our feelings in the countertransference, as these young people may have little language to tell us how they feel. We have to rely on non-verbal cues, and our feelings in the presence of the child, to understand them. Sometimes, I may have a more physical response to a patient rather than an emotional reaction. It may be a gut reaction of tension in my stomach, where I am picking up the anxiety of my patient, a dryness in the mouth that for me is more like fear, or a boredom or sleepiness in response to a disengaged child that is like a shutting down of my capacity to think. These bodily responses are most present when early pre-verbal feelings are being communicated to me by my patients. I might simply try and put these feelings into words, but in a generalised way, so they do not feel too persecuting to hear. I might suggest 'it must be so worrying' if I am feeling anxious, or 'these things can be so hard to think about' if I feel I am being shut out by my child patient.

The therapeutic relationship offers a safe setting where transference feelings can be explored and thought about, and new ways of relating can be discovered. As this exploration occurs, slowly session by session, the young person can discover in this new relationship a different way of relating, a new way of seeing the self and others that can then be tried out in other settings like home and school. To give a very simple example: a nervous compliant young boy who is fearful of angering his parents may begin to recognise his feelings of frustration in therapy and allow himself to express some annoyance to his therapist. He finds the therapist is receptive, even interested in exploring these feelings, and this gives him the confidence to try being assertive with his parents or friends, to discover whether this new side of himself can be expressed safely there too. This external change will probably only emerge after a great deal of exploration of the young person's feelings, his anxieties and conflicts, has occurred within the therapy, but it is sometimes the first sign to parents that the child is progressing. It is important that parents see themselves as part of the therapeutic work, too, and can welcome signs of this new self-confidence. If they are able to accept some therapeutic support for themselves as parents, as I discuss in the next chapter, it will help them recognise these changes, and also enable them to get through the rocky patches when the young person's behaviour can be more difficult, if negative feelings are being worked through in sessions.

Being exposed to negative feelings in the transference as a psychotherapist is painful, even though we know they are projections onto us from the patient's internal world. They feel real enough. In the process of the work, we may be faced with denigration, annoyance and rejection from our young patients as well as more positive feelings as the patient recovers. As a psychotherapist, I have had to find a balance, allowing myself to be touched by these feelings, recognise them, but not get taken over by them in an unhelpful way. Alongside the transference relationship, I work hard to maintain a therapeutic alliance with the young person based on the trust that has built up between us over time. This allows me to reconnect with the reality of our therapeutic task, alongside the powerful transference feelings that may have dominated a difficult session. In a very practical way, managing the endings of sessions is important in this process. Tidying a messy room together, or helping a young adolescent girl prepare herself to face the world again, can be helpful in reasserting the ordinary world for the young person in the face of this rather overpowering subjective reality.

Our emotional response to our patients in therapy, as it changes session by session, guides us to the changing quality of the relationship between us as psychotherapy progresses. I will explore this further in the next section on the process of change.

Working through: the process of change

In psychotherapy, we call the slow process of treatment that brings about recovery 'working through'. This phrase captures the experience of a gradual sequence of problems worked on, as they surface in therapy, following the logic of the unconscious mind of the patient. This is a different process than the more cognitive solution-focused therapies where the process is led in a more directive way by the therapist. This does not mean that as a psychotherapist I put aside the reasons for referral, the young person's behavioural and emotional distress. In fact, children constantly remind us of these issues with their difficult behaviour and troubled moods in sessions and in the external world, and regular reviews with parents remind us of their experience. But I have found that I can only discover the underlying causes of a child's difficulties by allowing the patient's free flow of thoughts to dictate the content of the sessions, rather than following my own agenda. There is often uneven progress in this therapeutic journey. Emotional problems when they emerge can cause a regression to earlier behavioural difficulties, and then there may be a leap forward when a challenge is faced, and the young person gains new confidence or self-understanding.

It may be helpful to think of three phases of 'working through': the early, middle and final stages of therapy, whether the treatment lasts three months or two years.

The early treatment phase of psychotherapy can sometimes feel bewildering. I often find it hard to make sense of the therapeutic material and my emotional responses to the child, and I wonder where it is all heading. Allowing this period of doubt and uncertainty is important, as gradually the mist will clear, and certain themes will emerge as central to this beginning phase of treatment. This gradual process of clarification was illustrated by a series of photos I took of a child's weekly play in the sand tray. She had asked me to take these as a record of her work.

> Jenny was eight years old. She was a slight shy girl, prone to outbursts of anger if she felt threatened, and she would often retreat into silence. She did not talk to me for weeks, so her play in the sand tray was her only direct communication for some time. After a few months, we set out the photos in sequence on the table, and I was fascinated to see how the pictures reflected the development of her therapy, which I had not realised until then. The first photos showed a chaotic muddle of animals and people which she had placed on the sand, static scenes that made no sense to me. The next series of pictures were more simple and clear, and showed a disaster scene and a group of characters unable to move. There was a family, a girl and her parents with several animals, and they were surrounded by crashed cars and planes, nose-dived into the sand. There was also a wizard, Mickey Mouse on a skateboard, and two wrestlers, but, she told me, these were frozen figures who did not move.
>
> I was still unsure how to connect this play with Jenny's own issues, but I thought she was showing me how her energy and imaginative world had become frozen, because she feared an emotional disaster, or she had experienced one in the past. I did not try to interpret, make any links with her own life, as I feared she would close down again. It was after six months into therapy that Jenny became more openly expressive, and her school, her friendships and her family were brought to life in fictional characters. This meant we could begin to make links with her own experience and I could help her think more directly about some of the emotional upsets she faced each week, and why they happened.

This piece of work shows the typical development of the therapeutic process. Over the weeks, themes come into focus in the sessions, reflecting the tensions in the inner life of the child and clashes with the external world. These tensions begin to be explored as the therapeutic relationship becomes a safer place to share and get help. Alongside the evolution of the content of the therapy is the development of the therapeutic relationship which is a key factor and barometer of change. Jenny kept herself emotionally distant at first, and I tried to fathom why. Was she wary I might be critical of her or intrusive, or was she afraid of exploding into fury if she allowed her jealous or angry feelings to come to the surface? Gradually, over the weeks, she relaxed as she felt safer with me, reassured that I would follow her play at her pace. Eventually we would become allies, searching together to understand her underlying brittle lack of self-confidence and her feelings of persecution and mistrust.

As I work, I am always trying to find the right words to develop a shared language with the young person, matching the child's view of the world and the culture of the family. Sometimes, special words or images come up in conversation that become a metaphor for the therapy, maybe quite humorously. Being weird, or like an alien, is how several young people have described themselves to me. Playing with these words and their different meanings became a focus for us, as we explore how they feel about themselves and how they see themselves in relation to others. The self-disgust or self-criticism of these initial feelings can soften into a more humorous self - caricature as the work progresses, although sometimes these self-perceptions can be hard to shift as I describe in the later chapter on adolescents.

This takes me to the middle phase of treatment when the patient and the therapist are building a picture of the young person's world and the problems there. I would hope to have engaged the child's curiosity and interest in this search by now, and to have made a therapeutic alliance with my patient (and the parents hopefully) that will see us through the stormy phases of treatment when the young person is testing my capacity to cope with anger and despair and make sense of it. As the young person's pattern of rigid defences relaxes, self-expression becomes easier, and this frees the child to develop emotionally. Themes surface and deepen over the weeks as problems are looked at from many different angles. Perhaps the best image for the therapeutic process is that of a spiral repeatedly turning, as problems are revisited and seen from a new perspective each time the spiral turns. A process of recognising, reflecting and understanding.

I know my particular pre-occupation as a psychotherapist is wanting to find out the reason why things have gone wrong, feeling this knowledge would help the child or adolescent gain insight. Yet this often is not possible, or we develop a hypothesis that makes sense to us but not to the young patient. Yet, for many young people, what matters is the present, their wish for friendship and happiness now. Making links with the past may seem irrelevant.

For others, it can be extraordinarily helpful, particularly in the later stages of psychotherapy, to look back at the past and see how problems began in the parents' childhood or maybe as far back as their grandparents' lives. Seeing these patterns can prevent a young person feeling so responsible for those difficult phases in family life. These can now be understood as part of the family story. As John Byng-Hall says in his interesting paper, 'Family scripts: A concept which can bridge child psychotherapy and family therapy thinking': 'For a child to appreciate that his parent's current behaviour is an attempt to correct their own hurt experience paves the way to forgiveness' (Byng-Hall 1986).

The final phase of treatment is often rewarding, even at times enjoyable. Young people become more self-confident and self-aware, as they internalise a more positive sense of self in response to the therapeutic work. They have found new ways of understanding and managing their difficult feelings and they can look back at the therapeutic work they have done and recognise the progress they have made. At this stage, psychotherapy naturally moves on to helping the young people work through the ending process, acknowledging their development and discovering, along with some sense of loss, the feeling of freedom and of being more independent once they end therapy. Of course, not all therapies progress in this straightforward way to a positive conclusion, and we will be considering, later in the book, disruptions and difficulties that can undermine the work.

References

Alvarez, A. (1992) *Live Company.* London: Routledge.

Alvarez, A. (2012) *The Thinking Heart.* Hove and New York: Routledge.

Bion, W.R. (1962a) A theory of thinking. In E. Bott Spillius (ed) *Melanie Klein Today: Developments in Theory and Practice*, vol. 1: *Mainly Theory*, pp. 178–186. London: Routledge, 1988.

Bion, W.R. (1962b) *Learning from Experience.* London: Heinemann.

Byng-Hall, J. (1986) Family scripts: A concept which can bridge child psychotherapy and family therapy thinking. *Journal of Child Psychotherapy* 12(1): 3–13.

Freud, A. (1966 [1936]) *The Ego and Mechanisms of Defence.* London: Karnac.

Freud, S. (1900) The Interpretation of Dreams. In J. Strachey et al. (eds) *Standard Edition of the Complete Psychological Works of Sigmund Freud*, vols 4–5. London: Hogarth Press, 1953.

Horne, A. (2006) The Independent position in psychoanalytic psychotherapy with children and adolescents. In M. Lanyado & A. Horne (eds) *A Question of Technique*, pp. 15–28. London: Routledge.

Klein, M. (1946) Notes on some schizoid mechanisms. *International Journal of Psychoanalysis* 27: 99–110.

Lanyado, M. & Horne, A. (1999) The therapeutic setting and process. In M. Lanyado & A. Horne (eds) *The Handbook of Child and Adolescent Psychotherapy*, pp. 157–174. London: Routledge.

Life, Animated (2016) *US documentary directed by R.R. Williams.* Brooklyn, NY: Motto Pictures.

Wilson, P. (1989) Latency and certainty. *Journal of Child Psychotherapy* 15: 59–69.

Winnicott, D.W. (1945) Primitive emotional development. In D.W. Winnicott (ed) *Through Paediatrics to Psychoanalysis: Collected Papers*, pp. 145–156. London: Tavistock, 1958.

Winnicott, D.W. (1953) Transitional objects and transitional phenomena. *International Journal of Psycho-Analysis* 34: 89–97.

Winnicott, D.W. (1960) Ego distortion in terms of true and false self. In D.W. Winnicott (ed) *The Maturational Processes and the Facilitating Environment*, pp. 140–152. London: Karnac, 1965.

Winnicott, D.W. (1968) Communication between infant and mother and mother and infant, compared and contrasted. In L. Caldwell & H. Taylor Robinson (eds) *The Collected Works of D.W. Winnicott*, vol. 8, pp. 227–238. New York and London: Oxford University Press, 2016.

Chapter 2

Creating a therapeutic setting

What is essential in setting up a room for therapy? It can be a rather anonymous room in a child mental health office, with a bag of play materials brought by the child psychotherapist, a spare room in a school, or a purpose-built therapy room. In each, it is possible to create a therapeutic space, as long as the child therapist has guaranteed privacy with the patient for 50 minutes, the room is reliably available each week, and it is a safe place to play and talk.

When I set up my independent practice, after many years in a busy public service, I had an opportunity to design my own therapeutic setting. I had a room built in the garden, the only available space, reached by a gravel path alongside the house. Inside, there is now seating for a family, a couch, a small child's table and chairs, a toy box with shared toys and a cupboard for children's individual toy boxes. And a toilet, an essential resource. It is interesting how this setting has shaped the experience of children and adults coming to the room. As they walk down the path, they notice the plants and flowers changing with the seasons, and I often find the imagery of growing things enters the children's conversations. The autistic girl, Mary, was fascinated by the pear tree outside the window, and she would comment on how many pears she saw there each autumn. It was one of the earliest signs of her growing interest in the outside world. Spiders, wasps and flies also get in uninvited, and make a challenging contribution to the therapy. I have become an expert in the cup and saucer method of removing them without tragic incidents while the children watch me with great interest.

I am fairly traditional in my technique, offering children a limited set of play or work materials adapted to the age of the child as I was taught as a trainee child psychotherapist. These include a drawing and writing pad, felt tip pens and pencils, a paint tray, sticky tape, string, a model family who represent the ethnic origin and size of the patients' family, likewise a baby doll of similar colouring and features, some families of animals, both domestic and wild, and some cars for younger children, and a soft ball or two. These are ideally kept in a box for each child which they make their own. The therapist looks after the box and brings it out each session. There may also be shared play materials like a doll's house or a box of Lego, and I have introduced some simple picture books about topics like anger or loss as these may help younger or less verbal children begin talking about their concerns. I have also set up a sand tray with figures that create a small world. This has proved a very useful medium for both adolescents and young children to set out an imaginary world and to play out scenarios. Teenagers and young adults are given a writing pad and felt tips for drawing, so they can draw, doodle or write their ideas if they wish, and these are kept in their folder. This can be helpful when talking is difficult. Ideally, the child psychotherapist makes few additions to the original set given to a young person, except to replace those that have run out, as these play objects and materials gather meaning over time. Too many toys and new additions can be a distraction. Sometimes, children bring their own toys too, which I allow, but I encourage them to take them home at the end of a session, keeping the boundary between therapy and home.

The firm boundaries of therapy are essential, as they create a sense of safety and predictability for the patient who may feel overwhelmed by inner turmoil. I keep to the 50-minute hour, except perhaps in the introductory meeting with parents and their child when more time may be needed. Children are seen weekly, at a regular time. Occasionally I offer twice-weekly sessions if the child is too troubled to cope with a long gap between sessions. I provide calendars for younger children before the holidays, so they can see how many sessions they will miss and when they will return. I rediscovered the value of this technique when a young girl, who had voiced nothing but disdain for me, asked with some poignancy if I could make her calendar continue for every month of the year so she could see how long she would be coming for. I had been seeing her for therapy for seven months and I had no idea until then how much she valued therapy.

Chapter 3

Making an assessment and starting the work

Meeting the parents

Meeting parents who are desperate for a solution to their child's difficulties is always challenging. They often arrive in despair and with the expectation that, as an expert, the child psychotherapist will have the answer to helping their child recover. They may also feel ashamed that they have failed in the apparently straightforward task of being a parent. When I meet parents, I know that I have to create a therapeutic alliance with them that will support the work with their child, but also disappoint them in their hope that I alone can bring about change. My experience is that individual work with a young person living at home cannot bring about recovery unless the parents are prepared to consider their contribution to the young person's difficulties and agree to some therapeutic involvement themselves. This might involve regular sessions with another therapist thinking with them about life as a family and their parenting, and attending regular reviews with me as a child psychotherapist. From the beginning, I stress the importance of both parents being involved in meetings about the child's therapy. Often meeting the therapist can be seen as the mother's task, particularly if the father is working long hours so he does not attend, but missing out on his perspective and involvement is a real loss to a rounded view of family life It is more difficult later to insist on his attendance, if he is not involved from the start of the work.

In that first meeting with parents, I explain how I work as a child psychotherapist and then I encourage the parents to tell me about themselves, their child's history and their experiences as parents. This is also an opportunity to hear the parents' perspective on the child's problem and how this has been shaped by their cultural, religious and ethnic upbringing. Every family we meet is different from our own experience, but the gap widens if the family is from a very different background from our own. Iris Gibbs (2009: 98) emphasises how different cultures can vary in their view of what constitutes the problem and its severity, for example around issues of separation and individuation in adolescence, and the acceptable level of aggression. Most parents struggle to decide what limits to set as their teenagers grow up, but

ns between generations may increase when parents have emigrated
 and their children are growing up with different values than their
 f origin. Exploring the parents' concerns enables the child psychotherapist to begin to get an idea of the family lifestyle before meeting the
young person in therapy.

The first interview with parents can give a picture of how the stress of
family life has impacted on their relationship as a couple, and whether they
have come closer or drawn apart with the strain. I will see how open they
are to exploring their family functioning and the possible reasons for their
child's difficulties. When parents are straightforward about the emotional
strain they have been under, the task is much easier, like this couple
described below:

> The parents asked me to see their son, aged 10, whose angry outbursts
> at school had alienated his teachers. He could be just as outrageous at
> home. The couple were open about their own emotional difficulties. The
> mother admitted that she often became infuriated with her children,
> particularly recently after her husband had suffered a period of depres-
> sion. They realised that their son was probably reacting to the unhappi-
> ness at home time but felt powerless to help him. I agreed to see him for
> an assessment of three sessions to explore whether psychotherapy
> would be helpful, but I also made it clear that they would benefit from
> some help as parents from a colleague. I knew that these rather anxious
> parents would need support to help their son better manage his feelings,
> while also exploring the impact that their emotional distress was having
> on their relationship with their son.

Taking a history

Asking parents to recount their child's history can lead to an emotional and
revealing discussion as parents talk about about the family history and
consider what led to their child's troubles now. I encourage the parents to
recall the child's developmental steps from birth to the present in detail.
I begin by asking how they felt as a couple when this baby was conceived
and about the birth experience. Memories of a painful birth can haunt the
mother for a long time, and may have made the initial bonding difficult.
I then move on to ask about the first year, their memories of their baby's
feeding and sleeping pattern, and how other siblings in the family
responded. The story continues as you hear how the infant began to
babble and to crawl, through toddlerhood to starting nursery and school.
I ask how the parents found these early years, whether the mother got
depressed with the birth of this child or with the next, and how the toddler
coped with arrival of siblings. Family crises, illnesses, parental bereavement

or unexpected separations all create difficult times for children and parents, that may continue to have an impact on the family now. Each child in the family will respond in their own way to family distress, one may become anxious and withdraw while another is more tense and excitable. The parents may not have realised these reactions until they think about it now, as then they were absorbed in getting through the family crisis.

I am interested, too, in the relationship between siblings and how each of them gets on with their parents. Are these children who can have fun together as well as the usual tussles, or has the rivalry between them made family life hard to endure? The position in the family of the child who is causing concern may have been a crucial factor in his or her development. Sometimes the oldest child is exposed to the most tension between parents, new to their role, and then might feel pushed out by the birth of the next child., The middle child can feel forgotten and the youngest can be bullied or babied by the others. On the positive side, the bond between brothers and sisters can be a strength that helps them survive when the family goes through stressful times, and the caring between them can mitigate the lack of attention by overstretched parents.

Talking to parents about their wider family and social network reveals whether they feel isolated or supported by family and friends. I discovered on a recent parenting course I facilitated that for parents who had recently emigrated here to England for work, that what they regretted most was the loss of their close family, and the community life they had as children. Children often tell us about a grandparent, uncle or cousin who they know they can go to for comfort, or who is a role model who they want to emulate. Relatives living close by can also offer a valuable escape route for teenagers when family life becomes too tense or offer a place to stay as a first step for an anxious young adult scared to leave home.

Taking a history is probably the only time I write notes in a therapy session, so I have the fine details to reflect on later. After the meeting I often draw a timeline for the referred child to make sense of how these events may have shaped development. This can be enlightening when you first observe a child's play:

> In her first assessment session, a young girl created a desolate scene in the sand tray, an empty place with a single tree, a half-buried caravan, and a bus turned upside down. There was a lone figure, but he was almost buried in the sand. I asked about the story and she said it was about a time 'a long time ago'. She told me that the half-buried figure was hiding from enemies. To me, her play suggested a trauma 'a long time ago', when she was little. I was able to put this together with the parents' description of how overwhelmed they had both been when their second child, a son, was born with cerebral palsy. This girl would have been two years old then. As her play

developed, over the sessions, I thought that the unhappiness this girl was feeling was connected with her feeling that she had lost her mother's love when her younger brother was born so disabled, as her parents were so unhappy and pre-occupied with his care. She imagined she might be responsible for this 'disaster', but she could not forgive her younger brother for coming between her and her mother, and taking away her sense of security and contentment. I did not yet share these ideas with my patient, but making these connections for the parents helped them remember just how distressing that time had been. They understood why their daughter could be so over-sensitive and provocative to her brother and this gave the mother the patience and understanding to work to strengthen her relationship with her daughter over time.

A wise family therapist once said to me, 'Always go back two generations to see how these problems began. The story of grandparents and great grandparents will carry the seeds of the current crisis'. Exploring the parents' history growing up in their families of origin, and their relationships with their parents, can reveal aspects of the parents' own unresolved unhappiness that may still be alive in the family dynamic, transferred across the generations.

There are one or two more questions that I find quite helpful in uncovering these stories. I might ask the parents what their life was like at the age of the child being referred. Parents often surprise me in their responses. Like the carefully dressed, well-spoken mother who described how she was a tearaway as a young person at the age their daughter was presenting difficulties. Her parents were at a loss how to handle her rebellion. Now she also was fearful that her daughter would go off the rails, as she felt she did not have an internal repertoire to handle it, remembering only her parents' helplessness with her.

Another important question I ask now, through hard-earned experience, is whether there is anyone else in the close family who has had emotional or mental health difficulties similar to the referred child. Several times I have found that an uncle, grandparent or cousin had depression or psychotic episodes, and there is an unconscious expectation that one or more of the children of the next generation will be the same. When these unconscious patterns are made evident to the parents, they can think about whether their anxiety has influenced how they have seen and responded to their child's problems.

It may be helpful to think of two broad categories of family problems I have seen. There are those families where the precipitating factors for the young person's distress are fairly clear. There may have been mental or physical illness, trauma and loss in their history and we have to understand how and why this particular child in the family was emotionally touched or damaged by the experience.

The other pattern I meet is parents who are bewildered by the strange young person growing up in their midst, and do not know why or how to help their child. I'm thinking of a young man I saw who had always found peer relationships difficult. He was highly sensitive to any change and struggled with a feeling that he did not fit in this world. The term Asperger's[1] was used to describe his presentation. This young person, like others I have seen, may have had neurological problems and would have been different from birth. Here the child psychotherapy assessment can provide an insight into how the child experiences the world and what difficulties are most troubling Then the task is to help the parents begin to understand the child's perspective and think with the therapist what other expert help their child may need. I would also want to think about their possible disappointment that their child has not fulfilled their hopes and help them consider their anxieties about the future.

None of this would be possible unless we can give the parents some hope that this painstaking exploration will yield results, and they are able gradually to develop trust in the therapist to support them and their child through this uncertain process of change.

Meeting the child for the first time

The first interview is often rich in material as if the child knows, at some level, that this is an opportunity to share long-held anxieties, and I often look back at the first interview and see that much I understood later was evident in the child's communication in that first meeting. It can also be frightening meeting a new therapist, however well the parents prepare their child. Children often expect us to be critical or punitive. Certainly this was Jack's fear when I was asked to see him at the request of his mother, because recently he had become very angry at school and thrown a dustbin lid at another child.

> Jack walked into the therapy room and stood still as if transfixed. He was a sturdy boy, wearing a duffel coat and scarf, about nine years old. I could see he was terrified at the prospect of meeting me, and I knew that we would be unable to talk while he was in such a state. I had put out the Lego bricks and play figures, so I suggested he build something to show me what was on his mind. He carefully chose a Lego figure representing a nurse and put a policeman's helmet on her head. It was clear that he feared I would be like a policewoman, dressed up as a nurse, apparently there to help, but actually there to judge him and maybe punish him too. I put these thoughts into words for him and he nodded silently. I then began to play Winnicott's squiggle game (1968) with him, suggesting that each of us draw a squiggle which the other turns into a picture, a way of starting a 'conversation' between us. Jack turned my squiggle into a bomb shelter. He then drew himself crouched

inside with his hands over his ears. There were bombs crashing on the outside surface of the shelter.

I could see from Jack's drawings that he felt under constant threat of attack. He was eventually able to tell me that he had lived alone with his mother since his parents separated, but his father continued to harass his mother with phone calls, trying to get him to be a go-between. Jack felt caught in the middle of this conflict. I understood now why he covered his ears in that first picture and hid away. He was trying to shut out the war around him, and yet he felt, in some awful way, responsible for his parents' unending arguments and was sure that I would blame him.

Recognising these initial anxieties is the first step in making emotional contact with a new patient. The young person will also be assessing you. Are you safe? Will you be patient and will you try to understand life from their point of view? Similarly, I can feel anxious seeing a new young patient for the first time. I wonder if I will be able to establish a sense of connection that will make it possible for the young person to talk openly about anxieties and concerns. The next step is to make clear how therapy works. As children or teenagers walk into the therapy room, I draw their attention to the drawing or play materials, explaining that these are there for them to use, as sometimes talking may not be their best way of telling me about their problems. I talk about the concerns that have led their parents to seek help, and say we are going to try and understand what has gone wrong and why. I explain that we all do things at times that we don't understand, but, like detectives, we can search for the clues together. To teenagers, I point out that our mind is like an iceberg. Much of it is hidden from our awareness, we can only see the part that emerges on the surface. I explain that we have three sessions together to try and understand these difficulties and see if therapy seems helpful. I also talk about the limits of confidentiality, how much I will share with their parents or carers and why.

In reality, children and teenagers learn about therapy from the experience of these first sessions, how we respond to what they say, how we make links and try and understand. I allow myself to ask questions more directly in this initial assessment phase as there is information I need to know to understand the child's predicament. At first, I encourage the young people to tell me about themselves, what's on their mind. I find that some know exactly what they want to talk about or they turn to the play materials or the paints to create something that will show me what is wrong. Others are more anxious or closed off or reluctant to talk about themselves. Then I may initiate the conversation, as too long a silence can make a child more anxious. I ask a child to draw a picture of the family or suggest we begin a simple game together. My aim is to discover what approach might help this young person feel comfortable in my presence and able to explore problems through activities or discussion.

I hope that by the third session, or sometimes I find I need up to five, we will have moved into a more therapeutic exchange where the young person feels free to come into the therapy room and start the conversation or the play where they wish. By then, I hope to have an idea whether this young person can use psychotherapy or whether some other intervention may be preferable. I make sure the child knows that this is our last meeting in the initial phase, and explain what my observations have been and whether I will be recommending therapy. We discuss the child's view about what should happen next with the assurance that I will take this to the meeting with the parents too.

The family meeting

A family meeting can be valuable when I have met a child three or four times but there is still something I would like to understand about the child's relationships in the family. From working closely with a family therapist, I have come to appreciate how valuable it is to see a prospective patient in the family setting alongside siblings and parents. If this meeting can happen during the assessment phase before you begin your therapeutic work, it is less likely to intrude on the early therapeutic work. Often a child's presenting problems can be seen more clearly, in the context of whole family. You may discover that the referred child's difficulty, say overwhelming anxiety, is evident in other members of the family, like one of the parents. This child may be highly sensitive to any concerns that arise, being aware of this vulnerability in the parent, so the increase in the child's level of worry becomes like a barometer for the family's well-being. Similarly, the anger or distress that the young person has expressed in the sessions may be voiced by others in the family too. Brothers and sisters in these meetings often reveal what has led to the current crisis and they can often bring a different perspective on the family dynamic, and the strains in the family as a whole.

Ideally, I meet the family with a co-worker, so we can share ideas and observations about the family. If there is a colleague who has agreed to support the parents, then this is an ideal opportunity to begin working together. Sometimes the parents refuse the option of a co-worker, or no one is available, so I have to work alone. Then I still adopt the more directive family therapy approach in this meeting, as the family are usually less anxious if they are given a clear structure to help them approach the problems together. I would begin by asking the family to introduce themselves or each other and to clarify why we have met, but then there are two techniques that I have found helpful.

The first is to suggest to the family that they draw a family tree over two or three generations, and we use it to look at family patterns that have developed over this time, to see if they shed some light on the problem the child you are seeing faces now. It is useful to get the children to draw the tree and ask the parents to tell them the names of their relatives and the facts about their past.

This way the parents end up telling the children about their family history and the children can ask unexpected but helpful questions.

The other approach is to focus on the immediate problem directly, like the issue of angry outbursts, but suggest it's a family dilemma, and get everyone's ideas on how it has developed and what can be done about it. What is important is to focus on the problem as belonging to the whole family, rather than the individual child you are seeing, so the young person is not seen as 'the problem'.

If I am working with a colleague, we tell the family that we will be taking five minutes out about 40 minutes into the session, so we have some time to think about their issues and give feedback to the family. This gives us an opportunity to make sense of the interactions and frame a thoughtful response before the session finishes. It also gives the family a brief time to talk together about any issues they wish to raise before the session ends. I don't have the benefit of this type of reflection if I am working alone until I discuss the work in supervision.

To give a flavour of an initial session, I will describe a brief excerpt from an initial family meeting I had with a co-worker. The parents were concerned about a young teenager Susan who, they said, bullied her nine-year-old sister, Anna. She had recently trashed her sister's room. Seeing the family together gave me a different perspective on Susan's problems.

> In the family meeting, we asked Anna, the younger sister, to tell us her views on the family difficulties. She described playing out with her sister and having fun, a much more positive view than we expected. It was clear that she had a warmer relationship with Susie than her parents realised. She admitted she got fed up with Susie's tempers, but she thought that Susie got most stressed when her parents were tense, particularly when they worked too hard. They were both pharmacists and worked long hours. It seemed that Susie had become the barometer of the family's anxiety and anger. Although she needed help to manage her moods and impulsivity, we suggested in our feedback that part of the problem was that the parents were exhausted, and it would help if they could create time to relax and take time out as a family. This insight changed my perception of Susie's problems and also allowed her to see that I understood her behaviour was part of the family dynamic as well as struggling with her own issues.

Making an assessment

Assessing the child's development

Anna Freud's discussion of developmental lines in her book *Normality and Pathology in Childhood* (1989 [1965]) is a helpful guide to thinking about how the child is progressing in key aspects of development, like becoming independent, caring for the body, playing and learning. This development is not a straightforward chronological process. The child may mature at different rates, socially, intellectually, physically and emotionally, and this uneven pattern can create difficulties in coping with life. Your assessment will need to consider how a child is developing in these different parameters, and whether there are areas of development where the child might need additional help.

Arriving at a formulation

Making an assessment is like putting together pieces of a jigsaw from the different observations you and others have made of the child or adolescent to build a picture of the young person's emotional life and experience of the outside world. This will include your observations of the young person as revealed in psychotherapy as well as his or her view about life and the family. Alongside this are the parents' views, the family history, the child's development in that family, and how the child is perceived outside the home, in school or with friends. These different aspects always have to be viewed in the social and cultural context of the family's life. What is impinging on the family from outside that is adding pressures on their life together or creating divisions between them? It is fascinating how these different perceptions of the child's life combine together or jar with each other, as you try to reach an initial hypothesis about what is underlying the child's presenting problems.

When working on a paediatric team in a hospital, I had to consider how early life experiences and the child's emotional state influenced the progress of a child's illness.

I was asked to see a child by the medical team where it seemed likely that stress in the child and the family were exacerbating a physical illness.

> Martha, aged six, was referred as she suffered from severe eczema which often led to periods of hospitalisation. She was referred for psychotherapy by the medical team because it seemed that her skin disease got worse when she became stressed and unhappy, but the cause of her distress was unclear. In other ways, her development was good. She was a clever girl and she had friends. Her drawings in the three assessment sessions with me showed her terrible anxiety about being attacked. In her pictures, she was surrounded by aggressive aliens and she defended herself with every type of weapon possible. My immediate thought was that she felt as if her body was being attacking her from within when the eczema flared up. Family meetings led by the social worker revealed that there were emotional pressures on the child too. The mother was vulnerable. She had been abused as an adolescent and was fiercely protective of her children, whilst also being intolerant of them expressing any anger towards her.

I met the mother and hearing her history led me to re-evaluate my focus on Martha's physical illness as the cause of her terror. I began to wonder how much she had identified with her mother's distress and fear, which she was unable to separate from her own anxiety. Any feelings of anger or anxiety towards her mother became a threat to their relationship, so they had to be suppressed, and they were held in her body where they exacerbated her skin disease.

Clearly all these elements, physical illness, emotional distress and family history, were important in thinking about this girl, as well as her developmental stage. At six, she would be desperate for ownership of her body and eager to explore the outside world, which her illness had undermined. I recommended weekly psychotherapy for Martha, as I felt she would benefit from a therapeutic relationship where she could work on these difficult feelings outside the family. In psychotherapy, she could work through these feelings in play and later in words. This would reduce Martha's need to use bodily somatic defences to deal with her anxiety, and this may prevent such severe attacks of eczema. The mother was also offered individual psychotherapy, so she could have help with her own distress, and separate her historical fears from her anxiety about her daughter's illness now.

Creating an assessment framework

A therapeutic assessment framework is a helpful structure to come to a formulation or hypothesis about a young person. Over time, it becomes second nature to think within certain parameters when writing an assessment, including the child's internal life, the external world, the family and social context, and recommendations for future help. The assessment outline may be determined by your work setting, and often there is a formal meeting with parents where your conclusions and recommendations are shared. This can be a valuable process for parents who will need time to think through the implications of your assessment for their child and themselves, before deciding the next step. I sometimes follow a similar process in private work, writing down my initial assessment so that parents are able to take it away and mull over the issues. There are so many aspects to think about when assessing children and teenagers that this is an area of work that will develop and deepen as you become more experienced as a psychotherapist.

Starting the work

Child psychotherapists often face a difficult time beginning treatment after an assessment, Children may talk openly about anxieties in those first weeks and then withdraw and stop talking. The drawings, the discussions and the stories dry up, a defensive response by the young person to the prospect of opening up further about painful topics. Often, this does not seem a conscious process, but the psychotherapist may then be faced with weeks of angry avoidance or dumb misery. The challenge is how to re-establish therapeutic contact with the young person faced with this anxiety about change.

In reality, the feelings in the room at this time, often not verbalised, may be the ones that the youngster has been struggling with for months or years, and has never put into words. The young person may be too distressed or angry to believe that anyone can really help or care. Taken this way, as a communication to us rather than a rejection of our help, it is easier to survive the feeling that one has nothing to offer. I recall this experience with a young woman I will call Jackie.

> Jackie, aged 12, had a facial disfigurement since becoming badly scarred in an accident several years earlier. She was referred to me when I worked as a child psychotherapist in CAMHS, a child and adolescent community mental health team, because she had become so uncommunicative, and avoided social contact. Jackie hid her face from me behind her coat in the first months of therapy, while I tried to talk to her about her unhappiness and her disbelief that I could help her. This finally led to some activity. She made some drawings that she pushed towards me. They were cruel caricatures of her and me, clearly annotated. I was the 'the-rapist' stabbing her with words, and she was an alien cartoon figure looking towards me with derision. I found myself writing brief notes back to her, the beginning of our conversation, acknowledging what I thought she felt and feared, and showing her that I would try not to intrude but be there to listen to her. Our exchange slowly led to some more humorous sketches, a lightening of her depression and the beginning of an exchange in words. She let me know how lonely she was and how she avoided being with other young people at school because she could not bear them to look at her disfigured face and feel sorry for her. Developing a relationship with me gradually enabled Jackie to take risks elsewhere and she began to relate to others more easily.

If the child psychotherapist persists with a will to establish a therapeutic contact with the young person, while recognising the anxiety this evokes, usually it is possible to find a way to explore painful issues together. But it is a slow process and it may have to be the child psychotherapist who holds the hope for the young person that change is possible during this time of despair.

Anxiety and disruptive behaviour in the early sessions

One of the anxieties of a new psychotherapist is how to work with a young person who becomes disruptive or very distressed early on in the work. The assessment sessions should help clarify whether a child, who has been impulsive or aggressive in the past, can manage psychotherapy safely. However, sometimes the early sessions are fairly calm and the child does not become angry or very upset until she or he is more intensely involved in the therapeutic work. With experience, it becomes easier to recognise early on the signs that a child is becoming very anxious, over-excited or provocative and needs help to calm down. Putting these feelings into words so they can begin to be talked about may help the young patient tolerate these feelings so they don't get out of hand. Setting clear boundaries and limits to behaviour also brings a sense of safety. It is important to be sensitive about what you say in the early months of work, as you will not know yet how your comments will be perceived by the child, and whether certain feelings and memories will trigger an emotional response.

If a child becomes excitable or challenging and I am worried that the destructive or over-excited play is escalating, I stop the activity or if absolutely necessary stop the session for a short time and take the child back to the waiting room to the parent or carer waiting . I know I cannot think clearly if I am anxious about getting hurt or losing control of the session. I discovered during my CAMHS work with several aggressive children that a painful kick makes me angry, and it is hard to manage my feelings as well as the child's fury. I learnt my first two lessons about the importance of saying 'No' early on, from a lively angry lad who flooded the therapy room with water from the small basin in the room, showing me just how out of control he got when he was angry. My supervisor suggested I interrupt the child's play if he was about to repeat the performance next session. I explained that I saw how he felt the first time, and he did not have to repeat it for me to understand. Instead, we should think about what made him so cross. I also learnt to help this boy manage his feelings better when he got angry and started to throw things, by asking how I could help him calm down, rather than saying: 'Do not throw that!' The first, more ego supportive comment supported the boy's wish not to hurt me, rather than connecting with his fury and his impulse to make me hurt too. It worked, and I have used it many times since as a tactic when I have felt under threat.

However, it is preferable if you are able to anticipate such difficult moments by making sure there aren't sharp scissors or metal objects in the room that can be thrown, if you are feeling nervous about a child's impulsiveness. I always do a quick check of the therapy room before a session to make sure that the drawers and windows are safely locked, telephones put away and computers safely kept at a distance if I have a quick-fingered child in the room. It is difficult to think if you are always trying to keep an eye on your safety and the child's. Similarly, if you fear a child may run off, you can ask for parent or helper to sit outside the room until the child becomes more settled in psychotherapy.

Of course, one hopes that interpretations, and putting feelings into words, will help reduce the need for the young person to act out in this way, but it is not always enough. Managing one's own anxiety and anger is a key aspect of this work. Talking through such difficult sessions afterwards in supervision is a relief as it gives us the emotional distance needed to understand our responses to the children, and to tease out the underlying causes of the child's behaviour.

Note

1 Asperger syndrome (AS), also known as Asperger's, is a developmental disorder characterised by significant difficulties in social interaction and non-verbal communication, along with restricted and repetitive patterns of behaviour and interests. As a milder autism spectrum disorder (ASD), it differs from other ASDs by relatively normal language and intelligence.

References

Freud, A. (1989 [1965]) *Normality and Pathology in Childhood: Assessments of Development*. London: Karnac.

Gibbs, I. (2009) Reflections on race and culture in therapeutic consultation and assessment. In A. Horne and M. Lanyado (eds) *Through Assessment to Consultation*, pp. 93–102. London: Routledge.

Winnicott, D.W. (1968) The squiggle game. *Voices: The Art and Science of Psychotherapy* 4(1): 299–316.

Chapter 4

Approaches to child psychotherapy with children of different ages

In this chapter, I will explore how we adapt our technique to the emotional needs of the child, through the stages of development, as the young person becomes more self-aware and perceptive of others, and begins to separate from the family and develop independent skills. Aspects of therapy remain the same. As Winnicott says:

> Psychotherapy has to do with two people playing together. The corollary of this is that where playing is not possible then the work done by the therapist is directed towards bringing the patient from a state of not being able to play into a state of being able to play.
>
> (1971b: 38)

We do this by offering a therapeutic relationship, a place to recover and understand what has gone wrong, to put feelings and thoughts into words so they can be thought about and integrated.

As young people gain confidence and a clearer sense of self as a result of the work in psychotherapy, their spontaneity and humour often returns and this allows them to relate more easily to their peers and family members. Our aim is to help the young person get back on the track where the thrust of ordinary developmental processes and family life will carry them through. Margot Waddell (2006) talks about the importance of the child's resilience, and I think that is what we are attempting to enhance. What changes through this development is how we use ourselves in the therapeutic relationship to meet the child's needs.

In the early years, we actively create a therapeutic space where the young child discovers how to communicate with us through play and interaction, often non-verbal, as the child may not yet have the capacity to put feelings into words. We are alert to the feelings we experience in the room with the child, and the clues these give us about the child's emotional state. In the relationship we offer, we respond to the child's need for two aspects of ourselves, a maternal reverie and paternal boundaries to facilitate this process and create a safe, stable setting. With the older child, the focus may be more on the emergence in the clinical material of unresolved early traumas and conflicts which have undermined the child's capacity to manage behaviour and relationships. As children grow, there is a clearer sense of the self and a defensive structure. As discussed earlier, these defences were self-protective responses once, when children were frightened or overwhelmed, but they can become rigid and limiting. Finally, in adolescence, the therapeutic relationship can be a safe place which the young person can use to explore problems and gain support in the process of finding a sense of self and separating from the family.

Thinking about the child's stage of development is a guide, but only that, as every young person develops at a different pace, and so often we see an uneven picture. A child who is intellectually and socially competent may feel quite fragile inside, covering up an immature emotional self, perhaps due to deprivation in infancy. The cognitive, social, emotional and physical aspects of the self develop and interact, creating the child's unique sense of self, and particular strengths and vulnerabilities.

With each young person, it is worth considering if there are particular creative materials that might interest them for their therapy box or file, alongside the usual play materials. We can never quite predict what will capture children's imagination, or what play materials they may use to recall earlier significant times of their life. One lad aged seven, whom I saw for psychotherapy, slipped between using Duplo toddler building bricks or Lego construction pieces, depending on his emotional state each week. He might become like a little toddler building a house with Duplo, or use Lego to become a young discoverer flying off in his plane. Each story met a different emotional need within him. The child psychotherapist responds flexibly to the changing emotional time frame suggested by the child's play. This way, the therapist is able to follow the child's intuitive exploration to make sense of what has gone wrong, and repair areas of unmet need.

The child's use of us as a psychotherapist may be as a paternal or maternal developmental figure, whatever our gender. Here, I am using 'maternal' to describe those qualities in us that are emotionally containing and nurturing, while 'paternal' describes the much-needed boundaries and assertive aspects of the therapist, holding one's own against the child's aggression or manipulation. The need for a clear therapeutic setting and boundary is relevant throughout the age range, although increasingly the young person may be able to internalise this structure and set boundaries for him- or herself.

Establishing boundaries provides a clear frame for the therapy, but at times, we may choose to cross these lines if we feel this may help the child. The usual rule is that the child's work and play materials must stay in the therapy room to protect the child's work and confidentiality, but also to separate the therapeutic setting from the child's daily life. However, sometimes, it may be helpful to allow the child to take something home from the session if there is a need hold on to something from therapy to ease the separation at a particularly vulnerable time in the treatment, or to share an important achievement with a parent.

The next four sections explore approaches to therapeutic work with the developing child, with key concepts that I have found helpful.

Parent–infant psychotherapy

As child psychotherapists in training, we observe the development of a baby over the first two years of the baby's life. Our weekly hour-long visits are written up in great detail for discussion later in seminars. We learn skills in observation, developing our understanding of both the baby and the mother's state of mind as the baby develops and their relationship grows. We also learn to reflect on our emotional responses, our changing counter-transference reactions to the baby's minute-by-minute responses to his new life. We draw on these observational skills throughout our work, but particularly in parent–infant psychotherapy. Our technique of intervention begins with this type of observation.

Therapeutic work with parents and infants is focused on building a relationship between parent and infant, observing the subtle, non-verbal communication between them. In this section I refer mainly to the mother as the key figure in the baby's life, for ease of discussion, but these ideas will be relevant to the father, grandparent, foster parent or another key figure offering this important early relationship to the infant.

A child psychotherapist can feel deskilled meeting a distressed mother and her crying baby for the first time in therapy, not knowing how to help. Yet we can offer a calm supportive presence which helps the mother find a way to understand her anxiety and comfort the baby. By observing closely, the therapist can assess the quality of the parent–infant relationship, seeing how the baby relates to the mother, how the mother responds and the quality of the relationship that is developing between them. If the father comes too, his presence will complete the picture, adding the extra dimensions of his responses to the baby and to his partner in her new role as a mother.

Our understanding of how parent and infant mutually contribute to their developing relationship, and become attuned to each other, has been informed by the work of child development researchers like Daniel Stern (1985) in the USA and Professor Colwyn Trevarthen (2014) in Scotland. Trevarthen has spent many years observing and videoing parent–infant interaction. His research shows that from the beginning the baby has a sense of self. The baby is 'relationship-seeking', trying to communicate, and there is a rhythm to this interaction. In a fascinating video of a tiny premature baby boy tucked inside his father's coat, (from a Channel 4 documentary *Baby Love* sadly not available now) Trevarthen shows how even a premature baby 'talks' to his father, leaving gaps for the father's response. He suggests that this rhythm of interaction is the channel for emotional communication, for mother or father and infant to feel close. He describes how the tiny premature infant has 'a space in his mind' for another person.

As Trevarthen says, sometimes parents don't realise their babies are talking to them. Then they miss out on the baby's cues and they don't understand what the baby wants and needs. Often these are parents who have not had the experience of sensitive parenting themselves as infants, so these types of responses do not come intuitively. I have seen parents who are over-active, overwhelming their baby, and others who are unresponsive, not seeing the baby's attempts to reach out to them. In our therapeutic work, we can help parents recognise these patterns and find this emotional closeness if we can develop a trusting relationship that makes it possible for them to accept our support.

I have written in detail about this work in a chapter 'The capacity to be alone' (2006). There I show how we can help parents develop this attunement. They can learn to observe and follow their baby's cues in their 'conversations' with them, leaving the baby space to think and respond. Usually, their baby is delighted by the parents' more sensitive interaction, and the infant's positive response gives the parents courage to persevere, although they may feel awkward at first, worried they will get it wrong. I always found it reassuring that according to Tronick's research (1986) we often 'get it wrong' as parents, and misinterpret the baby's response the first time. A high percentage of our interactions are faulty, and the infant has coping strategies to correct them, signalling to the parent or averting his eyes. Then the parent adjusts and gets it right. It is this capacity to make good, and to persevere, that builds resilience in parent–infant relationships.

Beatrice Beebe used video-feedback research to observe how mothers and infants are continually self-regulating their responses to each other, as their relationship develops:

> It is a 'co-constructed' process in which each partner makes moment-by-moment adjustments in response to the other's shifts in behaviour such as gaze, facial expression, orientation, touch, vocal quality, and body and vocal rhythms.
>
> (Beebe 2005)

She applies these ideas to parent–infant psychotherapy showing how video feedback can be used to help a mother become more sensitive to her baby's cues by watching these recordings of minute-by-minute interactions between herself and the baby.

Parents may ask for help because they are anxious about their baby not feeding well, sleeping poorly or crying too much, but the underlying issue will often be their wish for help in understanding their relationship with their new baby. The baby's arrival can evoke powerful feelings of excitement, joy and anxiety in new parents, and they can feel totally out of their depth. A brief intervention can sometimes be enough. Dilys Daws describes her work at a GP baby clinic (Daws 1999) talking to worried parents. She shows that problems posed by parents sometimes represent deeper emotional conflicts, yet the current difficulties can often be resolved in a few meetings. She helps the parents recognise that their own emotional issues are intruding, so they can find a different response when their baby is distressed. For example, a mother sees her baby crying and feels it is her fault, because she lacks self-confidence in herself as a mother, when in reality the baby is just signalling to her the need for a feed.

In this section, I will explore both shorter- and longer-term approaches to parent–infant psychotherapy, beginning with the important first meeting.

The first meeting

Meeting a mother and baby for the first time, I encourage the mother to tell me about her experience of caring for her baby, her worries and what she enjoys. While in conversation, I am watching the baby, maybe during a feed, seeing how the mother holds the baby, talks and listens for a response. I observe how the whole experience feels to me. Does the baby snuggle in close, watch mother while feeding, maybe reaching tenderly for her necklace or her shirt? These affectionate contented moments feel very different from observing an anxious baby whose body is held rigid, who maybe arches away from the mother's body, or lies feeding with eyes closed or only opened briefly. My impression is that the anxious baby cannot relax and has to hold him- or herself together, during a feed. Then I wonder what has led to the baby's anxiety. Is it just a bad day, or is feeding always that difficult? Are the mother and her baby always unsure of each other? Has it been difficult for the mother to build up a feeling of closeness to the baby from birth? Was the birth and the following months a difficult time? Exploring these thoughts with the mother, I note how available she is to thinking about the stresses in her relationship with her infant, and this will be some guide as to what type of intervention to offer at this time.

Parents usually have some fear of criticism and judgement when they come for help, feeling they have failed in some way. In this crisis, some parents allow you close, while others cannot bear to feel so exposed and it is hard to gain their trust. These more anxious parents may find it easier to allow themselves to receive help among others in a supported nursery setting, like that offered in many family centres. Here being part of a group of parents can feel less personal and persecuting, and parents gain help from being with others going through these early difficult months of parenthood.

One factor I have found to be crucial in shaping parents' self-confidence is whether they have support from their own family or friends or feel isolated. Mothers whose own mothers have died, or were absent or critical, often struggle the most, longing for maternal care and support with the new baby. It was as if the absence of this mother figure undermines the mother's belief in herself. As parent–infant therapists, we can sometimes help fill the gap, if our help is accepted as 'grandmother substitute'. Then, we can become an important source of support to both mother and baby through this early vulnerable time.

Short-term therapy with depressed or vulnerable parents

Unlike the brief intervention in the health clinic described by Daws, some parents may need several weeks or months of parent–infant psychotherapy, particularly if a mother has suffered from post-natal depression after the baby's birth. Research by Lyn Murray as far back as 1996 showed how brief input of only two months' counselling by health visitors with depressed mothers in the first year of the baby's life can help mothers recover a good relationship with their infants, with a good long-term outcome. There are now many parent–infant services developed by health visitors, nurses and child psychotherapists offering this type of brief intervention in UK.

I have found that, with brief therapeutic input, a mother is often able to gain confidence in her mothering, and the baby responds. Being alongside as a therapist, I can draw the mother's attention to what is happening between her and her baby, both positive and negative. Together we observe how the baby looks up. I encourage her to smile, to win the baby over, and suggest a gentle stroke is more comforting than anxious rocking. A baby boy who turned away and could not settle in his mother's arms, quickly recovered when his mother began to greet him warmly and gently. He was gradually able to relax and discover he was safe with her now, and their relationship grew. Using video feedback can be helpful here, and it is easy to do with the iPad or smartphone. When I showed one young mother a five-minute video which I took in the session with her agreement, she was totally surprised when she saw how often she missed her baby's attempts to get her attention and she became more responsive. She was young, impulsive but loving, and with this type of help, she discovered how to become more in touch with what her baby son needed from her.

Parent–infant psychotherapy with a couple

When parents arrive as a couple with their baby, the therapist works with the triangular relationship between them and the baby. It is interesting to observe who reaches out for the baby who cries, whether the parents are able to support each other or if there is competition for the baby's attention. Helping competent fathers stand back and support their anxious partners, rather than intervene, can be important if the mother lacks confidence. Equally important is encouraging the father to step in and offer to take the baby, giving respite to the mother, when the demands on her become too much. Attachment research shows that babies can have a very different attachment style with each parent.

The infant may be calm and content with one parent, and excited and anxious with another. This difference can be vital to protecting an infant's safety, when one parent, say the mother, is mentally ill. The presence of the involved father can sustain the baby emotionally and physically until the mother recovers and is once again able to take on the primary care of her baby.

Longer-term parent–infant psychotherapy: a holding relationship

Psychotherapy lasting for many months may be needed by parents whose lives have been emotionally troubled since childhood. Selma Fraiberg and the Infant Mental Health team pioneered this work in the USA. In her influential paper 'Ghosts in the nursery', Selma Fraiberg describes how the arrival of a new baby brings in ghosts from the past for us all:

> In every nursery, there are ghosts. They are visitors from the unremembered past of the parents; the uninvited guests at the christening. Under all favourable circumstances the unfriendly and unbidden spirits are banished from nursery and return to their subterranean dwelling place. The baby makes his own imperative claim upon parental love and, in its strict analogy with the fairytales, the bonds of love protect the child and his parents against the intruders, the malevolent ghosts.
>
> (Fraiberg et al. 1975)

However, for those parents who have experienced early trauma, or neglectful or abusive parenting, memories of these early experiences can intrude on their daily care of their child. A crying baby, who turns away, can evoke feelings of distress and rejection in the struggling mother who finds she cannot comfort her child, because she feels overwhelmed by her own feelings of deprivation. Early memories of her own unhappy infancy return, which have remained hidden from awareness until now. The 'ghosts' in these memories become like hostile internal figures haunting her. In those moments, the baby can become a persecutory figure evoking anger in the mother. She can feel frightened and out of control, fearful she will hurt the baby, and desperate for help with the feelings.

For these distressed parents, longer-term parent–infant psychotherapy can be invaluable, although this work by the child psychotherapist will need the involvement of a professional network because of the vulnerability of the parents and the risks to the infant. They can arrange for parents to receive additional family support during the day or a residential mother–baby unit. Ideally, the parents will be offered help with the daily care of the baby whose development can be monitored, alongside therapeutic input for themselves and their infants. I will describe parent–infant psychotherapy with one mother, Mary, from my work as a child psychotherapist at an inpatient family service at the Cassel Hospital (Dowling 2006).

There is a risk that parents who have suffered abuse will re-enact their history in the present relationship with their infant. Selma Fraiberg's work showed that those parents who are helped by psychotherapy to get in touch with the suffering they faced as a child can use this understanding to protect their own infant: 'It is only when a parent is emotionally in touch with her painful early memories of abuse and neglect, that she can be empathic and protective to her child, and prevent herself repeating these patterns' (Fraiberg et al. 1975).

> Mary, an older mother, had experienced a lifetime of difficulties but outwardly she coped well. She was referred due to her concern that she would not bond with her baby, and I was fortunate to meet her a few times before the birth. Her baby was born in a local maternity unit and the hospital staff were very concerned at the mother's lack of responsiveness to her baby when I visited her at the hospital. The baby was a few days old.
>
> When I arrived, both mother and infant were distressed. Mary told me she could not make herself look at her baby son in the cot alongside, or reach out to comfort him. She did not seem aware that he was looking at her through the plastic side of the cot, longing for contact. She told me that she knew she was not responding well to her baby, but she was scared she would not be able to meet his needs. The birth had been a shock as she felt she was not prepared for the baby emotionally, and his vulnerability terrified her. She was desperate for me to know just how awful she had found the first few days. My familiar presence helped. As we talked, she calmed, so did the baby. I could see the baby watching his mother through the sides of the cot, seeking a response from her. After some time, the mother relaxed, and with encouragement, she was able to take her son in her arms and look at him with some warmth, enjoying the close contact, maybe for the first time.
>
> Mary found her baby's vulnerability and neediness alarming. It evoked helpless feelings from her infancy when she was in the care of her drug-dependent mother who neglected her. Her childhood deprivation meant she had no internal map of motherhood to follow. It was like a foreign language she would have to discover, painfully, step by step with her baby. I realised it was not her resistance to caring that was getting in the way, or a fear of failure, but her inability to make contact with her baby in the simplest way; looking, holding, being there. She was relieved to have my support with her anxiety and anger at feeling so helpless in these early days, until she felt safer in this new relationship with her baby. Fortunately, this mother had the close support of her nurse in the mother–baby unit where I worked, and her own adult psychotherapist, who were both vital in helping her feel understood and contained. Mary was able to return home with her baby, feeling more confident in the loving

relationship she had established with him, knowing support was available in her community if she needed it.

As these clinical examples show, in parent–infant psychotherapy there is a triangular relationship, the presence of the psychotherapist offers a third person to reflect with the mother on her relationship with her baby. Within the sessions, we offer an emotionally holding relationship, where there is space to reflect together on how mother and baby are getting to know and understand each other.

Working with toddlers and children under five years

Selma Fraiberg (1996 [1950]) coined the phrase 'the magic years' to describe this phase of childhood when small children move between a passionate and curious interest in the real world, and their imaginative life of fantasy and magical thinking. She stressed the complexity of their emotional lives as they strive for independence and new skills. Their emotions can rapidly change from delight to despair, thoughtfulness to annoyance and frustration. These emotional upheavals can seem inexplicable to their parents, because young children show us through their behaviour, rather than tell us what is wrong. Toddlers' behaviour can trigger equally powerful emotions in their parents, who may find themselves suddenly furious or in despair with their toddler, as if mirroring these powerful feelings. In joint parent–toddler psychotherapy, parents can be helped to make sense of their toddler's behaviour and communication, and understand better what is happening in their relationship together.

A frequent concern is the toddler's anxiety about separation from the mother, which may become particularly intense at bedtimes. Encouraging the father to help with this separation by offering support and setting clear boundaries, when the toddler needs to sleep, can be helpful. This may be a harder task for a single parent mother to manage on her own, and the support and involvement of others, like grandparents, can reduce the intensity of these times. Similarly, the first child can feel rejected by the mother with the arrival of the next baby and will be relieved to have another familiar loving adult to turn to, a partner or grandparent, who can provide attention and comfort when the the mother is pre-occupied with the new baby.

Joint therapeutic work with parents and toddlers

Therapeutic work with parents and toddlers together is a development of the approach just described with parents and infants. In joint play sessions, parents are encouraged to play and talk with their toddler, while the child psychotherapist observes their relationship, how the small child plays and behaves, and the parents' response. This can be a hard experience for parents at first, if they are not used to playing and feel self-conscious being observed, but with practice it often gets easier and becomes rewarding. What becomes apparent is that some parents take over and direct the child's play, unused to following a child's lead, while others stand back, finding it difficult to get involved. Deprived or anxious parents, who had never played themselves as children, can find that developing this mutual play with the support of a child psychotherapist becomes a helpful way of developing a closer relationship with their toddler, that can be repeated when they are together at home.

To begin a play session, I encourage the toddler to select some toys from the toy box and suggest the parent sits alongside the child on the floor. I might join them, or stay in my chair while I suggest to the parent a response to the child's cues, to show their interest in the child's game. Meanwhile I talk to the parent about what the child might be communicating in the play with the farm animals, baby doll or toys. Gradually the parent begins to see the play from the child's perspective rather than an adult one. Parents are often totally surprised when they can see the play in this new way and the toddler is delighted to find that the parent is more responsive and interested. Often the theme of the toddler's play relates to some difficulty the child is facing, as exploration through play is how small children solve problems. I recall a father's astonishment when his two-year-old son, Sammy, began showing him in his play how pleased he felt to be spending more time with his father.

> We had been talking about the father's worries about his son earlier in the therapy session, and I knew the little boy was listening. Sammy began cuddling a small doll, then dressing it for bed, before getting on his father's lap and snuggling up to him to sleep. Once the father realised that his son was showing him how he enjoyed these close times together, that Sammy was 'talking' to him through play, it assumed new meaning for him. He felt he could get to know his son better this way

While the parents are playing with the child, I encourage them to tell me about the stressful times at home, maybe getting the child dressed in the morning or managing mealtimes. I know the toddler will be listening closely and will often comment on our discussion or show us a response through play. Then I encourage a three-way conversation, using simple language the child can understand, giving the parent cues to talk to the child about these worries, which the parent often finds easier in this shared arena.

Having time to think and talk about life with their toddler enables parents to make their own sense of why their relationship with their child has become strained at home. Sometimes, this links with their own childhood. A father faced with his child's tantrums, may become frightened of hitting him too hard, remembering how he was hit as a child by his angry father. Then, I might suggest meeting alone with the parents, so the father feels free to explore these feelings about his childhood before returning for another joint session with the child. It is often the therapist's capacity to listen and contain anxiety in this way, that can release the parents' capacity to think and understand these dynamics.

Winnicott's book *Therapeutic Consultations* (1971a) has many fascinating descriptions of such joint parent–child work. As a busy paediatrician and analyst, his sessions combined creative interpretations and practical advice for the parents with playful interventions with the child that opened the door to a different way of seeing things.

Individual psychotherapy with children under five

Once children reach the age of three, they are usually more able to separate from their parents or carers. Then they can often be helped by individual psychotherapy as it provides a safe place to express their feelings of anger and distress away from their parents, and to discover new ways of relating if this has been difficult in the past. In this section, I will discuss three key aspects of therapeutic work with children under five: communicating with small children, managing their difficult behaviour and understanding our relationship with the small child.

Communicating with small children

New child psychotherapists are often anxious about working with small children. They worry about how to talk to such a young child. In practice, small children are often very direct in letting us know what is wrong, through their play and behaviour. The skill is in our ability to tune into their communication, as the relationship develops, and show by our response that we can explore their problems together with them. Much of the child's early communication will be non-verbal. I describe in the vignette below how a small child, Sally, gradually discovered a way of telling me about her difficult life through the medium of play, and she used our therapy sessions to begin resolving her feelings about the loss and abuse that happened to her as an infant.

> Sally was a robust, unsmiling four-year-old who was referred for intensive therapy, three sessions weekly, when I worked in CAMHS, because she was very challenging of her foster parents due to her traumatic early history. It was agreed that she needed this intensive therapy because of her level of emotional deprivation and abuse. She had been sexually abused and neglected in her birth family during the first two years of her life. Sally would only go to sleep at night after a series of rituals: three stories, many kisses and increasing calls for

more. Sally spent many early psychotherapy sessions playing haphazardly with the toys she had collected from the box. She placed these around her as a barrier between us. She seemed lost and unhappy, silently keeping herself busy. She was also unsure how to respond to my expressions of concern about her worries, but she was clearly listening. After a while, there was a slight change in her play as she began naming and sorting the play materials she had gathered around her, while observing me, keeping me at a safe distance. I thought she was trying to create some sense of order in her world in response to my attempts to understand how she might be feeling.

I could not make sense of her early attempts to communicate with me through play which began several sessions later. I remember feeling despair as she tore paper into little pieces, dropping them onto the floor, watching closely for my response. Nothing I said about 'everything falling to pieces' and that 'nothing could be fixed' seemed to have any meaning for her. Finally, one week, she walked into the therapy room with determination and began playing at being Cinderella, the unhappy and neglected princess of fairy stories. Clearly, she had been puzzling between the sessions how to show me what was wrong. In her play-acting as Cinderella, she cleaned the floor, looking very unhappy, watching for my response. I talked about how she must feel, 'Poor Cinderella is doing all the hard work and nobody is noticing her or caring about her.' Later I added, 'Cinderella wanted a prince to come and love her but maybe, in your story, he was not kind.' Sally, relieved, turned and looked at me and said, 'This is a good story'. I think she meant she had found us a shared language for our work, and I felt relieved too. Many months later in the sessions, she replayed aspects of the sexual abuse that had disturbed her, but I realised that it was the experience of sudden loss and rejection by her birth mother and partner that had troubled her most at this time, not the actual abuse. As professionals, I don't think we had recognised this, because the sexual abuse seemed the more shocking.

Sally had discovered a way of talking to me about her past life through symbolic play and we both sensed a working alliance had developed. Her Cinderella play felt like one of those important 'moments of meeting' described by Daniel Stern et al. (1998) when something new takes place that transforms the relationship between patient and therapist and marks a development in therapy.

Each week over the coming months, Sally continued her Cinderella story varying the details, and I was slowly able to link her story with how she had felt when she was very little. I talked simply about how sad she was to lose her mother, and how upset and angry she was that her mother's boyfriend treated her badly.

As our relationship developed, Sally could safely express her frustration and sadness with me, particularly when I had been away on holiday. I did not like Sally in the early months. She was often imperious and bossy, but she softened once we found a way to talk. I could see how sad she was beneath the haughty exterior. She was angry that she could not go back and start her life again, a feeling shared by many children I have seen. These disturbing memories had made it difficult for her to relax and sleep at night and to reach out and play with other children at nursery, but now her need for bedtime rituals reduced, as these past experiences were integrated, and she began to make friends at school.

Unlike Sally, other children actively avoid play or they are too withdrawn to allow themselves to do so. Very depressed or deprived young children do not know how to seek out the emotional warmth they need. As psychotherapists, we have to be both patient and creative with these children to work out how to create a spark of interest in a relationship with us. It may take weeks before we are able to make real emotional contact with them. We have to reach out actively to these children, offering lively, warm interest, responding to any small sign of engagement to draw them out of their depression.

With the silent or withdrawn small child, I might initiate the play, do a drawing, find a simple puzzle, build a brick house, or bring out some animal puppets, trying to find what catches the child's interest. Sometimes, when children do start to play, they prefer to play on their own at a distance, listening and observing as the therapist shows as an interest in what they are doing. It can be hard to keep our attention alive, faced with such reserve, but we have to trust the therapeutic process and give it some time to work. We often do not see the slow process of the ice melting before the child begins to open up to us.

> I remember a little girl, three years old, I was asked to see by her adoptive parents in private practice. She walked awkwardly into my therapy room, her head turned aside, avoiding any eye contact or conversation with me. Her aloofness was distressing but determined. Despite wanting to keep me at a distance, she was interested in my picture books which she looked at, alone in the corner. Eventually, towards the end of the session, she showed me one of the books she liked, and we talked a little about it. After this, each week, she returned and read the same one book, as if establishing a safe ritual for us coming together. Her terror of closeness sat alongside a great curiosity about the world. This was how I understood her awkward side-turned head stance. It enabled her to look but not be looked at. This avoidance lessened as she felt more comfortable in my presence.

These children often engage first with the play materials in my room rather than me, and the toys they choose are not always the ones I expect. I have an ancient polar bear puppet with only one eye, who often interests children the most. I think they identify with his damage and his need for care. Picture book stories about children who are scared at night, or get angry, often interest children as they offer a way of thinking about their own worries, at a safe distance. Other icebreakers are finger puppets, and Russian dolls, the ones that fit inside each other with a baby inside. It's rare that I find a small child who is not tempted to take these dolls apart in order to discover the tiny baby figure inside. Incidentally, I watch closely now as this wooden baby doll is likely to be picked up by some child and slipped into a pocket.

Managing small children's difficult behaviour

The other challenge in working with small children is managing their impulsivity and oppositional behaviour. In contrast to the withdrawn child, there are young ones who are referred for therapy because their feelings spill out when they are overwhelmed, in panic attacks, temper tantrums or they become very disruptive. This difficult behaviour will be re-enacted in psychotherapy, often after a honeymoon period where the child behaves well in sessions while getting to know you. Once the therapeutic relationship develops, and anxieties about separation or control come to the fore, events in the session can suddenly trigger the child's anger or distress, and this can be very challenging.

The child psychotherapist has to be prepared to meet this outpouring of feeling with a mixture of firmness, understanding and sometimes curiosity. It can be helpful to say, as if mystified. 'I wonder what made you so cross just then, did you feel I was laughing at you?' The clear boundaries of therapy are very reassuring. By this I mean the reliability of weekly sessions, your stance as a therapist, trying to understand their behaviour, but also setting limits to their destructiveness. Stopping aggressive behaviour escalating is important. It frightens children if they are allowed to be too destructive and the therapist who is always on the move to keep the child safe cannot reflect on what is happening. If the child is likely to get aggressive, I reduce the play materials to only those that are safe, like the puppets, soft toys, drawing materials and a soft ball, and sharp objects are removed. If children experience their therapist as keeping them both safe from harm, and able to survive their aggression, their anxiety will gradually die down and, with your encouragement, they may be able to show you what's wrong in their play rather than act it out in this way. Ann Horne summarised this process for me: 'the child moves from activity to symbolisation, to play and words, and more play' (personal communication).

Our readiness to tolerate and try to understand small children's passionate and angry feelings is a relief to them as they often fear that they have become too much for those who care for them, and that their hating feelings will wipe out the loving ones in themselves and those that care for them. Their parents, too, may be dismayed by the strength of their small child's reactions and find it hard to set boundaries to help the child manage the angry outbursts. In psychotherapy, these childish feelings can be understood and withstood, but the work can be tiring and demands patience and resilience from the therapist, as the child's capacity to manage behaviour like this may progress slowly, almost imperceptibly over the weeks and months of treatment.

Understanding the therapeutic relationship with the small child

Small children are still very involved with their parents, and aspects of this current relationship will emerge in the transference relationship with you. We have to be careful not to take on an actively parental role, particularly with deprived children who seek this out, wanting physical closeness and practical care. My responses to children in therapy show them that I am only 'a problem solver', helping them think about what is wrong, and my job is to support those who provide the actual care, not take on this role myself. This can be hard for a child who is desperate for more intimacy with me. The child may come up close, seeking the physical comfort of sitting on my lap or asking me for hugs. Then I respond tactfully with warmth, and I offer other ways of finding comfort. I might suggest a child wraps up in a blanket or makes a den to hide in, somewhere in the room. The familiar sound of my voice talking to the child about these feelings can also be reassuring. One ingenious lad lay across my desk in these moments, near me but not on my lap. We both understood his action, without me putting him on the spot by talking about it.

Alongside this need for comfort, the small child will have to deal with a wide range of conflicting feelings in relationship to the therapist. Using our countertransference feelings, we try to make sense of what the small child is expressing and find a way to put it into words. I might say, 'It feels safer hiding away in that corner when you are upset', or 'it gets a bit scary when the cross feelings get too strong', or 'sometimes when you get too excited it's hard to stop'. It is important to identify the negative transference, the child's feelings of hatred, frustration and disappointment with adults, which may feel so unsafe to show at home, but which can safely be expressed in their relationship with the therapist.

Some of these feelings will be a normal part of their development. At this age, as the Oedipal phase sets in, small children can become passionately involved and possessive of their parents of the opposite sex, and quite rejecting to the same sex parent, or possessive of both, determined to get between them. When parents assert their right to be together as a couple, the small child can feel furious at the apparent exclusion, yet it is important for children to see their parents as a loving couple, and this helps them separate and begin to seek out their own interests elsewhere.

Through the child's play, many anxiety-provoking experiences can be worked through at a safe emotional distance in displacement. We may be given the role of the angry witch who always punishes children or we become the victim of a harsh teacher who hates naughty children. We have to play these roles with moderation, voicing the child's fears but never letting the play break down because it gets too scary. Here, the play is in the transitional space (1953), as Winnicott describes, understood by the child to be both real and not real, interlinking the external and internal worlds of the child. Children need us to keep limits to their play and manage their anxiety, so they are able to return next session without fear that the feelings will get too much to bear. Through these interactions, often repeated for many sessions, these stories become a way of processing feelings that have remained stuck and inhibited the child's curiosity and ability to make relationships.

Therapy with the younger school-aged child: latency

> Latency is battening down the hatches on the impulsivity of toddler-hood and being babyish – learning, mastering, leaving all that behind! Developmentally the child's thrust, therefore, is anti-therapy, anti- any challenging of the carefully constructed defences.
>
> (Ann Horne, personal communication)

Children of this age feel frustrated when we ask them to tell us what is happening or what they feel in therapy. They want us to understand them without having to spell things out. The early passions and the open expressiveness of the toddler and the young child often disappear as they move into the next phase of development. This is called latency in psychoanalytic thinking, and lasts from around five years of age to puberty. The transition to school and life outside the home can be challenging for children, particularly if their early years have been troubled and their development delayed. They may struggle with the demands on this age group: learning in school, making friends, developing new skills and managing conflict in their relationships. As child psychotherapists, we often see children whose anxiety about separation from their parents, or feelings of failure and inadequacy, may be masked by angry outbursts or an inability to concentrate at school or make friends.

This is an age, too, when parents or the school might seek help for a child who has caused concern for several years but is now too challenging to manage, and they are worried about the future. Some children we see may be more reserved.

They may have been assessed as having developmental difficulties like autism, ADHD, or they have learning difficulties that have impeded their social and emotional development and their capacity to make close relationships. Then child psychotherapy can offer an opportunity for children to understand these anxieties and learn to manage their particular vulnerabilities.

Latency children have a rich imaginative life but they are often highly defended from exploring these thoughts, so therapy can create a real conflict for the child. Their wish to feel better is set against a fear of exploring painful feelings that may be revealed in their play. Our technique is adapted to this. We work at the child's pace, recognising these anxieties but also staying focused on trying to understand the underlying problems. We make it evident that we believe there is a meaning to the young person's behaviour that we can discover together to help make life more manageable.

In this section, I will look at four aspects of therapy with this age group: establishing a working alliance, discovering the problem, thinking about delinquent and disruptive behaviour, and the work of exploration and consolidation.

Establishing a working alliance

Young schoolchildren will have built up a pattern of defences, a 'way of being', to deal with their anxieties. The prospect of change in therapy can feel like a threat to this equilibrium, so it can take time to build up a therapeutic alliance. Hiding in their shell or starting a fight may not improve the child's self-confidence, but it brings immediate relief to any threat posed to them.

By this age, children will have established an attachment style and an internal model of life from their earlier life experiences and relationships, and any new relationship will be perceived at first within this framework. The child psychotherapist may be expected to behave like a critical teacher, or a mocking adversary. In the early period of treatment, I will try to discover the child's fears about working with me. A child who is expecting ridicule will naturally hide his drawings or his play, and I will respect this. A shy child will flounder unless I start to play and invite the child to join in. The skill is to offer just enough input to help the child gain the confidence to play or talk, and then do only what is needed to encourage this to continue. If we contribute too much, the play will not reveal the child's inner world, but the expectation of what we might be looking for.

Developing themes – discovering the problem

Once a child has established a mode of 'play', and a way of communicating with the therapist, this pattern often becomes part of their shared interaction for many weeks, as I found with Steven.

Steven, an anxious eight-year-old, found the start of each session so difficult. He would always ask to play two or three games of hide and seek to help him manage these uncomfortable moments. Once I had 'found' him in his hiding place a few times, usually with some humour and exaggerated concern that 'I had lost him for ever', he relaxed and felt more comfortable. This was his way of processing the feelings of anxiety and relief that accompanied every separation, and his fear that I would not be the same on his return. Steven also began to use this game as an escape from deadening moments in therapy, when he did not know what to do. Then I had to negotiate hard to keep these games to a limit, so Steve could not avoid us thinking about these difficult moments and what they were about. He insisted that he should have extra hiding games after a holiday break and I agreed, showing him that I understood that dealing with his mixed annoyance and relief about my return after a long gap did make the first session back harder to manage.

As the children's play develops over the sessions, it reveals their deeper concerns. Some scenarios may be reality based, problems at school with friends, or siblings at home, heightened by unconscious anxieties. Others may show symbolically the fears and fantasies in the child's mind. You may be invited by the child to join a role play about a child in school with a harsh teacher, sit and observe the construction of a Lego castle under attack from an enemy, watch a prisoner trapped in a cell or see an alien landing on a hostile planet. These characters represent the child's inner world in a fantasy form and it is through these characters that you will be able to begin to make links for them with their underlying fears and conflicts, and what is upsetting them now.

Some of these stories are a clear communication to the therapist about what is on the child's mind. Diana created a story in her therapy sessions as a way of talking to me about her hopes and fears at the prospect of living with her mother again, after a period apart:

Diana was eight years old. She was living with her aunt but beginning regular visits to her mother in preparation for a trial return home. Her mother had been severely depressed, and was in hospital but allowed to spend weekends with her daughter under supervision. I was asked to see Diana for psychotherapy to offer her support through this trial period of rehabilitation. She was excited at the prospect of living with her mother again, and in her play, week by week, she created a shop that sold everything needed to set up a home: furniture, kitchenware, toys and a desk. It was poignant to watch her. She was hopeful about the future, and remembering the happy early days spent with her mother before she became ill. Unfortunately, her mother's mental state deteriorated under the pressure of anxiety about her daughter's potential return and she slowly began to slip into depression again. She stopped caring for herself and missed contacts with her daughter. Diana became disillusioned, recognising that the long-awaited return home to live with her mother may never happen. Her play in her sessions changed. The shop became a second-hand shop, selling off unwanted goods, and then it closed for good. Through this story, she expressed her anger, disappointment and sadness that she would not live with her mother again. Capturing these feelings in therapy enabled Diana to work them through, rather than feel overwhelmed by them as she had in the past. She was gradually able to accept that her hope of reunion with her mother was not to be realised, and that she would have to accept living with her caring relatives instead.

Despite her difficult life, Diana had developed a strong ego – by that I mean a strong sense of self and her capacities. She was secure in the knowledge that her mother had always loved her, despite her mother's periods of illness. These strengths gave her the ability to use the therapeutic relationship with me to think about and share her feelings and worries.

With other children, there is more confusion and uncertainty. They are unhappy, but they do not know why. They have not been able to shape their feelings and anxieties into meaningful ideas, and the therapeutic task is to discover and give shape to these distressing feelings. These children often leave us feeling bemused and uncertain what they are communicating. They may anxiously switch from one type of play to another and it can be hard to find the focus. This confusion will probably reflect the young person's inner experience of life being tangled, knotted up like a ball of string. For some children, their anxiety makes ideas and experiences rush through their minds, so it is hard to focus on one thing before the next anxious thought drives it away. Alternatively, the child may just feel a dull misery and a sense of emptiness, a feeling of depression.

Although a child like this may play for many weeks in an apparently undirected way, I have found, if I am patient, the play begins to take a meaningful shape as the child discovers how to communicate feelings and ideas within therapy. Gradually, some themes develop. A ball, which the child has thrown randomly about the room previously, is thrown to you with purpose, and a game develops. I might begin to wonder aloud, 'So now I can catch your ball. Will you catch it if I throw it back, or will the ball get lost?' This game represents a step forward, the child's capacity and wish to make contact with you. This is where we have to be creative, using our sense of what the child is communicating, to help the child continue to develop the play and its meaning. In his paper 'Reverie and metaphor', Ogden (1997) discusses how we can help patients 'come alive' through the creative use of metaphor in our attempts to capture the rich experience of the therapy. He suggests this is possible if we can maintain a receptive state he calls reverie. A simple observation might be all that is needed to capture the new sense of connection that the ball game brings: 'It's good to play a game together, for me to catch your ball and you to catch mine', maybe with the humorous addition, 'I can see how pleased you are when you're winning, too!'

While we are participating in this interaction as therapists, we are thinking about the underlying themes that the child's play or behaviour suggests. We are conscious too of the feeling tone of the relationship between us and if this has changed in the session. Ideas come to mind. Does the ball being thrown suggest a wish for some emotional contact with the therapist, but at a distance? If the child's play with the ball then gets increasingly frenetic and he aims it at the light bulb or at the therapist, is this an indication that a wish for closeness also brings a threat? The child may be fearful of becoming aggressive or needy, or being overwhelmed if he does get closer to the therapist.

Managing these heightened moments with sensitivity and firmness is a skill that develops. It is safer to capture the child's feeling of anxiety or anger early on, before any difficult behaviour escalates. I might say to an excitable young girl that I think that she is showing me how hard it is to manage exciting or cross feelings and stay calm. Often, the child is able to stop and reflect if we address these feelings directly, encouraging their capacity for self-control. Sometimes, we need to intervene actively to slow things down, but this usually gets less necessary as time goes on.

Thinking about delinquent and disruptive behaviour

A frequent reason for referral to child psychotherapy in this age group is for delinquent and disruptive behaviour, particularly among boys. I have always been heartened by Winnicott's ideas in his papers 'Delinquency as a sign of hope' (1968) and 'The anti-social tendency' (1956). Unlike many in society at the time, he saw stealing as an unconscious communication from the child, a positive attempt by a deprived youngster to claim back his mother's love which he feels is missing in his life. He said:

> At the basis of the antisocial tendency is a good early experience that has been lost.
>
> (Winnicott 1968)

Winnicott was more worried by the deprived children who do not express their needs in this way, as it is a sign they have given up hope. He developed these ideas while working with Barbara Dockar-Drysdale, who founded the Mulberry Bush, a residential special school for children with emotional problems, which I will describe in more detail in the final chapter. Winnicott's work showed his continuous search for meaning in children's behaviour, and of creative ways to respond to their communication.

Our therapeutic work has a similar aim. With these impulsive, acting-out children, we have to work hard to maintain the therapeutic frame, being firm to ensure safety in the session, while trying to encourage the children to think about what feelings are underlying their behaviour too. The therapeutic relationship eventually helps these vulnerable and often traumatised children feel secure enough to begin making this exploration about why they are in this state. Winnicott pointed out that the process of analysis is parallel to that of the mother–infant relationship, a shared experience. He was not an advocate of doing analysis to someone, but of it being a shared, co-construction.

Children who are delinquent or disruptive usually do not expect adults to try and understand why they keep getting into trouble, and often appreciate our attempts to make sense of their behaviour. We recognise that children may feel driven to behave in a way they don't understand, as these impulses may be unconscious. This was true of Peter who desperately wanted to be loved but reacted to any loss of attention with anger and distress because of his early deprivation. He was seen by a child psychotherapist in CAMHS who discussed him with me in supervision.

> Peter, aged nine, was always in trouble at school for provoking fights and he stole from his aunt and uncle who adopted him. He had been neglected by his birth family as a toddler, and then he felt an intruder in the busy home of his relatives, although they cared about him dearly. Peter felt he had no right to love now, but he longed for the affection that he had missed as an infant, and this led to his difficult behaviour. The therapist had an important role in helping the school and the family understand and tolerate his behaviour and provide the extra support he needed in the class room, while the therapy progressed. Peter gradually began to recover over the next two years, with weekly psychotherapy and the ongoing care from his adoptive family. Slowly, too, he began to believe he was loved by his new family and then his delinquency slowly reduced.

Exploration and consolidation

Once the main issues underlying the child's problem have been established, there may be many weeks and months where the child and psychotherapist together explore how the problems in the external world relate to the child's inner life and earlier experiences. In psychotherapy, the child has a chance to experience a different relationship where familiar tensions can be looked at from a new perspective, and new modes of relating can be tried out.

Simon, in his therapy, showed a similar capacity for change but I found his initial verbal aggression harder to tolerate than other children's physical outbursts.

Simon, aged 10, was the angry one in the family and at school. In therapy, we struggled to make sense of his simmering fury. He would provoke me with scathing remarks about something I said. When I was able to meet his habitual provocation with curiosity, rather than feel hurt or annoyed, it took the heat out of the moment and he became thoughtful too. I would say, 'Why do you think you said that? How did you think I might feel?' Gradually he was able to recognise his defensiveness. Expecting criticism, he challenged me first. Not wanting to show his hunger for affection, he covered up his vulnerability with a cool neutrality. In this initial phase, he came to sessions but he felt hopeless about any chance of change.

Ann Horne in supervision once suggested I say 'Ouch!' when the young person's verbal attacks on me really do hurt, registering the intended pain, but not getting too caught up with it.

As Simon began to feel more comfortable in the sessions, he could take some risks in showing me different sides of himself, including a rather ironic humour which I enjoyed. Eventually, he became more confident and outgoing outside the sessions with his peers, and he began making new friends. Then he could admit his hope that this change in him would last. Once he got the hang of therapy, he began to make links himself, recognising what had provoked his temper. Therapy became more like a joint project in the final months of the work.

With other children, the process of change can feel more fragile, more shaky. In a paper given at an ACP conference in 2000, Monica Lanyado (2001) described how she sometimes felt she was holding a child in her pocket in that delicate phase of therapy when the child is in the process of change, when the first new shoots are showing. I knew what she meant. At times, I can feel unusually preoccupied by a child, thinking about my patient between sessions, trying to make sense of the material in therapy. I sense a new aspect of the child's self is emerging, one that is more open to affection or thinking.

In retrospect, I can usually see there were signs of this change coming in earlier sessions. A boy who had been utterly self-absorbed became interested in caring for a baby doll, feeding it and putting the doll to bed, as if caring for an aspect of his infant self. A young girl sang a song, for the first time, another boy told me about a good time he had with his family. This felt like a gift after weeks of sullen negativity. These precursors to change can then become more frequent as the young person gains confidence that there is some good inside, as well as the demons. Even if there is a setback, due to an upsetting life event or even just a fear of change, we have both seen these positive qualities and we can be hopeful they will return.

When do we know the child is ready to work towards ending? During this period of working through, there is often a time of consolidation, when the new better experiences become an accepted part of the young person's life. Home and school are seen as happier places, and the young person is no longer so involved in therapy. In fact, it can feel a bit boring, life has become more interesting outside. It can feel a risk to suggest to parents and the child that enough progress has been achieved and therapy can work to a conclusion. Yet, as I describe in a later chapter on endings, important changes are achieved in this ending process, if a sufficient time is allowed for it.

Psychotherapy with adolescents

> I would there were no age between sixteen and
> three-and-twenty, or that youth would sleep out the
> rest; for there is nothing in the between but
> getting wenches with child, wronging the ancientry,
> stealing, fighting – Hark you now! Would any but
> these boiled brains of nineteen and two-and-twenty
> hunt this weather?
> (Shakespeare, *The Winter's Tale* III.iii.58–64)

As Shakespeare remarks, teenagers are a challenge, but they have an energy and adventurous spirit that we might envy as we get older. In psychotherapy, adolescence is seen as a second chance to rework unresolved aspects of development from early childhood, especially around separation and individuation. It is a time of major re-organisation within the adolescent's body and mind, one when previous insecurities can re-emerge and be worked through. Changes in physical, emotional and neurological development underlie this leap into the next phase. It is a confusing and exciting time for young people and their parents.

As psychotherapists, we can help adolescents make sense of the impact of this transition and explore why difficulties have occurred. Our change to a more conversational style in psychotherapy reflects this new phase when the teenager is developing an increased capacity to self-reflect and explore abstract ideas through language. I use humour more consciously too, to introduce ideas or to capture a mood and engage the teenager. The adolescent, who is now more self-aware, can take more responsibility for the therapeutic work. On the downside, we often have to work hard to keep their commitment to therapy when there is such a strong developmental drive for separation, away from parent figures and towards reliance on the peer group instead.

In this section, I will look at five main areas: psychotherapy with adolescents in crisis; the dynamic between the young person and his family; assessing risk in therapeutic work; the impact of the internet, cyber bullying and access to pornography; and finally developing resilience.

Psychotherapy with adolescents in crisis

Adolescents are often referred or refer themselves because they are frightened of the power and volatility of their feelings and their capacity to be destructive to themselves or others. They may have been struggling for years with a sense of being different, but the pressures to cope with teenage life propel them to get help now. They often feel they have become a teenager before they are ready, particularly if their early childhood has been troubled. They do not feel emotionally prepared to leave the comparative safety of latency to move into the uncharted waters of adolescence.

Becoming an adolescent can bring a loss of certainty. The belief in the solid structures of the adult world can crumble in the bid for autonomy and the need to create one's own identity. Uncertainties about sexuality and gender may have been under the surface for some time, and now become more challenging, as the young person faces new desires and a more fluid sense of self. The sureness of latency dissolves at a time when everything is up for questioning, but the need for encouragement and support remains. It can be very lonely if the young person no longer feels close to parents and siblings, and lacks friends for support. The adolescent may feel lost, alienated from the familiar self and not sure how to find a new sense of inner security. It can be hard to focus on the challenges of school work with these preoccupations, although for some studying is a welcome distraction from the powerful feelings and fantasies that beset their minds.

In psychotherapy, the young person can explore the anxieties of this turbulent phase. It will involve a search together with the therapist for the underlying causes of the present crisis, to make sense of the array of feelings that most teenagers experience: hope and excitement, fury and despair. This search for understanding can go back and forth, between self and other, past and present, and eventually look towards the future. The disillusioned adolescent may feel cynical about the prospect of change. Then the therapist has to hold the hope for both of them that things can improve.

In the early phase of psychotherapy, a picture builds up of the young person's inner experience of life, at school, at home, with friends and alone. Difficulties in current relationships often reflect underlying internal conflicts and uncertainties, like those faced by Terry, a young woman of 13 who was referred for psychotherapy because of social anxiety. I saw her weekly in private practice with periodic meetings with her parents at reviews.

> Terry, a quiet, serious girl aged 13, told me how she lingered on the outside of the group of 'popular' kids at school, not believing she would fit in, but not wanting to be seen alone. She had given up netball, her favourite sport, as she felt she played badly. An acute self -consciousness troubled her all the time and made social life an agony. Together, we were able to trace how this lack of self-confidence began with the onset of adolescence when she felt dismayed by the bodily changes of puberty, not feeling ready to face

becoming a young woman. She had always been rather shy and sensitive, so she was shocked by the sudden rages that went through her body when she felt cornered, although I think she felt enlivened by the energy it released too. There was also a new excitement and fantasies about romantic involvement with boys, but she could not believe that any boy would find her attractive and she hid her body in baggy clothes. In psychotherapy, over the months, she began to understand these feelings and she recognised how critical she was of herself. She had felt ashamed of how confused she felt about everything, unable to make decisions, until she began to realise that this uncertainty was normal in adolescence. As she gained confidence, she found a group of friends 'more like her' and she was able to venture out to some social gatherings.

As the adolescents explore their concerns in therapy, they begin to recognise how their past life experiences have shaped their perceptions of themselves and how they can misperceive the world because of their defensive approach. A teenager may come to see that it is an ongoing feeling of anger within and a lack of self-confidence that create the sense of persecution by teachers and parents, not external reality. Gradually, defences of splitting and projection can lessen as a young person gains a more balanced view of the inner strengths and vulnerabilities that shape our relationship to the world. The dreams, experiences and ideas explored in therapy, and those that arise in the week between sessions, all contribute to a process of re-evaluation. Gaps between sessions and holiday breaks are important, as it is during these times of separation, when the young patient has to manage alone, that these new ways of thinking and acting towards others can be tested out.

One idea adolescents have found helpful is that of recognising their 'changing states of mind', when they feel caught up in moods of despair, anger or excitement. As they observe their moods change, they begin to see them as less rigid and all-pervasive. I encourage them to think about why these states of mind developed, what triggered that mood today or the sudden flash of emotion in the session. This approach often appeals to their curiosity, as many teenagers are fascinated by how their mind works.

A young man I saw in therapy would often arrive in a fury, hating everyone including himself, but if he allowed himself to think about what had upset him, an argument with his Dad or a disagreement with his girlfriend, then his mood would shift. He would become more reflective and sad. This led him to think about his mind and his thoughts, and how easily he dismissed good experiences in favour of misery. Watching this pattern, week by week, provided a framework for his recovery, a way of integrating loving and destructive feelings, and recognising and accepting ambivalence. He discovered that life was a mixed bag and he had some power to shape its outcome.

Sexuality is an important theme in adolescent psychotherapy. Here, a young person can explore the new feelings of desire, jealousy and sometimes self-disgust and shame that emerge in the move towards the first adolescent intimate relationships. It is perhaps with adolescents that we are most conscious of our gender as psychotherapists, and how this shapes the psychotherapeutic process. The young person's transference to the therapist will include feelings emerging from adolescent sexuality, and from earlier infantile dependency needs. As an older psychotherapist now, I am more removed from the erotic transference, but I recall my self-consciousness with young male patients, drawn to me by the transference, but increased by my youthfulness, and the fantasies this provoked. It may be difficult, at first, to talk about sexuality and how this emerges in the relationship with you as a therapist, but with help in supervision, and following the lead of the young person, it becomes possible to find a language to explore this together. I recall an eroticised transference developing with one of my adolescent female patients. Her relationship with me was a complex mixture of excitement, seeking my admiration and annoyance that she felt like this. This was complicated further by a fear of merging with a maternal figure at the times when she felt as needy as a small infant because of her early deprivation.

The teenager and his family

Helping a young person disentangle his own issues from those belonging to his parents or the family history is an important part of the therapeutic process. Bringing up teenagers can be a real challenge for parents as it will evoke unresolved issues from their own adolescent years. It will remind them of how they struggled then with their aggression, sexuality and the need to separate from their family of origin. The tensions that can develop between fathers and their sons and daughters, or mothers and their teenage children, will have their source in both generations. In the assessment, a decision will need to be made with the parents whether it would be preferable to explore the conflicts with their son or daughter in family therapy, or whether individual work for the young person is more appropriate. Either way, it is important to have the parents' support and willingness to respond positively, as their teenager seeks a new way of relating to them. Regular reviews, involving the teenager where possible, can be a place where these changes can be thoughtfully negotiated on both sides.

The relationship between teenagers and their siblings can also become turbulent as they each reach a new phase of development. Friction can be intense between rivalrous siblings or it can be a source of support if they can find a way of sharing interests, and spending time together. Talking about these ambivalent feelings towards siblings, the jealousy and love they feel for each other, is often a central theme in therapy. These sibling relationships are often the model for other relationships with peers at school and later staring work

Young people observe their parents as they grow up and often feel responsible for their parents' arguments or unhappiness. They may feel they did not deal well with a crisis that hit the family when they were younger, like the illness or death of a sibling or a parent's depression. These early memories can haunt young people, leaving them blaming themselves for situations they probably did not understand fully and they had no power to change. This is particularly likely if these past painful events could not be talked about in the family at the time, as feelings were still too raw. Helping the young person review these past times from their position as teenagers now, and think about how it might have been for them when they were younger, can bring both a relief from this self-criticism and a new under-standing of their parents' response. I recall talking this through with an adolescent girl, Sarah, who remained troubled many years after the death of her sibling.

> I was asked to see Sarah aged 15, in my private practice, by her worried parents because of her low mood. She was eight years old when her sister died after a serious illness. It was difficult for Sarah to talk about her memories of sister's sudden illness, which were shadowy and painful. She told me how guilty she felt about being the surviving daughter, and angry that she could not enjoy her teenage years, as with each new experience, she would remind herself that her sister was not there to enjoy it. In psychotherapy, she began to explore her confused memories of her sister's illness and death, and how she missed having her sister there to share her life now. These conversa-tions made it possible for her to go home and talk to her parents, who had not known how to start this conversation. Her guilt about being the surviving daughter softened, and she began to take up new opportunities and allow herself to have some fun. I was aware though, when we finished this brief piece of therapy, how this difficult process of mourning would continue and how, at each stage of her life, she might revisit this loss of her sibling.

As this work shows, adolescents may need to have their own confidential space in therapy to work out their problems, but the therapist needs to understand the parents' perspective and family dynamics too. The therapist working individually with adolescents will hear about the changing family dynamic as the work progresses, and they can then consider with the parents, when they meet, how to support the young person maturing and becoming more independent.

Repetition of trauma in adolescents

Adolescents are more likely to 'act out' their feelings, trying out new roles and identities, and the peer group can be a safe place to do this. Neurological changes in the brain lead to new impulses of aggression and sexuality, and the desire for excitement and risk. Unexpected feelings can lead to impulsive behaviour, and at times the young person may feel out of control. Margaret Tonnesmann (1980) drew our attention to the risks of adolescent re-enactment during this adolescent phase, a repetition of unresolved early trauma. It is important to differentiate when a young person's behaviour is a revival of earlier trauma or a response to a new crisis brought on by present life challenges. Knowing the teenager's early history in some detail can explain an unexpected change in an adolescent's usual sense of confidence or a phase of turbulent behaviour.

I was asked to offer brief psychotherapy to a young man who found himself terrified at the prospect of leaving a safe boarding school to go to university. His mother had died from a drug overdose when he was a small boy and he had been brought up by caring foster parents and placed at a boarding school where he had become quite self-assured and progressed well. He was intelligent and determined, but it was as if the ground had opened up beneath him at the prospect of leaving this safe haven. He was shaken by early fears and separation anxieties that he remembered from the distressing time of his mother's illness and death. In psychotherapy, he bravely broached these early traumatic memories, which he had kept at a safe distance all this time. Now he understood the source of his separation anxiety surfacing at the prospect of leaving a safe refuge, and this helped him regain his self-confidence about leaving his school and making the move to university which he so much wanted.

This young man had felt his future and his sense of self was in jeopardy if he could not make the transition to university he so much wanted. I felt this anxiety from his whole demeanour as much as from what he said to me. Being in touch with one's countertransference is a crucial guide to recognising risk, even though the objective evidence is not immediately obvious.

Assessing risk

Being aware of risk is crucial in psychotherapy with teenagers, particularly if they have a history of self-harm, suicide or psychotic episodes. Careful assessment early on can help clarify if the young person is able to manage this treatment. Psychotherapy is a painful and confusing process, and it may not be the treatment of choice if a young person is too emotionally vulnerable or isolated. Knowing the young person has a stable family and/ or a strong professional network around him is a crucial factor. If the adolescent psychotherapist is working as part of a team, the anxiety and assessment of risk to the young person can be shared.

Working privately it is difficult for the psychotherapist to be responsible for both the care management of a young person at risk, and provide treatment, as the therapist does not have easy access to the resources of the community team, and cannot offer 24-hour support. The pressure to look after the young person's safety does not leave the therapist the mental space or freedom to think therapeutically. It shifts the balance. If I am very worried about a young person's mental state, I explain I will need to contact their parents and the GP, and maybe seek the advice of a child psychiatrist, as their safety is my priority.

Teenagers may directly let you know of their suicidal wishes, or they may imply that they are feeling suicidal by their tone or behaviour, as if waiting for therapist to put these feelings into words. The young person's anxiety can be projected into you, so you are the one left worried, although the teenager may minimise any concerns. Then the therapist has to pursue the issue to ascertain whether this is an idea only, or if the young person has actual plans to self-harm. There is a danger with emotionally volatile adolescents, that the psychotherapist becomes the one who cares about the young person's safety and feels responsible, rather than the young person. If the balance tips this way, then it is important to consider whether the treatment is viable. From the beginning of treatment, I make it clear to young people with a history of self-harming that, if I am worried about them, I will share my concerns with the family and professionals, and this takes priority over confidentiality. This creates a clear containing boundary that protects me as a therapist, as well as my patient.

Risk-taking can become a perverse, exciting game that registers the young person's despair, but it also makes those close to the teenage suffer, including the therapist. This can become an ongoing challenge when working with disturbed young people. The task is then to help them face the choice between the perverse excitement of self-harming behaviour, or moving on to recognise their despair and guilt, and what provokes it. Honestly facing these issues needs some courage and it becomes easier as the relationship with the therapist becomes more secure.

The impact of the internet, cyber bullying and access to pornography

The majority of the adolescents we see will have a life on the internet. The virtual world is like a third area for us to conceptualise, alongside the external world and the internal world. For many teenagers, it is an essential part of their life, and their education. Yet it also brings added pressures, particularly for a vulnerable or isolated adolescent. Many of these are gender specific too. For young women, there may be peer pressure to share every aspect of their social life on social media, and this leads to further pressure to compare and conform to the behaviour they see there. Young girls take photos of themselves, post them online where others see them, and can compliment or sneer. Before long, everyone in their class will have seen an embarrassing picture. Being part of the 'popular' group in school is so important to many, particularly those with less social confidence, and ridicule like this can make going to school a humiliating experience. Cyber bulling, publicly ridiculing others online, is now an offence, but it is very hard for schools to monitor and it can be a traumatic experience for those going through it. Teenagers can feel they have no way of dealing with it. Either they shut off the internet, which feels like exclusion from their peers, or remain on it and face the painful minute-by-minute endurance test of the conversations there about them.

Parents too can feel out of their depth. This technological change was not part of their youth, and learning how to set appropriate boundaries and to master the technology can take a lot of skill. Younger child psychotherapists may feel more comfortable with this ever-changing technology and will have built up strategies to manage its intrusive aspect, as well as valuing its positive side. As an older therapist, I feel out of my depth at times. It is like I am running to keep up with changing ideas although I live in a technically minded family, so I am always being 'upgraded'.

For the younger, socially anxious, vulnerable adolescent we often see in psychotherapy, the challenges of social media are great, as they may not have the emotional maturity to deal with this level of complexity. I worked with two teenagers in psychotherapy, one who was overwhelmed by the demands of the internet world and another who had escaped into it, to avoid the complexities of a social life.

> Patricia, aged 11, was only slowly adjusting to the physical and emotional changes of puberty and the transition to secondary school. She was not ready to think about her sexuality, her body image or boyfriends. She could see her peers revelling in the excitement of daily snapshots of themselves, dressed up, dancing, spending time with boys, and she felt stupid, embarrassed that she could not keep up. In therapy, we explored her anxieties about not feeling a part of this peer group, yet desperately wanting to. I encouraged her to hold on to and value other aspects of herself, her artistic qualities, her conscientious hard work and her dreams for her future, but she felt these did not give her the status with her peer group she wanted. Therapy became a refuge, where she could try and work out what she felt was right and wrong in the shifting world of social media and allow herself to set boundaries. A place where she could find herself. It was painful to watch, as she slowly developed the ego capacities she needed to face these external pressures, and the capacity to think about their impact on her, and what she wanted for herself.

In contrast, Thomas, a reserved young man found the retreat into gaming on the internet easier than facing the pressures of the social life at school. The excitement, competitiveness and intellectual challenge of these hours of playing met a need in him, but they still left him feeling empty and alone. Thomas was desperate for the intimacy of a relationship with a girl, and scared how easily he could be pulled into watching pornography as a way of meeting his sexual fantasies and desires. He worried about approaching a girl he liked. We explored these anxieties in sessions, talking about his fears of being too jealous and possessive if he did start seeing a girl. Thomas finally began a relationship with this girl and he began to learn about a different side of himself; the myriad of feelings that could be part of a first love. Its tenderness, aggression, annoyance, desire, even boredom. This relationship also gave him the security to separate from the draw of the virtual internet world and build a life for himself at college.

Perhaps the saddest aspect of the internet is how easy it is for deprived and disturbed young people to become caught up in the criminal world of pornography and sexual exploitation, either as victims or as perpetrators, or both. For many years, I have supervised child psychotherapists at an agency working with young people involved in sexual abuse, mostly teenage boys. Their stories remind me of the neglected and deprived young men I worked with as a social worker, who were often caught up in delinquent behaviour. The difference here is the addiction to the perverse mixture of sexuality, power and violence involved in online pornography to fulfil an unmet need, when relationships are troubled at home or there is a lack of affectionate concern. Some of these young perpetrators, mostly adolescent boys, have been sexually abused as children and are re-enacting this experience of trauma. Others feel lonely, angry and rejected, and this sexual exploitation of others online or actual sexual abuse is a way of feeling powerful, getting revenge or pleasure seeking. This excellent local therapeutic service offers assessment of young people referred by the police, followed by therapeutic work with parents and longer-term individual psychotherapy for the young people,

The therapeutic team there are particularly skilled in developing an alliance with the young perpetrators. They offer them a safe setting to think about their offending, trying to understand the meaning of their sexual offending within the context of their whole life experience. Often it is the young person's anxieties and relationships in their current life that led to the offence, although earlier trauma or abuse may have been underlying precipitators. If the parents are willing to be involved in therapy, this reveals the family context that contributed to this breakdown and therapeutic work with the parents is offered. Often parental relationships are under stress or broken down, so there is the loss of the father's presence and the comfort of a loving parental relationship. The young people then withdraw to find their own solutions in the internet world or use inappropriate sexual behaviour to give the excitement and contact they are missing. In these exploitative relationships online, mostly with young girls, the young men externalise the feelings of shame and abasement that arise from having been bullied themselves or from memories of their own humiliation and abuse. Encouraging parents, or carers, to understand their predicament and become more involved in providing support in the daily lives of these young people is vital, as well as offering individual psychotherapy to help the teenager explore and understand his behaviour.

Developing resilience

To conclude this discussion of adolescent therapy, I would like to return to Margot Waddell's (2006) paper in which she explores the development of resilience in adolescence. She questions why some young people, faced with the complex troubling experiences of adolescence, refuse to join the group culture of bullying, while others turn to sadistic taunting of more vulnerable young people. She suggests that this can be traced back to early infancy when a small child needs to have these aggressive, excited and vulnerable feelings understood and made manageable by their parents. If not, the more vulnerable infant will have to resort to primitive fight or flight defences as a defence from these powerful feelings. Later, as a teenager, this young person may have to project the hurt received from others onto an external victim who is punished, while the adolescent who has a strong sense of self has sufficient confidence not to resort to this behaviour.

Margot Waddell also looks at the wider social context: the family, school, society and the culture that encourages or contains these more destructive feelings. She describes how the individual can develop 'an internal gang', aspects of the self that are intolerant of any vulnerability or need. In psychotherapy, we often see young people who are cruel and punishing to themselves and undermine their own progress, as well as bullying others. Helping these young people in therapy to develop resilience, by providing a second chance for those feelings to be tolerated and understood, is an important aspect of our work as adolescent psychotherapists.

References

Beebe, B. (2005) Mother–infant research informs mother–infant treatment. *Psychoanalytic Study of the Child* 60: 6–46.

Daws, D. (1999) Brief psychotherapy with infants and their parents. In M. Lanyado & A. Horne (eds) *The Handbook of Child and Adolescent Psychotherapy*, pp. 261–272. London and New York: Routledge.

Dowling, D. (2006) The capacity to be alone. In M. Lanyado & A. Horne (eds) *A Question of Technique*, pp. 54–68. London and New York: Routledge.

Fraiberg, S. (1996 [1950]) *The Magic Years: Understanding and Handling the Problems of Early Childhood*. New York: Simon & Schuster.

Fraiberg, S., Adelson, E. & Shapiro, V. (1975) Ghosts in the nursery: A psychoanalytic approach to the problem of impaired infant–mother relationships. In L. Fraiberg (ed) *Selected Writings of Selma Fraiberg*, pp. 100–136. Columbus, OH: Ohio State University Press, 1987.

Lanyado, M. (2001) The symbolism of the story of Lot and his wife: The function of the 'present relationship' and non-interpretive aspects of the therapeutic relationship in facilitating change. *Journal of Child Psychotherapy* 27(1): 19–33.

Ogden, T. (1997) Reverie and metaphor: Some thoughts on how I work as an analyst. *International Journal of Psycho-Analysis* 78: 719–731.

Stern, D. (1985) *The Interpersonal World of the Infant*. New York: Basic Books.

Stern, D. et al. (1998) Non-interpretive mechanisms in psycho-analytic therapy: The 'something more' than interpretation. *International Journal of Psycho-Analysis* 79: 903–921.

Tonnesmann, M. (1980) Adolescent reenactment, trauma and reconstruction. *Journal of Child Psychotherapy* 6(1): 23–44.

Trevarthen, C. (2014) Stepping away from the mirror: Pride and shame in adventures in companionship. In C.S. Carter, L. Ahnert, K.E. Grossman, S.B. Hardy, M.E. Lamb, S.W. Porges & N. Sachser (eds) *Attachment and Bonding: A New Synthesis* (Dahlem Workshop Report 92), pp. 55–58. Cambridge, MA: MIT Press.

Tronick, E.Z. & Gianino, A. (1986) Interactive mismatch and repair: Challenges to the coping infant. *Zero to Three* 6(3): 1–6.

Waddell, M. (2006) Grouping or ganging: The psychodynamics of bullying. *British Journal of Psychotherapy* 23(2): 189–204.

Winnicott, D.W. (1953) Transitional objects and transitional phenomena. *International Journal of Psycho-Analysis* 34: 89–97.

Winnicott, D.W. (1956) The anti-social tendency. In D.W. Winnicott (ed) *Deprivation and Delinquency*, pp. 120–131. London and New York: Tavistock, 1984.

Winnicott, D.W. (1968) Delinquency as a sign of hope. *Prison Service Journal* 7(27): 2–9. A talk given to the Borstal Assistant Governors' Conference, held at King Alfred's College, Winchester, April 1967.

Winnicott, D.W. (1971a) *Therapeutic Consultations*. London: Hogarth Press. Reprinted by Karnac, 1996.

Winnicott, D.W. (1971b) Playing: A theoretical statement. In *Playing and Reality*, pp. 38–52. London: Tavistock.

Chapter 5

Reflections on brief psychotherapy

Child psychotherapy has often been associated with longer-term open-ended psychotherapy, for children with complex problems, but we have always offered a range of brief interventions, adapted to children's needs. Brief psychotherapy uses familiar therapeutic skills, but the therapy is more focused and limited in scope.

An example of early brief intervention was devised in the 1920s, by Donald Winnicott when he was working as a paediatrician at Paddington Green Hospital. He needed to make rapid assessments of the many infants he saw every day, so he devised an ingenious approach. While the mother was talking to him with her baby sitting on her lap, he placed a shiny spatula on the table nearby. He was interested to see how freely the baby reached out for this glittering object, and then went on to explore it, curiously and playfully. This would be a healthy response. If the baby ignored the spatula or became too anxious to reach for it, he was alerted to some interference in the baby's natural capacity to play, which he could then explore further. I have described this simply, but Winnicott writes in detail about what he discovered in these observations of infants in this set situation in his paper 'The observation of infants in a set situation' (1941: 66)

Winnicott developed another playful but serious brief intervention for the initial meetings with the young children he saw in child psychiatry, which he called the squiggle game (1964–68). He thought that the first therapeutic meeting held a special significance for a child or adults seeking help and what happened there was often a crucial communication. He drew a squiggle, a quick drawing which he invited the child to complete, and then the child did a squiggle which he made into something. The child's drawings were a spontaneous response, often shedding light on the deeper issues underlying current problems, communicated in a way that the child could not have put into words. He said they sometimes made 20 to 30 drawings in one session, and that gradually the significance of these shared drawings became deeper, and the child felt they were important communications. He said:

> In this work the consultant specialist does not need to be clever so much as to be able to provide a natural and freely moving human relationship

within the professional setting where the patient gradually surprises himself by the production of ideas and feelings that had not previously been integrated into the total personality.

(1968: 299)

A comment that holds true of all our therapeutic contact with children.

The therapist's role is to provide an emotionally holding environment within which this emotional experience can be integrated. These sessions are described in his book *Therapeutic Consultations in Child Psychiatry* (Winnicott 1971) and provide a fascinating insight into how helpful interventions can emerge in a playful interaction with a child in one consultation or two.

The consultations offered by Dilys Daws (1985) for parents and infants at a GP baby clinic, discussed in the previous chapter, is another example of a brief intervention. Many other short-term treatments have been developed since, including the under-fives consultation service at the Tavistock Clinic, and a walk-in clinic for adolescents at the Brent Centre for Young People.

A brief intervention that I found to be particularly effective was the parenting assessments we carried out as a part of the Court Assessment Service at the Cassel Hospital (Dowling 2009: 26). It met the Court's need for rapid assessments of the parents' potential to engage in a psychotherapeutic treatment programme. The aim was to help them resume care of their children, while also engaging the parents in thinking about their parenting and their motivation for change.

Parenting assessments

These out-patient assessments carried out on the Family Service were completed in two sessions, the first with parents and children together, and the second with just the parents. The children, who had previously been separated from their parents as a result of serious concerns about their care, were re-united in this meeting. A child psychotherapist and an adult psychotherapist working together led the interviews. There was a firm structure to the sessions, which could be both chaotic and emotionally intense, as parents often struggled to manage their excited and anxious children for the hour. Having two psychotherapists made it possible for us to see the detail of the interaction within the family, which we could think over together afterwards when we were drawing up the assessment. In the first session, while the family played or talked together, we observed how the children related to their parents and each other. We looked for the parents' strengths and vulnerabilities, and their alone capacity to respond sensitively to their children. When the parents returned a fortnight later, we encouraged them to think about the challenges of that first session, how their children might feel about returning to their care. and what help they might need as parents. These were highly emotional meetings for the parents. They knew that their potential as parents was being assessed, but these assessments could be the catalyst for change, helping them face difficulties in themselves that had been denied or avoided previously, and so make it possible for them to work towards their children's return to their care.

Technique in brief child psychotherapy

Brief therapy is more focused and limited in scope than open-ended longer-term work, and this can be an effective approach in many settings. Children and adolescents can make good use of six, twelve or eighteen psychotherapy sessions, particularly if they are in crisis and want help, or if the idea of longer therapy is too intimidating. A brief intervention is more likely to be effective if the problem is a more recent development in response to internal or external pressures, rather than a serious developmental issue that the young person has faced for many years. It would also not suit children who have complex emotional issues or the deprived and neglected children who need long-term psychotherapy to establish a secure relationship and internalise a positive self-image. All these factors would need to be considered in the assessment. Sometimes parents hope that brief work will be sufficient, when only a longer-term intervention will help a seriously troubled child.

The importance of maintaining a clear focus to the therapy has been stressed by Lanyado (2009) in her chapter 'Brief psychotherapy and therapeutic consultations'. She points out that the therapy can be diverted to other life issues affecting the child, but this will undermine the potential to achieve the aims that have been agreed. Setting clear goals with the child and parents, or adolescent alone, at the beginning of treatment, can be a useful focus, and Goal Based Outcomes measures are an effective tool for this approach. The current level of the problem is measured when therapy begins and then again when the work is reviewed or completed. Cathy Troupp (2013) in a paper discussing the use of these measures suggests that the therapist may consider having double goals, an internal and a behavioural goal. An internal change might be 'feel more confident with my friends' and a behavioural change would be 'be able to go for a sleepover'. The value of Goal Based Outcomes is that it is a collaborative project between the child and psychotherapist and it gives the clinic useful feedback on outcomes.

In brief work, the psychotherapist is likely to take a more active role in engaging the young patient and ensuring key issues are addressed, but the therapeutic relationship remains a central aspect of the treatment and can be more intense because of the limited time available. Time limits shape the therapy, with a clear beginning, middle and ending phase of the work. The therapist has to be very aware of the developing transference relationship, how the young person relates to the psychotherapist in the sessions, to understand the patient's state of mind. It is likely, though, that this will not be directly addressed with the patient by the therapist as they will not be working at this deeper level because they are parting relatively soon. However, a small change in one aspect of a young person's life can have a ripple effect in other areas, like the achievement of a sleepover described by Cathy Troupp can be a milestone for a young person who has been unable to spend a night away, due to separation anxiety. Attention is given throughout the treatment to the fact that there is an ending date, and this allows feelings about loss and separation to be anticipated and worked through, often in a very helpful way.

Child psychotherapists working in Child and Adolescent Mental Health Services (CAMHS) offer a range of brief therapies: parent–infant psychotherapy, single consultation sessions with parents, joint assessments with other professionals in a multi-professional team, assessments for child psychotherapy and brief therapeutic interventions to support young people through a crisis.

More recently, there has been the development of short-term psychoanalytic psychotherapy (STPP), a manualised intervention (Cregeen et al. 2018) developed for severely depressed adolescents which is now offered in many CAMHS clinics. This model offers 28 weekly sessions of psychotherapy to adolescents, alongside 12 supportive sessions for their parents. The IMPACT study, the first large-scale research into short-term child psychotherapy in the UK, showed that significant improvements were achieved with this model: 85% of adolescents receiving STPP no longer met diagnostic criteria for depression one year after the end of treatment, there was a 59% reduction in anxiety symptoms, 43% reduction in obsessive-compulsive symptoms and a 45% reduction in functioning impairment (Midgley et al. 2017). Another review by Abbass et al. (2013) suggested that the STPP approach may be effective as a treatment for children and adolescents across a wide range of common mental health disorders.

The need for a flexible and economic therapeutic response in a variety of settings has been a catalyst for change in child psychoanalytic psychotherapy, and this has led to a range of valuable developments in brief work. Some of these will be discussed further in the final part of the book. The challenge has been to maintain the key aspects of the psychoanalytic approach – the recognition of unconscious aspects of our behaviour and relationships, and the importance of developmental factors in children – whilst also offering a time-limited approach.

References

Abbass, A.A., Rabung, S., Leichsenring, F., Refseth, J.S. & Midgley, N. (2013) A psychodynamic psychotherapy for children and adolescents: A meta-analysis of short-term psychodynamic models. *Journal of the American Academy of Child and Adolescent Psychiatry* 52(8): 863–875.

Cregeen, S., Hughes, C., Midgley, N., Rhode, M. & Rustin, M. (2018) *Psychoanalytic Child Psychotherapy: Principles and Evidence in Short-Term Psychoanalytic Psychotherapy for Adolescents with Depression. A Treatment Manual by Simon Cregeen*. London: Routledge.

Daws, D. (1985) Two papers on work in a baby clinic: Standing next to the weighing scales. *Journal of Child Psychotherapy* 11(2): 77–85.

Dowling, D. (2009) Thinking aloud: A child psychotherapist assessing families for court. In A. Horne & M. Lanyado (eds) *Through Assessment to Consultation*, pp. 26–43. London: Routledge.

Lanyado, M. (2009) Brief psychotherapy and therapeutic consultations. In M. Lanyado & A. Horne (eds) *The Handbook of Child and Adolescent Psychotherapy: Psychoanalytic Approaches*, pp. 233–246. London: Routledge.

Midgley, N., O'Keefe, S., French, L. & Kennedy, E. (2017). Psychodynamic psychotherapy for children and adolescents: An updated narrative review of the evidence-base. *Journal of Child Psychotherapy*, 43(3): 307–329.

Troupp, C. (2013) 'What do you want to get from coming here?' Distinguishing patient generated outcome measures in CAMHS from a bespoke sandwich. *Child and Family Clinical Psychology Review* 1: 19–28.

Winnicott, D.W. (1941) The observation of infants in a set situation. In D.W. Winnicott (ed) *Through Paediatrics to Psychoanalysis*, pp. 52–69. London: Hogarth Press. Reprinted by Karnac, 1992.

Winnicott, D.W. (1968) The squiggle game. In C. Winnicott, R. Shepherd & M. Davies (eds) *Psycho-analytic Explorations*, pp. 299–317. London: Karnac, 1989.

Winnicott, D.W. (1971) *Therapeutic Consultations in Child Psychiatry*. London: Hogarth Press.

Chapter 6

Engaging with parents

Introduction

Parents lose confidence when they have difficulties in their relationship with their children or when they see their child is struggling with life and they do not know how to help. Meetings with a child psychotherapist or a fellow professional to think about their concerns can bring a fresh perspective, and offer a reflective space to think, away from the intense emotions of family life. Many factors will have shaped their relationship to their child. The child's personality and position in the family, the history of the child's development and the parents' experiences as children which, as Selma Fraiberg says, can intrude on their family life now.

> Even among families where the love bonds are stable and strong, the intruders from the parental past may break through the magic circle in an unguarded moment, and a parent and his child may find themselves re-enacting a moment or a scene from another time with another set of characters.
>
> Fraiberg et al. (1975)

Add to this the impact of life events on the family, the parents' relationship as a couple and the temperaments of their other children, all influencing the development of a young person.

In this chapter, I will consider some of the clinical issues that arise in therapeutic work with parents. This will include working with the parents on the impact of their early life on their parenting, the tensions that can develop in the couple relationship, thinking about life events and how they affect family dynamics, and a consideration of the more serious risk factors the parent worker may face. The child psychotherapist may work with the parents directly, alongside their work with the child, or prefer-ably a colleague can take on this role so that parents have their separate space to explore the issues involved. This allows the child psychotherapist to focus on the young person in treatment, knowing that the needs and concerns of the parents are being looked after by the colleague. As mentioned in the earlier chapter, ideally the father is involved from the beginning of treatment, if he is still in contact with the child, although separate meetings may be more appropriate if the parents are living apart. The child psychotherapist will still meet the parents at termly review but with this colleague present, so both the parents' perspective and the child's can be considered. Meetings with parents may be regular fort-nightly sessions, monthly or termly, but they are crucial to ensure that parents understand their role in helping their child recover. This work with parents, alongside child therapy, may occur in the public or volun-tary sector within a multidisciplinary team, or in private practice. When the child psychotherapist is working with both the child and the parents, the support of colleagues and supervision is perhaps more important to provide the thinking space necessary to be clear about the complex dynamics between these two related areas of work.

Therapeutic work with parents as a support to child therapy

When a child begins psychotherapy, parents need to be prepared for a period of change as their relationship to their child and the family dynamic will inevitably shift in response to this intervention. There are likely to be difficult periods, particularly in the early months of treat-ment as the young person often becomes more distressed or angry at home or at school, as the concerns that led to referral begin to be explored in the therapy. Parents will discover that they too need to respond differently to help their child manage these emotional times and the relationships with siblings. The therapy with the child, and that with the parents should be seen in parallel. The child's work in psychotherapy will shed new light on relationships at home, and parents can feed back their observations and experience of the young person in the family. A close working relationship between the child and parent therapists creates a containing environment for the therapeutic work, and ensures that the tensions that inevitably rise when the parents are struggling with a difficult child can be understood as they arise.

This approach would not be accepted by all child psychotherapists, as some believe that young people need to be present at all meetings with parents so that they do not feel they are being talked about behind their back. I think this is true of some adolescents, and older teenagers may not need parents involved, but my experience is that most young people in conflict with their parents want them to have help in their own right. They do not want to be involved in all their discussions, as long as their confidentiality is respected.

Discovering the parents' perspective

In parent psychotherapy, we encourage parents to bring their concerns and observations as the starting point for each session. The parents' arrival is often rich in material for the psychotherapist. Observing how the parents greet you, how they respond to each other if they come as a couple, and how they present the issues that are worrying them, will bring the reality and vitality of their relationship with their child into the room. I recall one couple's arrival:

> The father slumped in his chair as he sat down, and remained silent, while his wife was eager, sitting forward in her chair, wanting to tell me about a recent crisis with their son.

It would have been easy to become absorbed in listening to mother's stories, but I was concerned how to address father's powerful communication through his silence. I was aware that it could mean many things; his despair that this session will be of little use to him, his sense of guilt and helplessness about another fight with his son who had once again provoked his father into fury. Or did it reflect the tension between the parents as a couple, at odds because of their differing perceptions of their teenage son?

These various ideas came to my mind, as I listened to the mother and wondered how to bring father into the conversation, to hear his perspective. What was most obvious was their contrasting presentations. The father's slow, faltering attempts to describe the painful unrelenting conflict with his son made me wonder what was being re-enacted here, in the father–son relationship. I asked the father' about his experience with his father as a young teenager. I wondered if his son's frustration had triggered off memories of his own adolescent rows with his father, as this could have unconsciously intensified his anger with his son now. I knew that if this was a repeating pattern, I could help the father stand back from his adolescent self by bringing it into the open, and this might help him empathise with his son from a new perspective.

Emotions are often intense in the early weeks of parent therapy, as the parents have usually tolerated much before asking for help. Initially, they may just need to talk through their troubling experiences with their son or daughter, sharing the anxiety, anger and the confusion caused by their child's behaviour and relationship with them, past and present. Sometimes we can help this exploration by asking for clarification or by putting 'hard to express' feelings into words. The therapist works at building an alliance and keeping a sense of balance; helping parents to separate the young person's real difficulties from those that are part of normal development. Parents may also not realise, until you point it out, their child's strengths and resilience as well as the vulnerabilities.

Defences in the parents

Parenthood brings to the surface unexpected and powerful feelings that appear to defy the logic that has served parents so well in other aspects of their adult lives. A father may have the capacity to manage a large team in an engineering firm but be thrown by his small daughter's angry remark that she hates him, which makes him feel utterly useless and reminds him of other times when he felt rejected or inadequate. This new vulnerability often needs to be covered up by a defensive front, but this may prevent a parent from exploring these difficult feelings and understanding them. A mother may retreat into silence, or a father become very strict when he feels undermined in this way. In therapeutic work, we need to respect these defences, but also provide a space in the sessions to explore whether this self-protective behaviour is interfering with their capacity to parent. It can be a relief to parents to discover just how normal these responses are for any of us, faced with the difficult task of being a parent.

The influence of the parent's early history

As parents begin to trust their therapist, and emotions are more at an equilibrium, they often develop a curiosity and interest in the dynamics that have shaped their lives. Seeing how family life has impacted on their child, they begin to question how their early lives have shaped them. They discover how their child's behaviour triggers emotions and memories from their own childhood often creating tension and distance between them. Couples may have never told each other forgotten but important issues from their childhood. Sharing their histories in the parent–infant sessions can help parents make sense of their differences, which may have been tolerated but not understood until now.

Adult attachment research (George et al. 1985) has shown how parents' experiences of being parented in childhood influences their parenting, and how these patterns endure. Parents' internal models of relating, as described in attachment research, fall into four patterns: secure, anxious, avoidant and trauma-based attachment styles. This pattern of relating is likely to be repeated in their relationship with their children. So, parents, whose own parents avoided showing and facing difficult feelings, will have internalised this way of behaving. They will respond in a similar avoidant way with their children, unless they recognise the impact that these early experiences had on them as children growing up. However, those parents who have had very troubled early lives but are able to reflect on these experiences, and be in touch with how they were emotionally affected by them as children, are able to avoid repeating this negative pattern of parenting with their own children (Main et al. 1985). Parents can be helped to consider how they relate to their children and whether this has been affected by the way they were treated by their parents, Martine contacted me to arrange some parenting sessions as she was concerned that that she was unwittingly driven towards repeating her parents' behaviour. From her description, Martine's parents sounded like they were avoidant in their style. She recalled how they disliked any intimacy and lacked sensitivity in their responses to her:

> Martine, a calm thoughtful woman, was bemused by her angry reactions to her son, Alan, a toddler who could be quite naughty and challenging. I was surprised too by her annoyance and irritability towards her little boy and wondered about their origin. She told me that her parents had been firm disciplinarians, not interested in discussing feelings. Her father particularly, would not countenance opposition from her. Martine wanted to parent differently but she found that her impulse was to be severe when her son was disobedient, and this only exacerbated her son's behaviour as then he bit and scratched his mother. It was as if Alan sensed his mother's uncertainty and was testing out what she would do. Once Martine recognised this repeating pattern, and talked about these early memories, she was better able to keep calm when her son had tantrums. These recollections put her in touch with the fury and frustration she had felt as a child about not being free to express her feelings, and she was determined that her relationship with Alan would be different.

Echoes of the past

Parents can find a particular stage of their children's development more difficult to manage as it highlights a stressful period in their past. This is particularly true of adolescence. Parents often feel uncertain how to deal with their teenagers' volatile moods and sexuality, particularly if adolescence was a difficult time for them. On parenting courses I have led with a colleague, parents are often surprised how their own experience of growing up has shaped their responses to their teenagers at home now, and this makes the tension in these relationships easier to understand. Like the mother who remembered her sexual adventures as a teenager, and realised that now she had become very controlling of her daughter, not wanting her to repeat this pattern. It was a relief when another parent pointed out that this mother's daughter was having a more stable start than she did, and so she was less likely to seek out comfort through sex. When parents shared their experience with others, in groups like this, often with rueful humour as well as frustration and sadness, they did not feel so alone with their concerns and were not so quick to blame themselves for their current difficulties in the family.

The influence of upbringing and culture

As child psychotherapists, we bring the social and cultural expectations that shaped us to our work with families. It can be difficult to know to what extent our reactions to a family, who is very different from our own, have been triggered by our cultural history. Thinking of a recent, straightforward example, my reaction to a teenager's refusal to join the family for meals was very different from the parents' unconcerned response, because in my family there was a firm expectation that we children would be there, so I took for granted that this was an important aspect of family life. Having led parenting courses abroad in Asia as well as the UK, I have been fascinated by how much we have in common across cultures in our hopes and fears for our children, but I have also seen how profoundly we are shaped by our culture in response to gender roles, our expectations of our children and family life. Exploring these issues openly with parents can help clarify their own internal pressures, as well as help the therapist recognise the differences in outlook. Couples who have been brought up in different cultures can find they have conflicting views when they become parents. Tensions arise when their children reach an age when these differences become evident and parents find they have differing expectations of them according to their religious and cultural beliefs. Thinking with the couple about these differences may help them negotiate a consensus to prevent the children's behaviour becoming a point of conflict in the family.

Projective processes in families

A familiar pattern we see in psychotherapy is that 'the ill child' who is sent for therapy carries the projected, unresolved anxieties of the parents. Talking to parents about their families of origin can reveal these patterns, as in the example below where a father's anxieties from his past were exacerbating his son's emotional difficulties.

> Recalling his childhood, the father described memories of his younger brother who was withdrawn and disturbed, and was later diagnosed as suffering from Asperger's syndrome, a disorder on the autistic spectrum. He realised that this had made him fearful that his son would develop a similar condition. He had become highly sensitive to any aspect of his son's behaviour that reminded him of his brother, and then he lost sight that his son could be warm and outgoing, although he was socially awkward at times. Talking this through, he realised how different the two of them were, and his responses to his son changed, became freer and less anxious.

The impact of life events on child development

Life events impact on the whole family, but each person will see the event in their own way and may be surprised by how others react. In child psychotherapy, we hear children's perceptions of events, and how this shaped their view of themselves and others. The experiences may be as ordinary as the birth of the next child or traumatic events like serious illness, death or a disaster in the community. When parents think back to stressful events in the child's history with their therapist, they can sometimes discover why their child's development was disrupted at that time, leading to longer-term problems. If a teenager becomes intensely anxious when starting secondary school, it is useful to trace back to see if there were earlier sudden separations or traumatic losses which may have made the young person particularly sensitive to later transitions as they can trigger those early feelings of fear and loss again.

At the termly reviews with parents, the child psychotherapist and the parent worker, if there is one involved, can help parents reflect on what may have precipitated the child's problems, as well as reviewing the child's current progress. If parents discover likely causes of their child's difficulties, it can change their perception of their child's misbehaviour now they understand the underlying meaning of the child's distress. They can empathise with their child, rather than feel so provoked when problems occur next.

> Marcus was worrying his parents because of his cruel behaviour to his younger sister. They were relieved to understand what had led to his jealous attitude towards her when this was discussed at his regular review meeting, six months into treatment.
>
> Marcus aged six had an explosive temper, like a younger child, and he was very jealous of his little sister. He would sometimes physically hurt her if his parents were not looking. When the parent worker and I discussed this with the parents at a review, they told us that the birth of their second child had been particularly stressful because the new baby was premature. His mother was in mourning after the recent death of her mother, so she found it difficult to cope with two needy infants when she was grieving.
>
> We asked about family life at the time of his sister's birth. The parents remembered that Marcus, then three years old, was distressed by his baby sister getting all the attention. We talked about how he had suddenly lost the exclusive attention of the parents. Not understanding the crisis, he might have felt that he was the cause of his mother's unhappiness, that his mother did not love him as much any more. The parents admitted that they had been exhausted and anxious, and they had not been aware how miserable he was. Marcus lacked confidence and he had continued to be intolerant of his sister, and unable to deal with anger and jealousy with his peers. Understanding these factors made it easier for the parents to

tolerate Marcus' unreasonable behaviour and help him manage these feelings, while he continued to bring these difficult emotions to therapy. Progress was slow, as these were deep-seated feelings, hard for him to accept and work through, but the parents were more hopeful now that they too could help him, and that change was possible.

Living with a seriously ill or disabled sibling

Recently I have seen several young people for psychotherapy who have grown up with a seriously ill or disabled sibling, referred by their parents because of their concern about the effect that this has had on their children. I have realised how challenging this experience can be for the 'well child'. Young people think they ought to cope because they do not want to add to their parents' distress, but feel they have no place to take their fury or sadness about their sibling's illness and its impact on them. One young adult told me he had sometimes felt 'invisible' at home when he was younger because all the attention was given to his critically ill brother. His brother died when my patient was 14, and this added to his difficulties in mourning as he felt his brother was idealised by parents after his death. He sometimes felt like a poor substitute in their eyes. These are highly sensitive issues to discuss with parents as they know they could not protect their child from these stressful events. Yet when these difficult times are discussed openly, it can be a relief to the angry or depressed young person in treatment, who may be expressing the unresolved grief for the whole family. Family meetings may be the best setting for this discussion, ideally with the support of a family therapist, as everyone in the family will have memories and distressing feelings from these past events that were hard to share at the time.

Working with the parents' relationship as a couple and its impact on family dynamics

The parents' life experiences and expectations of their children shape the family milieu around the child. At times, the parents' relationship may suffer as a result of tensions between them and within the family. If they can be helped to discover together the underlying strains and support each other through these difficult times, a sense of equilibrium can be maintained for the whole family. The therapist working with parents, has to be sensitive to the boundaries of this work as the parents are not being offered therapy in their own right, but if the agreed focus is always on the well-being of the child in treatment, then there is a clear limit that all recognise.

There is often a dynamic between tensions in the couple relationship and the difficulties experienced by the young person in treatment. If there are unresolved conflicts between the parents, they can be drawn into over-close relationships with their children as a defence against intimacy in their own relationship. This is particularly likely when the children reach adolescence, with its accompanying resurgence of sexuality and aggression. The parents can become caught up in intense Oedipal relationships with their teenagers, to avoid the pain of their separation that has to occur at this age. Pairings can occur, a mother and son become emotionally over-close, leaving the father feeling excluded. Alternatively, a pattern of violent excited rows can develop between father and teenage daughter, leaving mother on the sidelines.

Young people are drawn into these pairings or sometimes try to provoke them, siding with one parent against another. This interferes with their need to find their own separate identity outside the family, so necessary as they grow up. We see in their own therapy how often young people feel trapped in these over-close ties. They would prefer their parents to be affectionate and close, and feel guilty about the parent who has been sidelined. Helping parents recognise and address these dynamics, thinking what may have caused the rift between them as a couple and what could bring them closer, can reduce divisions in the family, and free the young person to separate emotionally. In contrast, sometimes a distance develops between the father and his children because of his work demands or his role in the family, I have often meet boys in therapy who yearn for this closer relationship with their father as they grow up, and they are so encouraged if their fathers become more involved in the family, and maybe share some individual time doing activities together.

Another concerning family pattern we observe as therapists is when unresolved hostility and disappointment in a couple's relationship is projected onto a particular child in the family, who is then criticised and disliked. This enables the couple to stay together, joining in their concern or condemnation for their child who is seen as 'the problem'. The root of the disturbance may not be evident when the child's psychotherapy begins but it can become apparent in the work with parents over the months. I learnt this early on in my child psychotherapy career when I was working at the Cassel Hospital, an NHS residential resource which then offered treatment to families. I was seeing for psychotherapy a young girl who had been given harmful medication by her parents, while her parents had their own individual therapeutic treatment. She was a victim of induced illness syndrome. I wrote about this more fully in an article 'Poison glue' (Dowling 2008).

> In the work with this family, what emerged was that the angry but secretive attack on the child was an enactment of the fury and disappointment in the couple's relationship. Each felt neglected and mistreated by the other, but their desperate need of each other made this impossible to acknowledge. Both parents experienced neglect and abuse as children and, inevitably, they failed to meet each other's needs. This family needed

the safety of an in-patient setting to work with this severe level of disturbance. Here both parents and child received psychotherapy as well as nursing support with the demands of caring for their child. Their daughter slowly recovered in her own treatment and the parents worked hard to regain her trust and rebuild their relationship as a family.

Although this was a very serious breakdown of care, the pattern of a child in the family carrying the anxiety, depression or hostility that cannot be acknowledged between the parents is one frequently seen in therapeutic work with parents. A child may create difficulties to draw both parents together, sensing the distance that is developing between them, by getting into trouble or becoming ill. Either way, the child creates a distraction from the parents' arguments with each other. This is usually an unconscious process, not evident until it is discussed with the parents and the child in treatment. Parents have to face the painful fact that their difficulties are the underlying source of tension in the child, and the therapist working with the parent may be faced, at first, with hostility or denial rather than recognition. This is difficult work for the therapist who may fear that it can undermine the alliance with the parents that has protected the therapeutic work so far. However, working this through with the parents can change the dynamic in the family and relieve the pressure on the child who has felt responsible for holding the family together.

Challenging aspects of therapeutic work with parents and dealing with risk

Tensions can develop between parents and therapist that have the potential to undermine the continuation of the psychotherapy with a child. In my experience, these conflicts occur when the child's psychotherapy appears to represent a threat to the status quo and the parents' sense of emotional stability. A parent may be emotionally dependent on a child and so cannot tolerate the separation which occurs when the child becomes more independent due to the therapeutic work. There may be concerns that the parents' emotional difficulties are affecting their care of their children. These are disturbing and difficult situations for the child psychotherapist, who would usually need the support of a supervisor to help navigate these complex issues and clarify the dynamics involved.

Often it is possible to anticipate such difficulties in the assessment stage of the child's psychotherapy and to be cautious then as to whether the parents can tolerate the emotional challenges of this work, but this is not always the case.

One example of this occurred when I was working with a little girl who could not separate from her mother to go to nursery, as they were both reluctant to give up their closeness. In this case, resolution was possible because the parent was able to acknowledge her fear of loss, but I felt in a precarious position trying to balance the mother's needs and the child's as I describe below:

> Manel was four years old when I saw her for psychotherapy in the CAMHS service. She was very shy and nervous, and she found it difficult to separate from her thoughtful but depressed mother to go to nursery. The mother was a recent immigrant to this country and felt lonely and isolated in England, so she was desperate for her child's companionship. As Manel began to gain confidence in therapy and became more robust, the mother felt she was not needed by her daughter any more. She feared and resented the changes she saw in her daughter, although she also loved her and wanted the best for her.
>
> When the mother and I met for a termly review, the tension between us was high. I felt I had become a rival in her eyes for her daughter's affection, or an external authority who would intrude in her family life and enforce change. I was working alone in this case in private practice, and I wished I had a colleague who could help us manage these dynamics. In the review, I empathised with the mother's feeling that she was losing the closeness to her daughter and commended her commitment to bringing her to therapy despite her anxiety about the outcome. I saw that a compromise was needed and suggested we work towards ending the treatment as the little girl was now in nursery every day. We agreed to allow time for some final farewell sessions, so this piece of work ended better than I had feared. It was important for her daughter to see her mother and I working together, as I think she felt the growing tensions between us, and this was making her anxious and unsure about seeing me for therapy.

More serious conflicts can arise if the therapist is concerned that aspects of the parenting that have become apparent in the child's psychotherapy or in meetings with parents are causing harm to their patient, either emotionally, physically or sexually. These situations are more challenging if they occur in my private work as I do not have the support of the team around me to help me think things through, or the same sense of authority I felt working in the public services. However, I have found that when I can voice these concerns openly and the parents accept the need for change, then all may be relieved that these worrying issues are out in the open and can be addressed.

> I recall working with a 17-year-old girl who had become irritable and withdrawn and stopped studying after a long period of steady progress in therapy. Eventually she was able to tell me that her father was drinking too much, since recently losing his job. This was leading to violent rows between her parents and angry outbursts from her father towards her and her sister. I explained to my patient that I wanted to meet with her parents to raise these concerns with them. She agreed

with some relief, as she had felt increasingly anxious and not sure what to do, so I did not feel I was breaking my agreement of confidentiality with her. Fortunately, my relationship with these parents was sufficiently strong, as I had known them for a couple of years, so they were able to admit that this was true, they had been going through a difficult time, but it was now resolving and they said they would try to stop their distress spilling into the family.

It becomes more problematic in work with younger, more vulnerable children, when the parents have serious emotional difficulties and are reluctant to recognise their neglect or harm to the child. Child psychotherapists are likely to face this situation at times when they are working in the community offering parent–infant psychotherapy or therapeutic work with children considered at risk. Then they have the difficult task of managing their role in monitoring the child's well-being, while continuing to offer psychotherapy to the child. Seeing one's role as a part of team around the child, rather than carrying the responsibility alone, lessens the burden on the individual therapist in direct contact with the child. Support from managers and the team helps to balance one's concerns for the parents, who are also vulnerable, and the concern for the child's well-being When there are professionals alongside, looking after the families' needs, they can share the responsibility for managing the risk, and this difficult task becomes more manageable. The value of this team approach will be discussed further in the next chapter.

Therapeutic work with parents in an in-patient setting

I used to find it particularly demanding when I was working with adolescent mothers and their babies who were seen as at risk, in the Family Service at the Cassel Hospital (Dowling 2009). My anxiety and concern for both teenage mothers and their babies sometimes made me doubt my judgement. In these situations, the young parents' sense of being judged and monitored was high but it was still possible to maintain a therapeutic alliance if the young parent was determined to continue caring for her child, and recognised the previous failures in her care. I found that adolescents were relieved when I was clear about my concerns and the aspects of care they needed to change. As child psychotherapists, we are not accustomed to being so direct, even confrontative with parents, but sometimes it's necessary and helpful to address the highly ambivalent feelings that parents have towards their children and the potential for these to be acted out in a harmful way.

I have written about the value of this open dialogue with parents in our work at the Cassel Hospital (Dowling 2009) where families were assessed at the request of the courts because of concerns about their children's care. At assessment meetings and subsequent reviews, detailed clinical reports written by child psychotherapists and the rest of the team were openly discussed with the parents and their views sought. These difficult meetings were led by an experienced child psychiatrist who was able to work with the complex issues raised by the professional team and the often distraught emotional response of the parents. This detailed exploration of the families' difficulties could often bring about change because the concerns about the children and their consequences for the parents were so plainly mapped out that parents knew the commitment they had to make in order for their child to be eventually rehabilitated home.

As a child psychotherapist working privately now, I do not have the resources to work with such complicated family situations or this level of concern, so I am careful at the assessment stage not to accept referrals if they are too complex. If I am worried about a child being at risk, I inform the parents that I need to liaise closely with those most involved with the child and the family: the GP, the school, maybe the mental health worker for the parents or the social worker if they are involved, so that they are aware of my concerns and can monitor the child's development and well-being, alongside my therapeutic work.

Reaching out of the family into the community

The dynamic between the internal world of the children we see in therapy and their life in the community is a central theme in psychotherapy. We have to balance our focus as child psychotherapists on our therapeutic relationship with the child in the room, with the value of looking outside and considering issues raised by the external world. Understanding the young person's environment becomes more important as the child's social network widens to involve the extended family, school, friends, and the family's social, cultural and religious community. I often ask the parents for the child's school reports as this is offers an independent view of how the child is progressing with school work and friendships. Knowing if the child faces discrimination for being 'different' at school is important as these ties can become fraught with tension. Similarly, if the young person has to deal with issues of gender or disability, then knowing how these are seen in the extended family and the wider community becomes more important as the young person's social life moves outside the family.

Nowadays, as I have discussed earlier, the virtual community online may be as much part of the adolescent's world as the physical world outside. The parents face the difficult task of helping the young person set appropriate boundaries to this contact while recognising its central role in the young person's social life now. It is a difficult balance for the parents to negotiate, and one where they may value support to avoid the internet becoming the focus for conflict at home and for adolescent rebellion in the family.

For the isolated child, gradually making links in the community may lead to new friendships and a developing feeling of self-worth. When the time feels right, a psychotherapist working with the parents may help them to think about how to encourage the child to make these first steps to a social life. Brownies, football club or sleepovers can be a crucial point of emotional growth. In psychotherapy, this progress can be supported by helping the child with the anxiety, reluctance and excitement involved in making these transitions and new connections.

Joint meetings with the parents and the young person in therapy

There may be times, often later in psychotherapy, when its useful to arrange a joint meeting with the young person in therapy and the parents to explore issues that are becoming contentious to avoid a crisis occurring at home. There may be conflicts about the internet, homework or taking on responsibilities at home. If there is a parent worker then it is useful to do this meeting jointly. Then the child's psychotherapist can take more of a back seat so as to interfere as little as possible with the ongoing therapeutic work. Sometimes, this meeting might even involve siblings too.

> I recall a time when two teenage girls, one of whom I was seeing in therapy, were driving their mother to distraction. They were expecting her to run the home single-handed while she was in full-time work, leaving their clothes, cups and plates for her to clear away. She told me, after one of her daughter's sessions, that she was in despair. I discussed this with my patient and she agreed with my decision to arrange a joint meeting with her mother and sister, where these issues could be negotiated. Both girls agreed the tasks they would do at home, as well as also agreeing a non-violence rule between them as their arguments were another source of agitation for their mother. This took the heat out of arguments at home and allowed my individual therapeutic work with her son to continue in a less stressed environment.

These interruptions to the routine of weekly psychotherapy need careful thought as they will be interruptions to the therapy. The benefits have to outweigh the cost, and the timing must allow for sufficient working through of the issues with the young person raised before there is the next holiday break in therapy.

References

Dowling, D. (2008) Poison glue: The child's experience of Munchhausen syndrome by proxy. *Journal of Child Psychotherapy* 24(2): 307–326.

Dowling, D. (2009) Thinking aloud: A child psychotherapist assessing families for court. In A. Horne & M. Lanyado (eds) *Through Assessment to Consultation:*

Independent Psychoanalytic Approaches with Children and Adolescents, pp. 26–43. London: Routledge.

Fraiberg, S., Adelson, E. & Shapiro, V. (1975). Ghosts in the nursery: A psychoanalytic approach to the problem of impaired infant–mother relationships. In L. Fraiberg (ed) *Selected Writings of Selma Fraiberg*, pp. 100–136. Columbus, OH: Ohio State University Press, 1987.

George, C., Kaplan, N. & Main, M. (1985) The adult attachment interview. Unpublished manuscript. University of California at Berkeley.

Main, M., Kaplan, N. & Cassidy, J. (1985) Security in infancy, childhood, and adulthood: A move to the level of representation. *Monographs of the Society for Research in Child Development* 50(1–2): 66–104.

Chapter 7

Pleasures and challenges of working in a team

The challenge of teamwork is to create a working environment that supports therapeutic work and the professional team, while being open to new ideas and change. Many child psychotherapists will be part of a multidisciplinary team, whether they are working in the NHS or the voluntary sector. Others may be working privately but be part of the professional networks that develop around therapeutic work with children and families. Whatever the team setting, it is helpful to be aware of the dynamics that develop between those working together, and the impact of therapeutic involvement with troubled children and families on the functioning of the team.

Psychoanalytic thinking can help us understand our response to the team environment with its recognition of the unconscious processes that develop within a group working together and how this can reflect the dynamics of the families we treat. In her famous paper in 1959 'The functioning of social systems as a defence against anxiety', Isabel Menzies Lyth (1959) discussed how both individuals and institutions develop defences to protect themselves from the pain and anxiety of their particular work. She observed how rota systems had been set up on a paediatric ward which prevented nurses from being allocated to caring for particular children. This stopped them developing close relationships with the sick children and getting in touch with the pain of their suffering. These defences become counterproductive, undermining the capacity of those nurses in their caring role for the children. She proposed that the rota system should be changed to allow each child to have a special nurse, and that the organisation should provide reflective meetings where these underlying anxieties could be talked about openly. This would help the staff team process the painful feelings endemic to the work. Her ideas, of course, are just as relevant to our work as child psychotherapists. There is the need for us to look closely at the defences we create in response to the emotional pressures of our work and the importance of therapeutic teams becoming containing environments which have reflective spaces for the staff to think about their work.

When we join a team, we bring our own personal and professional history which shapes our expectations and response to the work group. The team too will have a history. Like a family, it is always in a process of change, but it has a culture which often persists despite these changes. Our interaction with the team, and our approach as child psychotherapists, will be influenced by all these factors. In this chapter I will look at the experience of a child psychotherapist in a team from four different perspectives: as a new member of a multidisciplinary team, working with complex cases, coping with risk and the reflective process in a team.

The multidisciplinary team

A multidisciplinary team in child mental health can include psychologists, social workers, nurses, psychiatrists, family therapist and child psychotherapists, each bringing their particular specialism to the team. They work together to consider the physical, social and psychological needs of the child, assessing need and offering treatment. The child psychotherapists will work alone and jointly in a range of work including assessments, consultations with parents, parent–infant psychotherapy, as well as brief and longer-term child and adolescent psychotherapy.

The different professional approaches and philosophies in a multidisciplinary team bring a creative tension but they can cause division when the group cannot agree. The potential for rivalry in interdisciplinary teams is shared by other disciplines. James Herbsleb, Professor of Software Research, ironically sums this up as the universal principle of interdisciplinary contempt (1996). There is a considerable literature on multidisciplinary team dynamics and a recent publication *Psychoanalysis, NHS, and Mental Health Work Today* (2017) edited by Alison Vaspe looks at a range of issues facing mental health teams in the NHS.

Iris Gibbs (2009) points out the potential for collaboration in a multidisciplinary team, a setting that can offer different perspectives on culture and life experience. A child psychotherapist working with a young person from a different cultural and ethnic origin can enlist the expertise of others to consider the assessment and the most appropriate intervention for the family. But it can also be a challenging environment. In any team setting, there will be competition for resources, conflicting ideas about clinical approaches and mixed views about strategy initiatives put forward by management. All these will influence the team's relationships with each other and need to be thought about if the team is to function well.

Joining a team

I worked for many years as a child psychotherapist and as a manager, but I still remember my anxiety when I first joined a team as a trainee in a new post in a CAMHS team. I was their first child psychotherapist and there was considerable reluctance from some of the multidisciplinary team to make space for a psychoanalytic child psychotherapist who would offer therapy to some 'chosen' children, working intensively and over long periods. This was seen as very different from the time-limited problem-solving approach that they offered. I felt rather lonely coming from a busy close-knit social work team, but I slowly developed good working relationships in this very different environment and I came to appreciate what an adjustment it must have been for the team taking on a new member with a psychoanalytic approach.

Finding one's place in a new work setting takes time. In many CAMHS teams now, resources are so limited that child psychotherapists do not have their own desks or regular rooms for seeing children for psychotherapy. A trainee child psychotherapist joining a team can feel deskilled, and there is a danger that the expertise and experience the trainee gained in previous work are left behind. Yet a new arrival has fresh eyes and can often see problems that others take for granted, where the tensions are in the team, and how much emotional sharing and support there is between the professions, as well as the more practical anomalies that could be improved. The question is where to take these thoughts and feelings? A reflective space is needed where these issues can be explored.

The importance of a containing environment

A consistent theme in Winnicott's work (1984) is the need for a resilient environment for parenting children and for therapeutic work. He considered that the more challenging the child's pathology, the greater the need for a robust environment. He thought that deprived and anti-social children need to express their hatred, and that this anger can ripple through the professional network, affecting all those involved in the care of these children. As discussed by Menzies Lyth, a crucial function of the team is to offer containment to help manage these difficult feelings. It is much harder to remain thoughtful if the work setting does not feel resilient. In my experience, a sense of safety as a child psychotherapist is derived from supportive relationships within the team built up over time, an effective supervisory system, clear child protection procedures to ensure an appropriate response and the support of management in dealing with risk.

Another contributor to resilience is maintaining a reasonable workload. When our capacities are over-stretched, our ordinary work becomes a burden. Vulnerable children and their parents, reliant on us for support, are vigilant and pick up our anxiety and become more challenging if we are under stress.

Britton suggests that

> the more primitive mechanisms and defences against anxiety are being used, the more is every professional contact likely to become a scene for action and for the professional to yield ... to re-enact an unconscious situation.
>
> (Britton 1995: 52)

If there are too many challenging children in our caseload, our capacity to think about them can be compromised by the disturbing feelings that flood into us in each session. Then we can react impulsively rather than thoughtfully, if there is a crisis.

Complex cases create complex dynamics

Another factor in the daily work of a child psychotherapist that can precipitate conflict with others in the multidisciplinary team or within a professional network is the difficult dynamics that develop around highly emotional complex cases, particularly those involving children at risk. These tensions between the professionals often mirror those in the family at the centre of the work, but they are not recognised until everyone sits down together to discuss their differences.

Typically, professionals identify with their own clients, seeing life from their perspective, often becoming defensive on their behalf. This was my experience working with a difficult schoolboy, alongside the teacher and the parent worker:

> The young lad was creating trouble at home and at school with his disruptive behaviour. I was feeling inadequate in my role as his psychotherapist, as he was highly defended and hard to reach in the sessions, the work was slow to progress, and his behaviour was not improving. The school emailed the parents regularly to tell them about the child's misdemeanours and the parents would forward these emails to me, feeling criticised and powerless themselves. The parent worker in this case, a colleague I knew well, held the hope that my involvement would help the troubled boy in time. We convened a joint meeting with the parents and the school teacher where I explained the little I was beginning to understand about their son's unhappiness, and my colleague supported the parents, recognising their frustration but also suggesting ideas to help them listen closely when he was distressed, as this was likely to reduce his misbehaviour. She also reaffirmed their attempts to be firm but understanding of his demands. I wrote to the Head of the school describing my work and my hope that therapeutic help would help the boy gradually learn to manage his feelings better, so he would not be such a handful in class.

Until we met to think together in the meeting, the 'blame' for this boy's behaviour swung between us all. As the child's therapist, I felt critical of the parents and teachers, who did not understand just how depressed he was and how he struggled to manage each day in school. The class teacher was critical of the parents for not setting clear enough boundaries for the child, and the parents felt everyone was critical of their parenting and did not realise just how demanding and difficult he was at home. The tensions between the adults reflected the anger, anxiety and conflict within the child. They could have escalated if we had not talked them over and recognised them as projections that could be managed more thoughtfully. Without this type of shared communication, distrust would have increased between the adults involved. The young boy may have been excluded from school for his aggression to other children, the parents would have felt more hopeless, making my task as a therapist reaching out to the boy more difficult.

If such differences can be discussed openly and the anxieties contained, the multiple viewpoints of a team approach can bring a depth and breadth to the clinical work not possible if one person is working alone. A child's emotional problems are usually the result of many factors interacting, so this wider viewpoint makes it possible to see the multi-layered aspect of the child's difficulties. In large professional meetings, the most crucial information often comes from those who know children best, like foster parents, family support workers or teaching assistants. These contributors may not speak up as they have the least status and may not be confident in this professional setting. It is important to ensure that their voices are heard, if vital pieces of the jigsaw are not to be lost. The child psychotherapist listening to these different perspectives can often act as an advocate for the child, explaining the child's perspective and struggles in daily life.

Issues of confidentiality

Working closely with the network can create dilemmas for the child psychotherapist who wishes to protect the young person's confidentiality. My compromise is that I explain to all involved, including the young person in treatment, that I will share the themes but not the content of the therapy, and feedback what I can to my patient. In practice, this means giving a careful summary of the issues relevant to those involved. Ideally, I will bring some contribution from the young person in treatment too. With teenagers, it is often helpful to involve them in meetings with their parents, social workers or care staff, but they may be reluctant to attend if life is still very difficult for them.

When a therapist is working as part of a clinic team or a therapeutic setting, it is more helpful to consider that confidentiality is kept within the team rather than by the individual worker, and often families feel a commitment to the clinic or institution as a whole. Parents are made aware when the therapeutic work begins that details of therapy are usually shared with both the supervisor and the therapeutic colleagues in clinical discussions, in order to provide a good service to them.

Writing succinct but informative records for the shared online records of a Mental Health Trust is another learning curve for a newer child psychotherapist. Parents have access to their children's records, as long as this does not create risk to the child, so these records need to be written by the child psychotherapist in a way that respects the parents' perspective and protects the ongoing work with the child.

Managing risk

When you are anxious about the level of risk in the children or families you are seeing, it is important to feel you have the support of the team around you. We develop informal support systems with our colleagues but we also need formal systems of supervision and management where the clinical responsibility for decision-making in situations of risk is clearly delineated. When there is concern about a child's welfare, a child psychotherapist needs access to an experienced child care practitioner who has time to talk things over and can clarify the procedures. This senior colleague can support the therapist in offering a caring but firm approach to ensure the young person comes to no harm.

Risk is not always easily identifiable. If there is high profile risky behaviour, like a young person's suicide attempt or abuse to a young child, then the response is clear, and senior professionals can be brought in to make an assessment of what input is needed. It is less straightforward when the child psychotherapist faces a worrying situation each week that never quite reaches crisis level. Such as a child turning up for sessions looking dirty and uncared for, or a teenager showing an ongoing low-level misery or self-harm in therapy sessions.

Taking take these concerns to supervision can help the child psychotherapist to clarify the level of concern and how to respond. Often there are policy directives dictating online forms that need to be completed to register concern. This is a necessary practice to alert the professional team but not a solution in itself. It is hard to capture the level of risk by ticking boxes on a risk form. The child psychotherapist may be left after a therapy session with a feeling of deep anxiety that is hard to pin down, a gut feeling or an intuition. It is likely that these are countertransference feelings in response to powerful non-verbal communications from the young person that cannot yet be to put into words. A detailed discussion of recent sessions and events in the young person's life with senior staff can help identify the issues underlying the young person's distress. Sharing concerns can bring a sense of perspective. There is a danger that by bearing the worry alone, the child psychotherapist ends up taking the worry home with it still unresolved.

Issues of risk reveal the defences that develop in us as workers and as a team. Under stress, we can become emotionally detached to protect ourselves from too much anxiety and distress, or we can rush into action to deal with our anxiety. It is difficult to stay in touch and think about painful or complex feelings, particularly if the distress is being denied by our patients too. I recall one such situation when I was reluctant to report a young man who was saying in an offhand way he felt suicidal sometimes. He did not want me to make this public as he feared his parents would overreact, and I felt similarly anxious not to be seen as overreacting in some way. Talking this over with colleagues, I realised I had become caught up in his denial and lack of care for himself, and that this could spiral unless I took action. I explained to him I would be telling his parents and his GP of my concerns. The fact that I had taken his concerns seriously helped him recognise his need for help, and he was able to tell his parents about his deep unhappiness.

A similar type of defensive response can develop in a team when it is besieged by too much pressure or distress. The group can develop a level of detachment or become too rigid, so that the level of risk and need of the families we work with is not recognised. Another reaction to increased work pressure is to take on too much, an omnipotent attitude of 'we can manage against the odds', and a denial that some staff have become too emotionally overloaded by difficult cases to work effectively. If the team meets together in regular team meetings, it provides an opportunity to consider together their level of stress and the effect it is having on them and their work.

A reflective team

When the team is stable, it may function well with a collaborative approach, but with the loss of a well-liked and experienced manager or member of staff, changes to practice or cuts in resources, the team's morale and thinking capacity may deteriorate. A regular reflective team meeting can be a place where the life of the team can be discussed and these pressures can be identified and understood. Sadly these meetings tend to get cancelled when work pressures are high, or it can become focused on practical issues and the strains facing the staff are ignored. When there is time to reflect on the working process, and the team trust each other enough to talk openly and honestly, it becomes clear how defences emerge and splits develop, often along familiar lines within a team, and between professional groupings. Thinking about these dynamics can help a team manage the tensions that arise.

The idea of a culture of enquiry developed by Tom Main (1989) is illuminating here.

He was a psychoanalyst and Director of the Cassel Hospital from 1946 to 1976. He saw the culture of enquiry as a key aspect of the therapeutic community developed in the in-patient psychiatric hospital. Staff and patients were encouraged to be curious and explore every aspect of their working life together, in order to understand the unconscious processes that influenced their emotional life, their interpersonal relationships and their place in social groups. Different aspects of the community life were discussed at a range of meetings and in individual psychotherapy sessions. Although this approach developed in an in-patient service, I think it is a helpful concept for thinking more broadly about the life of a therapeutic team. It taught me to listen closely to how staff talked about their patients as well as what they said.

> I heard a family nurse talk sadly, at a handover meeting, about a new mother's renewed anxiety and roughness bathing her baby, and the baby's distress. I was the mother's parent–infant psychotherapist, and I realised that her mental health was deteriorating, and that she needed additional support with her baby's care. I sensed in the nurse's sadness that she had picked up how distressed this mother was about her state of mind, and that the mother felt guilty about the aggression she had shown towards her baby. I also realised that by spending much of my time in my therapy room, I had neglected to talk to this nurse, so I had missed the informal opportunity to ask her how things were going with our shared patient.

Working relationships are crucial in any work setting. If a team is encouraged to be curious, and talk about their relationships in reflective meetings, these gaps or conflicts will be recognised and available for further thought. At the Cassel, the team working with a family attended regular nurse–therapist supervisions, led by a senior nurse and therapist. Here the child psychotherapist, adult psychotherapist and nurse talked about their experience of working with a family, but also how well, or not, they were working together. Thinking together about this process always shed light on the family disturbance as it was reflected in the team relationships. Often there was 'splitting', one member of the team favoured by the family, and another felt rejected and useless. This alienated worker carried important feelings of failure and inadequacy that mirrored those of the parents. Once this process was recognised, the dynamics were rebalanced within the team and they could return to work in a more balanced way with the family. Lydia Tischler, a consultant child psychotherapist who worked at the Cassel, has written about this approach in her chapter on 'Nurse–therapist supervision' (1987).

Similar patterns of splitting can happen in many therapeutic settings. I have seen how therapeutic work with adolescents can create conflicts within a professional team, some feeling more tolerant of the teenagers' acting-out behaviour while others feel critical, thinking the teenagers should take more responsibility for their behaviour. Both of these emotional responses hold some truth, but this paradoxical position is hard to maintain in a team, as it creates so much doubt and uncertainty. Yet, it is only by taking into account 'the good and bad' aspects of the split that realistic decisions can be made about the young people's treatment.

For professionals to talk openly about their feelings, and 'comfortably' disagree with each other requires relationships of trust which take time to build up between workers. This is easier when the team feel well supported in a good management structure. In times of crisis, or when attitudes became very polarised, the team may feel their own resources are not enough. Then it can be helpful to have the involvement of an external professional consultant to help the team understand why, at this particular time, they are finding it hard to function together successfully.

Working independently

In this chapter, I have talked primarily about the experience of working as part of a team. However, to conclude, I would like to think briefly about child psychotherapists who work alone in a setting like a school, or privately in the community, who have to create their own team of supportive colleagues who can share ideas and concerns, and who appreciate the contribution of a psychotherapeutic approach. The complexity of work with children and families and the level of risk involved makes working alone particularly hard. Since starting in private practice I have joined colleagues locally so that I am now part of a local team of independent practitioners, and I receive clinical supervision, both individually and in this peer group, to think about my work. Over time, this team has become part of a network of professionals working locally with children, and we have linked in with local schools, children's centres and the local CAMHS service. We now feel more integrated into our community in our therapeutic work, and I feel well supported in my practice.

Conclusion

Writing about 'The multidisciplinary team' (2009), Gabrielle Crockatt emphasises the importance of a multi-professional approach to mental health work with families because of their complex and wide-ranging needs. She cites evidence collected by Dr Zarina Kurtz (Kurtz et al. 1996) to support this. Recognising how hard it can be to work together as professionals, Gabrielle Crockatt suggests that we need to develop our capacity for effective co-working. The ideas I have discussed in this chapter are some that might contribute to making this more multi-professional approach more effective.

References

Britton, M. (1995) Re-enactment as an unwitting professional response to family dynamics. In M. Bower (ed) *Using Psychoanalytic Ideas for Child and Family Social Work*, pp. 49–59. London: Routledge.

Crockatt, G. (2009) The child psychotherapist in the multidisciplinary team. In M. Lanyado & A. Horne (eds) *The Handbook of Child and Adolescent Psychotherapy*, pp. 101–113. London: Routledge.

Gibbs, I. (2009) Reflections on race and culture in therapeutic consultation and assessment. In A. Horne & M. Lanyado (eds) *Through Assessment to Consultation*, pp. 93–102. London: Routledge.

Herbsleb, J. (1996) A sytematic survey of CMM experience and results. In H.D. Rombach (ed) *Proceedings of the 18th International Conference on Software Engineering*, pp. 323–330. Washington, DC: IEEE Computer Society.

Kurtz, Z., Thornes, R. & Wolkind, S. (1996) *Treating Children Well: A Guide to Using the Evidence Base in Commissioning and Managing Services of the Mental Health of Children and Young People*. London: Mental Health Foundation.

Main, T.F. (1989) *The Ailment and Other Psychoanalytic Essays*. London: Free Association Books.

Menzies Lyth, I. (1959) The functioning of social systems as a defence against anxiety. In I. Menzies Lyth (ed) *Containing Anxiety in Institutions: Selected Essays*, pp. 95–121. London: Free Association Books, 1988.

Tischler, L. (1987) Nurse–therapist supervision. In R. Kennedy, A. Heymans & L. Tischler (eds) *The Family as In-patient*, pp. 95–107. London: Free Association Books.

Vaspe, A. (ed) (2017) *Psychoanalysis, NHS, and Mental Health Work Today*. London: Karnac.

Winnicott, D.W. (1984) *Deprivation and Delinquency*. London and New York: Tavistock.

Part 2

Hard times

The challenges of child psychotherapy

Chapter 8

Facing despair, doubt and anger – and finding hope

In his book *At Home in the World* (2016) Thich Nhat Hanh, a Buddhist teacher, describes how, as a young boy in Vietnam, he wanted to reach a beautifully coloured dead leaf in a deep clay pot of water. He stirred the water 20 times with a stick, but he could not reach it, so he threw the stick away in frustration. He returned a few minutes later, and the leaf was floating on the surface, so he could take it easily. The teacher tells this story to explain his belief in the value of the unconscious for solving problems that our conscious thinking mind cannot solve on its own.

In psychotherapy, much of the understanding emerges from the unconscious mind in both patient and therapist, the thoughts and feelings that arise from their interaction at this deep level. My experience is that there is an inherent healing process enabling the mind to recover, if the will to change is strong enough. With children, we can add the drive to develop and grow, while recognising that this is not straightforward as there is also a resistance to change in all of us. And there is an inherent human need to be loving and loved, to be in a relationship with others and the world, which we have to seek out in the withdrawn or alienated young person.

When I first thought about writing this chapter, I was thinking of the intensely difficult times for the patient in therapy when change seems so hard to achieve. Now I am writing it, I am also aware of the times when psychotherapists feel angry and despairing in their work. In this chapter, I will try to understand these aspects of therapy. There are times when our patient appears to have lost hope and becomes stuck in repetitious patterns, or attacks any progress in a self-destructive way. We also can lose our sense of direction in the therapeutic work and doubt our capacity to help the young person. So how does hope arrive in therapy? Often it is unexpected, and sometimes it can be challenging too, as patients can resist progress and fear the possibility of change.

The loss of hope

Many of the troubled children and adolescents we see have long-standing emotional difficulties that are inextricably entwined with troubled times in their family. They often feel that their problems are insoluble, reflecting a sense of chronic despair in the family. They may have been too young to understand the troubling events at home that led to their feelings of distress, but when these memories begin to surface in the sessions, a feeling of despair can pervade the therapy. The young person loses hope that therapy can resolve anything and, at times, may not want to attend sessions, or may withdraw and become resistant to any interpretations.

Facing a young person's despair and anger, session after session, can undermine one's confidence as a therapist, even though we know that it is only by being in touch with these feelings that we can understand the young person's loneliness and confusion, and find some clarity about the reasons why. Time can feel like it is slipping away if this continues for many weeks, and this weighs heavily as the young patient is missing out on important years of his or her life. I saw two teenagers for therapy, both severely depressed, angry and lonely, whose therapy often seemed caught in this type of impasse.

Both these young people had retreated from the world to the family, which was both a refuge and a place of persecution. They struggled to make friends and they had lost touch with their peers. They were missing out on schooling, despite being clever and articulate. They were both scared by adolescence, as they felt that a gulf separated them from normal young people of their own age. They were now trying to emerge from these states in psychotherapy. These young people had been given different diagnoses: Asperger's, social anxiety and depression, but one common factor was their parents' fear that they would not recover.

These parents had family histories of depression and trauma creating an underlying pessimism about the possibility of their children being well and happy. The youngsters appeared to have identified unconsciously with their parents' anxiety about their future which had compounded their own fears of growing up. Therapy offered a place away from these family projections where these issues could be explored, so the adolescents could find their own sense of self and a sense of purpose, separate from their perceived identity in the family. The parents desperately wanted a different life for their children from their own deprivation and were committed to seeking help for them.

Feeling stuck, faced with these youngsters' chronic unhappiness, I had to work hard to keep my thinking lively and sustain some hope in the future. I was struck by the powerful image of the Dementors in the story of Harry Potter, dark frightening figures who sucked the life and the spirit out of any person they captured. In these characters, J.K. Rowling (1999) brought to life the despair of those who are overwhelmed by depression. I think my feeling of impasse was partly a response to this desperation, but also a result of my inability to form a coherent diagnosis and my uncertainty how to help. When I started to explore the literature and think about their clinical material, I began to see their chronic state as a retreat into a black hole of despair, like Francis Tustin's (1972) description of the autistic retreat. She saw this as a grief response to a traumatic separation from the mother. I thought these teenagers also feared that becoming independent would feel like a traumatic rupture, rather than a gradual and meaningful move towards individuation and freedom.

Whatever the historic or developmental difficulty that had led to their current crisis, these youngsters saw themselves as too damaged and different now to become like other teenagers. They felt alienated from normal life. As one teenager put it: 'I'm weird, I always will be'. Adolescence offered them a chance to discover their own identity as separate from that projected onto them by their parents, but it felt an enormous risk dealing with the challenges of separation, heightened aggression and sexuality when they felt so vulnerable. They were highly ambivalent about taking this next step while they were still mourning and in grievance about a childhood they felt was stolen from them. My therapeutic task seemed to be to allow this mourning, but also to question their almost perverse enjoyment of despair at the expense of ordinary day-to-day living, as shown by Anna whom I discuss below.

Anna was a young woman, aged 16, whose misery and despair seemed to pervade her being. When I first met her, she was thin and gaunt, and she seemed to drag herself into the therapy room. Anna told me about her paranoid fears of living in a persecuting world. She was fearful of her thoughts which were endlessly pre-occupied with fantasies of poisoning others or killing herself. She felt estranged, unlike other young women. She wanted to overcome these fears and, in calmer moments, she knew that she was clever, articulate and had a supportive, if troubled, family who were determined to help her recover.

Anna's father's family had suffered from poverty and unemployment, and the men drank too much. Anna remembered her father's rages when she was young, and how these had frightened her, although now her father was calmer, in a settled job as a lab technician, and no longer drank. Anna's mother was a quiet, anxious woman who worked as a teaching assistant. She was rather isolated, fearful of the conflict in her family, and unsure how to relate to her sharp-tongued daughter.

For many months, Anna struggled in therapy to find a way to talk about her horrific thoughts. She drew pictures of herself as a frightening witch, a thin starving figure, or a homeless girl on the streets. Gradually, we looked at the feelings behind these macabre images, her fury that she found exciting and frightening, and her stubborn refusal to allow herself to be emotionally nourished by those close to her. She watched endless horror films on her laptop at night that fed her macabre fantasy life. There were also moments of warmer interaction with her brother, Tod, and her mother, and this gave her a sense of connection with life and some hope.

Eventually Anna began to explore the past. She described herself when she was younger, feeling starved of attention, alone and scared, unable either to be angry or to ask for affection. The sadness of these memories softened the harshness of her self-criticism and tempered her guilt about her rage and her distrust of others. She became more reflective and, in discussion, we began to bring together these different aspects of her life experience and how they had shaped her negative images of herself and others. While we were having these conversations, she began to feel more hopeful and this helped her achieve more at school and make tentative steps towards friendship with her peers.

For young people like Anna, the therapeutic relationship is a safe setting to face their anxiety about feelings that had been too overwhelming for them or their family to manage alone, and it gives them a space to try out being different. What also helped this adolescent was her parents' willingness to think about their own painful histories in parent support sessions and to recognise how their anxieties had made them overprotective and doubtful of their teenagers' capacity to grow into healthy young adults.

Another aspect of working with these troubled young people is that they are so ambivalent about change, they can create a tortuous interaction in the sessions, so the therapist can feel blocked from offering help. This defensive behaviour covers up what Glasser (1998) describes as core complex anxieties, a fear of either becoming too close and merged with those they depend on, or of being rejected and abandoned by them. Peter, the other teenager I referred to, led me in a punishing dialogue as I struggled to get to know him in psychotherapy:

Peter, aged 14, was unhappy and isolated but he could not allow himself to talk about his fears and conflicts in therapy. He was so fearful of intimacy that he could only initiate a self-defeating interaction, denigrating me and others, while telling me in despair that he felt so alone. I often felt useless, angry with him for mocking me and keeping me at a distance. If I tried to draw out his achievements, I was seen as ignoring his unhappiness. If I drew attention to his self-criticism and disparagement of myself and others, he saw it as an attack. When we had a lighter session with some humour between us, he ended the session with a scathing, 'So I hope you enjoyed that'. He could not believe in his capacity to grow up or my wish to help him. He was a talented German speaker and when he did get an opportunity to go to Germany with a group of students, he turned it down. It felt so unsafe to take a step forward.

For Peter, therapy was a very slow process. Crab-like, he moved sideways to move forward. In time, he bravely began to face his aggression towards others and himself and he recognised how this covered up his anxiety about being loving and being loveable. He appreciated my persistence and concern and he slowly became more open, talking about his feelings, and this enabled him to respond more warmly to others and to recognise that he had something to offer and talents to develop.

Surviving hatred

Working with these young people can generate powerful feelings of dislike, despair and hopelessness in us as psychotherapists which we may find hard to process and not retaliate. As Ann Horne points out in her paper, 'Brief communications from the edge: Psychotherapy with challenging adolescents' (2006 [2001]):

> In the countertransference we find ourselves in touch with fundamental primitive fears, cruel and punishing superegos, immature atoll-like egos, and defences designed to deny intimacy, attachment, affect and pain. We need to cope with not-knowing – often for long spells – and to think both developmentally and psychoanalytically, recognising when the opportunity of becoming a 'new object' glimmers, yet in touch with the dangers inherent in this for the patient.

We have to find a way to survive their hatred and ours, precipitated by their destructive behaviour. As Winnicott says:

> However much he [the therapist] loves his patients he cannot avoid hating them and fearing them, and the better he knows this, the less will hate and fear be the motives determining what he does to his patients.
> (Winnicott 1947: 195)

I recall the feeling of relief and recognition when I read these lines, discovering that my feelings of hatred for a few young patients and some of their parents had a place in our work and could be understood. Winnicott's contribution in his paper 'Hate in the countertransference' was to use his own experience as an analyst to map out the dynamics of hatred as a necessary part of his work. He describes the therapist's countertransference to the primitive hatred of severely disturbed children, and the more ordinary ambivalence of motherhood and work with less disturbed patients. He also talks about how hard it is for foster carers (and therapists) of separated and deprived children to put up with the children's anger, as they test out their carers' ability to survive, once they have seen some hope of a future there.

Stuck in despair

Inevitably, there are times in therapy when the aims that seemed so clear at the beginning become harder to achieve, or temporarily get lost in the circuitous journey towards understanding and change. Therapy that begins with some hope then becomes stuck. This occurred in the mid phase of therapy with the young girl, Jenny, whom I discussed earlier in Chapter 1. Her play evoked feelings of paralysis, isolation and despair which left me unsure how to respond. Her stubborn refusal to speak more than a few words created a feeling of inertia and apathy in me. I was puzzled. Was she communicating a depression that had begun in infancy, or was she sitting on a fury which she was scared to express, because it felt so pervasive and destructive? Or both? I will attempt to describe this below.

> Jenny rarely talked to me in these midway sessions, but there was such unhappiness in her peaky, blank face that I was left feeling sad and bemused for a long time after she had gone. Every week, Jenny rolled up her sleeves and set up a scene with the figures in the sand tray. Her sandscapes were detailed but her stories never developed. She had chosen a small rabbit who I think represented her and was present in each story. She would build a small town with a mother and a child waiting for a train, some farm animals nearby but nothing ever happened. Then a pair of fighting boxers, a crocodile and a gorilla from the toy box were placed carefully in the centre of the scene. They were threatening, but unable to move. There was a wizard but I was told he had no magic, he was just a statue. The rabbit was always there, observing but not moving either. I thought Jenny was showing me how she felt so emotionally immobilised by her unhappiness. Nothing could change, develop or grow.

Christopher Bollas' concept of 'the unthought known' (1987) suggests a way of understanding this young girl. He said that patients let us know and feel in the countertransference their early experience of being an infant, through their moods and way of relating to us. He called it 'the unthought known', because it is familiar, 'known' to the patients, and has shaped their way of experiencing the world since infancy. But these emotions cannot be communicated in words because they were preverbal feeling states. If the therapist can find the language to talk about this experience, then the patient discovers that these long-known but confusing feelings can be recognised and understood.

These ideas made sense to me of Jenny's experience. I thought her infancy and early childhood was a bleak lonely time when she felt she could not reach out to be comforted by her parents and somehow she felt responsible for this, that she was unloveable. These thoughts seemed plausible when I talked to her parents as her mother said she had post-natal depression for a year after her daughter's birth, so the bond between them had been slow to develop. She recalled that, when Jenny was little, she had always found separations difficult, as if she was anxious about losing this late-developing attachment.

In her play, Jenny seemed to be in touch with an early paralysing depression. I tried to link this experience with the characters in story, a safer territory to discuss her feelings. I said the rabbit must be sad because she was so alone and she had no one to play with, and she might be frightened of the scary figures too. She wished someone could come along and help her. I continued this dialogue over the sessions and gradually these brief observations of mine became a narrative she expected, and it helped her begin to bring her story to life. When the therapist can recognise patterns, like I attempted to do here, and the child's play becomes comprehensible, it then becomes possible to work through some of these unresolved feelings from the past which are preventing the child from developing emotionally.

Hope and the fear of change

Hope when it arrives in therapy can be elusive. It may appear briefly in sessions then disappear, or grow so imperceptibly you do not notice it at the time. Only retrospectively can you see when it began. Some children show new hope briefly, but then they don't want you to see it as you might ignore those unhappy feelings which still trouble them.

As a therapist you will notice signs of progress. There is a warmer feeling in the relationship between you and your young patient. The child may spend a quiet contented moment playing in the sand tray or will tell you about a happy time with a parent or friend at the weekend. A youngster may laugh spontaneously for the first time and becomes less watchful as sessions become more relaxed. Teenagers become interested in their appearance. They are more independent and find a new sense of purpose in life. Sometimes you discover that there is progress in school or better relationships at home, but the young patient does not tell you, fearing that the good times will not last, and they will be disappointed again.

It is interesting to reflect on what brings about these positive developments, although it is likely to be many factors coming together. A young person can find security and understanding in the new relationship with the psychotherapist, and this makes it possible to look at other important relationships more positively and realistically. A young woman, reflecting on her therapy with me, told me that our work together had helped her look back at her relationship with her mother and sister in a different way. Instead of simply feeling rejected, she now recognised that she had been quite challenging in her behaviour to them, so she could appreciate now their attempts to rebuild a relationship with her and respond more warmly to them.

From a sadder perspective, a new sense of hopefulness can be too much for some deprived and disturbed children as it creates a sense of longing for what might have been if their life had been easier. It can feel like too little too late, and so it cannot be appreciated. I experienced this painful response from a young boy I saw when I worked in CAMHS whose relationship with his single mother was fraught, as she was so depressed and easily irritated. He had been through periods of neglect and experienced abuse from his father in early childhood. Memories from these times were painful and he kept them at bay with bravado and threatening behaviour. He took to therapy with enthusiasm, loving the attention and understanding, but this new relationship with me evoked unbearable feelings of longing for the care he had missed in the early years, and he could not rely on receiving this in his family life now. I began to see signs, first in his play and then in his provocative behaviour towards me that, if I did not intervene, he would erupt into violence in the sessions from the frustration and pain. I sadly decided to bring the therapy to a premature ending to protect him from becoming destructive and the therapy breaking down. He had a support worker in school and I felt that his worker could offer a less intense but supportive relationship which would be more helpful to him in the long term.

Consolidating progress

When young people make progress in therapy and it is sustained, I think it is important that this development is recognised by the therapist. This balances the poor self-image and the harsh self-criticism that has been their image of themselves for many years. A new sense of hope and security in the therapeutic relationship can lead to a further phase in recovery; the beginning of concern for the therapist and others, fair play in games, and a more generous response to their siblings. At this stage, children often want to mend the play materials they have damaged, as a gesture of reparation, and I help them in every way I can with ample supplies of sticky tape and glue. The fact that a torn poster will always show signs of the fury when the child tore it up is a reminder that the reality of the past cannot be got rid of, only repaired. Young people begin to take responsibility for what they have done wrong and try to mend relationships. At home, teenagers often want to take on a more mature role and a new position in the family, and it is important that this is recognised and admired by their parents and the siblings too, where possible.

Looking after oneself

Working with high levels of distress and anger in our young patients and their families is demanding and can lead to burn-out unless we take care of ourselves. I worked for many years with severely disturbed families, but the toll of this work was ameliorated for me by working in a supportive team in a well-functioning therapeutic community. However, I have spoken to other child psychotherapists working primarily with very disturbed 'looked-after' children who have found it too much, seeing one distressed and disturbed child after another. It may only be when a therapist is talking things over with a colleague, or in supervision, that this stress is recognised. This is the time to take steps where possible to ensure that there is a better balance in the work, a manageable mix in the caseload between the more troubled children and those who are less disturbed, and a realistic limit to the number of therapy sessions each day. Recognising these pressures, I think what makes this work sustainable is seeing how well children can use psychotherapy to recover from emotional disturbance and a traumatic past. The emotional scars and deprivation are still there, but the children have found the hope and resilience to look forward and wholeheartedly engage in the task of growing up.

In this book, I have made occasional references to Buddhist thinkers, Thich Nhat Hanh and Shunryu Suzuki. Like other child psychotherapists, Monica Lanyado (2012), Graham Music and Maria Pozzi Monzo (2014) to name a few, I have found Buddhist philosophy with its emphasis on awareness of the present moment, and treating the suffering side of the self and others with compassion, a helpful philosophy in my work. The stillness and self-awareness I aim to achieve in meditation seems similar to me to the reflective self we aim to develop in our patients. I don't directly teach these ideas to the children I work with, but I have found that on a hectic day or in a stressful session, a few minutes of quiet helps me recover my equanimity, and this may be a useful tool for others too.

References

Bollas, C. (1987) *The Shadow of the Object: Psychoanalysis of the Unthought Known*. London: Free Association Books.

Glasser, M. (1998) On violence: A preliminary communication. *International Journal of Psycho-Analysis* 79(5): 887–902.

Hanh, T.N. (2016) *At Home in the World: Stories and Essential Teachings from a Monk's Life*. Berkeley, CA: Parallax Press.

Horne, A. (2006 [2001]) Brief communications from the edge: Psychotherapy with challenging adolescents. In M. Lanyado & A. Horne (eds) *A Question of Technique: Independent Psychoanalytic Approaches with Children and Young People*, pp. 128–142. London: Routledge.

Lanyado, M. (2012) Transition and change: An exploration of the resonances between transitional and meditative states of mind and their roles in the therapeutic process. In A. Horne & M. Lanyado (eds) *Winnicott's Children*, pp. 123–140. London and New York: Routledge.

Pozzi Monzo, M. (2014) *The Buddha and the Baby: Psychotherapy and Meditation in Working with Children and Adults*. London: Routledge.

Rowling, J.K. (1999) *Harry Potter and the Prisoner of Azkaban*. London: Bloomsbury Children's Books.

Tustin, F. (1972) *Autistic States in Children*. London: Routledge.

Winnicott, D.W. (1947) Hate in the countertransference. In D.W. Winnicott (ed) *Through Paediatrics to Psychoanalysis*, pp. 194–203. London: Karnac, 1992.

Chapter 9

Learning from mistakes, losing my way and the value of supervision

When I was a trainee child psychotherapist, I felt disheartened when I read case studies because each one seemed a perfectly formed piece of work. There might be periods of crisis that had to be resolved, but overall the children made steady progress. The psychotherapist never made mistakes. In contrast, I felt I was muddling along trying to make sense of children's play or conversation and how it explained their symptoms and underlying problems. It was hard to be patient, to follow Bion's precept (1967) to begin each session 'without memory and desire' so as not to interfere with the therapeutic process, to see what emerged and make sense of the whole. I was aware I made mistakes, a clumsy interpretation at the wrong time, or I got caught up in the emotion of the session and 'acted in' by responding impulsively, without proper thought. What I have learnt since is that psychotherapy is a craft that is refined over the years, and our mistakes can prove to be opportunities for learning on the way. As Suzuki says in *Zen Mind, Beginner's Mind*, 'in the beginner's mind there are many possibilities, in the expert's mind there are few' (Suzuki 2011 [1970]: 1)

The beginner brings a fresh mind to the work and asks questions which can be invaluable to the more seasoned practitioner. Psychotherapy has a clear technique but it's also an unfolding process with no right and wrong answers. Doubt is part of the process.

In this chapter, I will look at those aspects of psychotherapy where I have tripped up most often, the timing and response to young patients, setting clear boundaries, ending therapy too early, as well as the positive value of listening to the unconscious and learning from one's own experience.

Understanding our mistakes

Perhaps the first glimpse I had of this way of viewing psychotherapy was from a book by Patrick Casement called *On Learning from the Patient* (1985). Casement, a psychoanalyst, describes how he listened to the feedback from his patients in shaping the direction of their therapeutic work together. From their responses to his 'conversation' with them, he discovered what helped and hindered their search for meaning and recovery in psychotherapy.

Similarly, by listening closely and observing our young patients' responses, we can learn from our mistakes. We can recognise the times when we are not closely attuned to our patients and correct ourselves. I remember working with a thoughtful young man who was struggling to find the words to tell me how he felt. I jumped in and said what I thought he felt. He looked annoyed and shrugged his shoulders and I realised that I had, in my impatience, interfered with his attempts to explain himself, and apologised. I had sensed his uneasiness about talking about himself and, in my attempt to help, I pre-empted his own attempts to clarify his thoughts.

Another dilemma is *pacing*: when to comment and when to stay silent, just observing and listening. Sometimes, I am told if I have got it wrong. I recall that one young lad complained, 'You leave me to do all the work, while you just sit there and watch'. I realised he felt left alone, and that we were no longer working together to understand what was troubling him. This reminds me of Beatrice Beebe's research on mother–infant interaction which shows how often parents misunderstand their infants, and how the process of repairing these small misunderstandings contributes to the development of a secure attachment with their small children. Our ability to learn the 'language' of the children we see in therapy, recognising when we get it wrong, helps develop our relationship with them, particularly as children appreciate our close attention, and value the idea of us searching together to understand their problems.

Michael Parsons suggests we can learn from the times our mind wanders off in therapy, or when we act in a way that surprises us. He suggests that if we look closely at the minute-by-minute developments in a therapeutic session, we will find that those thoughts that appear to come out of nowhere are an unconscious response to a communication from our patient. Looking closely at our responses to the patients offer insights into the patients' preoccupations. In his paper 'Raiding the inarticulate: The internal analytic setting and listening beyond countertransference' (2007), he says:

> The analytic encounter may stir up elements that belong to the analyst's psyche which, rather than impeding the analytic encounter, can actively enrich it.
>
> (p. 1441)

Parsons gives the example of a conversation with a patient which set him thinking about his own work, and these thoughts gave him a new way of considering what was on his patient's mind. The patient's comments had set off a train of thought about his fascination in developing ideas as an analyst but also his sorrow about the limitations of what he could achieve in his lifetime. This put him in touch with the patient's sorrow of a life 'half wasted', and his fears of his future not being fulfilled, which the patient had not yet been able to put into words:

> the sense of loss and curtailment, and the sorrow at not having been able to be who he might have been, do not make their way fully into words. I comprehend them more, as yet, through the psychic work on my own situation that this analysis provokes in me.
>
> (p. 1454)

Parsons stresses the importance of the analyst feeling free to let his mind 'raid the inarticulate':

> The freedom of self-experience within the internal analytic setting is the basis for that kind of inwardly directed listening which I described earlier as the analyst being an analytic listener to herself.
>
> (p. 1445)

Like Parsons, I have come to trust the unconscious connections that my mind makes, the unexpected thoughts and feelings that surface when I observe a child with the evenly suspended attention (1912) that Freud recommended for analysis. If I think these thoughts have value, I will try them out, make a suggestion about what I think the child is showing me, not minding at all if the child says I am mistaken. It can start an interesting conversation:

When I looked recently at the dark gloomy shapes in a picture painted by a girl in therapy I thought of the nightmare figures she might be seeing in her sleep. When I suggested this to her, she brushed me away saying it was just the background colour. I accepted this, wondering still if my idea was wrong, or my timing. Maybe she was not ready yet to share the fearful thoughts these images had suggested to me.

Learning by experience

Child psychotherapy is taught on an apprenticeship model as it has to be learned by experience. The child psychotherapy trainee in psychoanalytic training in the UK is in a placement in a child mental health setting for four years. The trainee will be supervised by an experienced practitioner in a wide range of brief and longer-term therapeutic work with children and adolescents, and with their parents. There is also intensive work where trainees see three children, one under five, one latency and one adolescent, three or four times weekly for a year, and in one case two years. The purpose of this is to teach the child psychoanalytic psychotherapist the minutiae of the therapeutic process, and to work with the transference and countertransference in the relationship with the patient. This complex work is supported by our own experience of receiving equally intensive psychoanalysis during the training which provides a safe setting to learn about our inner world, and to reflect on our emotional responses to our patients.

As apprentices, we inevitably make mistakes in therapy, maybe holding back and saying too little, or jumping in and interpreting too early. We allow a little girl to become too chaotic and disruptive in the session, and then find it hard to stop her running out of the room. We learn the importance of putting boundaries on a child after we have had to clear up following a messy session when toys were thrown everywhere, or water and sand were spilled on the floor. Particularly if the next child is expected ten minutes later, and the room has to be tidy by then.

Therapy can become confusing and difficult to manage as the child begins to express the disturbance that brought him to treatment. Parents often tell their child to 'Be good' on his way to the session. I gently challenge this, explaining that I am looking forward to whatever their child brings to the session, as that is what it is important for me to understand. Parents look ruefully at me afterwards, if I come out looking exhausted or rather dishevelled, as their child has given me a hard time. I think also they also feel relieved that I have discovered just how challenging their youngster can be.

Uncertainty at the beginning of therapy

Managing uncertainty is one of the more difficult aspects of this new craft, as parents and other professionals expect us to be 'experts', so we feel we should know what to do. At the beginning of therapy, it is most likely that the therapist will feel unsure where the child's work in sessions is leading, even after coming to a provisional diagnosis in the assessment. Staying with this uncertainty, rather than reaching prematurely for clarity, is necessary but uncomfortable. It is likely our initial assessment of the child's problems will be modified and become more complex as the therapy progresses.

It is particularly anxiety-provoking when a child's challenging behaviour continues to disrupt life at home or in school, and the value of the therapy is being questioned. You cannot hurry the therapeutic process despite the pressure on you for change. It takes time for a child to develop trust, to find a way of communicating with you about what is wrong, and to begin to discover a new way of being. In this early phase, when you are unclear where the play or conversation is leading, you may feel your responses to the young person sound clumsy and awkward, or you miss a cue which later seems obvious. Usually children are quite forgiving when you get it wrong as they sense you are trying to understand and make some genuine emotional contact with them. Gradually, a child's play or behaviour will take a shape that begins to make sense to you both, and then the difficult behaviour will probably lessen. Like little Sally whom I talked about in Chapter 4 who, after several months, finally found the Cinderella story as a way of telling me about her deprived and abusive past. Then her anxiety lessened and her behaviour improved. Until that time, her carers had to put up with her endless bedtime rituals and her angry outbursts which were exhausting. Fortunately, they had the support of their social worker who helped them find patience with Sally until we made some progress in therapy.

Another anxiety is when to agree to a child's demands in a session when you are not sure if what the child is asking of you is helpful to their treatment. I find I have to rely on my sense of what is right at the time:

> A young girl in therapy asked me to play the role of a child being taunted by teachers and school mates, while she pretended to be one of the persecutors. I could see that she wanted me to know what it felt like to be ridiculed and teased, as she had been. Then she wanted me to play a cruel and controlling therapist, shouting at her, the helpless child. I felt uncomfortable in this role, but I could see it meant something to her. I agreed, somewhat cautiously, to be 'horrible' to her, and in role, I felt the cruel thrill of this type of bullying. Afterwards I said it could be exciting to be so unkind, particularly if someone is making you jealous or cross. She was relieved I understood her desire for revenge, as she was often cruel and then felt guilty afterwards. Then she was able to move on and leave this play behind. She had wanted me to understand how difficult it was at times not to give way to these destructive impulses.

I won't agree to a role-play if I think the child is drawing me into too intimate, seductive or abusive behaviour, even if I understand the impulse that has led to this action.

On one occasion a young boy aged eight who I had been seeing for some time, set up a bed on the floor of the therapy room and asked me to lie down and join him there. I refused and helped him find a soft toy to cuddle instead. I think he wanted the closeness of a mother and baby contact, which I knew I could not offer, but I also feared that this could lead to the wish for an excited seductive interaction with me which would be wrong.

Acting out or acting in

The difficulty of managing intense feelings in therapy is that there is a pressure on us to act, so that sometimes we respond impulsively in a session and then regret this later. This was my experience soon after I qualified as a child psychotherapist and began working with parents and infants at high risk at the Cassel Hospital. I was unprepared for how anxious and distressed I would feel, seeing a mother treat her child unkindly. In an assessment session, I observed a mother I will call Sheila who become increasingly rejecting to her toddler. I stopped the session as I found it intolerable to watch, as I describe below:

> In a parent–infant assessment session, Sheila was becoming increasingly unkind towards her two-year-old daughter. Every time her little girl approached her asking to play, she would find something critical to say to her, and the child's hopefulness collapsed. It reached a level of cruelty in her rejection of the child which I could not tolerate. Very distressed, I abruptly stopped the session and asked the mother to leave and take her child back to nursery, and then I burst into tears. With the friendly support of an experienced family nurse who came to see what was wrong, I was able to recover and ask the mother to come back alone, so we could talk over what had happened. The shaken and sobered mother was then able to think about her anger towards her daughter and how unhappy and frightened her little girl must have felt. Sheila then told me that when her daughter was three months old, she asked her mother to look after her, as she had felt too depressed to care for her. Since her toddler had returned to her care a few months ago, she had felt too guilty to show the affection her daughter was seeking. This made her upset and angry, and unkind. This was history repeating itself as Sheila's mother had placed her in her grandmother's care for some months as a small child. After Sheila returned to her mother, her relationship with her was always a difficult one. Now she was fearful of getting close to her daughter as she was so unsure she could be a good parent to her.

I think we both felt that surviving this encounter had enabled us to discover a dynamic that was important for her as a mother, how her guilt and despair about ever creating a loving bond made her push away her daughter in a cruel way. Sadly, but appropriately, this mother eventually decided to place her child for adoption and find psychotherapy for herself, as she knew she would not be able to offer her child the nurturing care she needed, soon enough to meet her needs.

Thinking over this experience, I realised I had rejected Sheila in the same way she had rejected the child, reacting to the intense unmanageable feelings in their relationship, rather than managing them in a more thoughtful way. I think that a similar chain of rejection can be played out within professional networks. Children or teenagers and their parents can get caught up in violent rows and reject each other, and the professionals involved are sometimes propelled into mirroring this behaviour. They give in to the parents' demands to remove their children from home because they have identified with the feelings of hopelessness and anger in the family, rather than containing these distressing feelings. In Chapter 13, I describe a consultation service for professional child care teams to help them recognise these projective processes and prevent them from distorting the decision-making about the children and their parents.

As I have gained experience in joint therapy with parents and children, I have realised how challenging this work is, because we identify with the powerful and conflicting feelings of both mother and child, and we have to find a balance inside ourselves. I can now prepare myself a little better for the complex feelings involved. I recognise how quickly vulnerable parents become angry and overwhelmed when they are unable to comfort or calm their children, and I can intervene to help them respond thoughtfully, and protect their children from these difficult feelings. As a fairly new psychotherapist, I needed the support of the experienced team around me to help me put right my impulsive response to that mother and toddler, and turn it around to a helpful exploration of the parent–infant relationship.

Ending psychotherapy too early

Judging the right time to end therapy can be difficult. We may be subject to many pressures in making this decision, from parents, our team and the managers pre-occupied by waiting lists of children needing therapy and the scarce resources to deal with them. When psychotherapy is time-limited, the ending date will have been decided at the beginning, and there will be an agreed focus of work. More complex and long-term developmental difficulties in children often need open-ended, longer-term therapy and then it can be difficult to decide when therapy is enough. If we prematurely end longer-term work, we are likely to discover that difficult behaviour patterns return, and the young person becomes increasingly anxious about the future. This would indicate that the ending is happening too early and further consolidation is needed. I have made this mistake. Seeing that a young person has become more settled and self-confident, I have made a decision to end therapy too early. This was partly because resources are so limited, and there were other children waiting for therapy. But I think this pressure had come from within me, rather than the child or the family, as I have not wanted to perpetuate the therapy longer than the child needs. Realising my mistake, I was able to extend their therapy which went on to a successful ending, as I describe below. For Fergus, the too-early ending had threatened to undermine the progress he had made in psychotherapy.

> Fergus, aged 16 years, had been in weekly therapy for two years when we agreed a planned ending phase of two months. During this time, his old pattern of reckless behaviour returned and he became uneasy in sessions and reluctant to talk. I think, in retrospect, he felt I was ending therapy because I was glad to get rid of him because of his early challenging behaviour, rather than waiting until he was ready to finish. His renewed difficult behaviour was an unconscious communication of his anxiety about being forced to end psychotherapy too quickly. Once this was recognised, we made a new plan to continue for another six

months and then review, by which time he was ready for a planned ending and he made a more confident departure from therapy.

In Chapter 10, I will discuss the many issues involved in ending therapy in more detail.

The value of supervision

Dealing all day with children's disturbance, questions of risk and the concerns of distressed parents and carers, the child psychotherapist needs the support of a team where it feels safe to share concerns and uncertainties and ask for support when necessary. Equally important is the role of clinical supervision, individually and in a peer group where possible. Here, the psychotherapist has the opportunity to reflect on the dynamics of the therapist–patient relationship and the emotional experience of the session.

Monica Lanyado talks about her experience of supervising child psychotherapists in her book *Transforming Despair to Hope* (2018). She describes how the supervisor helps the therapist think about experiences in the session 'that are on the edge of consciousness' and very much the stuff of inchoate emotional communication.

The supervisor helps the therapist to 'hold' difficult and disturbing experiences being expressed by the patient. This combination of experience and reflection within the supervision session can then become part of the conscious awareness of the supervisee when he or she returns to the clinical situation.

The traditional approach is that the therapist writes up the therapeutic hour with the patient in a detailed process recording, including any thoughts and feelings that have come to mind during the clinical session or in the process of writing. As the therapist recounts the session, the discussion of the clinical material brings the relationship between the therapist and the young patient alive in the room. This becomes a mirroring process that enables the supervisor to get a feel for what is happening in the therapist–patient relationship and to offer a different perspective on the dynamics of the sessions. Ideally, this is a two-way process. There is a free flow of ideas between supervisor and supervisee that leads to a new ways of looking at the clinical material.

Lanyado talks, in particular, about the shared exploration of those difficult times when the child psychotherapist has been intensely involved in working with the despair of severely traumatised young people. She describes those moments in supervision when she has been able to recognise signs of transformation and hope in the clinical material, and how sharing this with the therapist has brought a new understanding to the work.

The learning and development that comes from struggling with difficult patients in psychotherapy is passed on in supervision, as Ogden points out:

> [The] psychoanalytic supervisory relationship is … an indispensable medium through which the psychoanalytic knowledge is passed from one generation of psychoanalysts to the next.
>
> (Ogden 2009: 31)

There is also the excitement of learning and developing with one's peers, sharing experiences and new ideas. I value this aspect of peer group supervision which has been a source of support in my therapeutic work through the years. These groups can take place in the work setting or in a gathering of child psychotherapists living locally. Often child psychotherapists join one of these groups when they qualify, or set one up with fellow trainees, and they may remain in these monthly groups for many years. No one leads, the person presenting their work for discussion takes on that role. There is a special quality to thinking together as a group about a challenging case, where each practitioner will bring their own perspective, feeling comfortable to be open with peers about the uncertainties and complex responses we have towards disturbing or confusing case material. Often I discover that the mind of the group is larger than the individuals involved, and a situation that felt impossible to understand at first, gradually makes sense as we all put together our ideas, sparking off each other's thinking. For this to work comfortably, it helps to have a group most of whom know each other well, and of course, a supply of tea and biscuits as nourishment after a day at work.

References

Bion, W.R. (1967). Notes on memory and desire. *The Psychoanalytic Forum* 2(3): 271–280.

Casement, P. (1985). *On Learning from the Patient*. London: Routledge.

Freud, S. (1912). Recommendations to physicians practising psycho-analysis. In J. Strachey et al. (eds) *Standard Edition of the Complete Psychological Works of Sigmund Freud*, vol. 12, pp. 109–120. London: Hogarth Press, 1958.

Lanyado, M. (2018). *Transforming Despair to Hope: Reflections on the Psychotherapeutic Process with Severely Neglected and Traumatised Children*. Abingdon: Routledge.

Ogden, T.H. (2009) On psychoanalytic supervision. In T.H. Ogden (ed) *Rediscovering Psychoanalysis: Thinking and Dreaming, Learning and Forgetting*, pp. 31–49. London and New York: Routledge.

Parsons, M. (2007). Raiding the inarticulate: The internal analytic setting and listening beyond countertransference. *International Journal of Psychoanalysis* 88(6): 1441–1456.

Suzuki, S. (2011 [1970]). *Zen Mind, Beginner's Mind: Informal Talks on Zen Meditation and Practice*. Boulder, CO: Shambhala.

Chapter 10

Working towards an ending

Introduction

In the early months of therapy, Simon a six-year-old began every session by running in front of me to hide in a corner of my small therapy room, Once I found him, he would repeat the game, and he would have continued playing 'hide and seek' all session if I had not stopped him. It was not fun. It was his way of coping with seeing me after a week's separation, managing the complicated feelings of wanting and hating, evoked by my absence. After that, he became withdrawn and sullen, but I could sense his overwhelming sadness. He curled away in the corner or kicked the door, saying he did not need my help. Endings of sessions were similarly hard for him. He watched the clock, counting down the minutes to the end, then ran out the room a few minutes early so he could leave me before I left him.

Beginnings and endings of therapy sessions are often moments of heightened anxiety for children who have experienced many unhappy and unexpected separations in the past and whose relationships are full of conflict now. Like Simon, they fear that past disappointments in relationships will be repeated with their therapist. They defend themselves by hiding their vulnerability and need. But there is also a germ of hope suggested in the 'hide and seek' game, a wish to be found, for this new meeting to bring some warmth and pleasure. Many children we see in treatment have experienced multiple and traumatic losses. In psychotherapy, there is an opportunity to look at past feelings of anger and distress in a safe relationship at the child's pace. When the ending phase of therapy is planned and anticipated, children can be helped to work through and overcome their fears about separation. They can then anticipate their future with more optimism. In this chapter, I will consider the impact of unresolved loss on children, planned and unplanned endings in therapy, when to finish therapy, the ending process and preparing for the future.

The experience of unresolved loss

John Bowlby, a British psychologist, psychiatrist and psychoanalyst, studied children's responses to loss and separation from their key attachment figures.

From his observations of young children separated from their parents in hospital or institutions, he delineated three phases of reaction to their loss: protest, despair and detachment (1960). The protest is due to the child's anxiety about separation and the threat of loss. The despair is an expression of child's grief, and the detachment is the child's defence against the pain of loss. If there is the opportunity for a new relationship, there then can be the re-establishment of a new attachment and recovery.

James and Joyce Robertson worked as researchers with Bowlby in his studies of children experiencing separation and loss. They fostered children and they found that the children they cared for were less distressed during the period of separation because they were there to comfort and support them through the experience. At this time, the impact on children of separation and loss from key attachment figures was not recognised. Hospitals in the UK discouraged parents from visiting their children during long stays in hospital. Weekly or even monthly visits from parents were common, and in extreme cases parents were only permitted to view their children through a window. The belief was that parental visits 'unsettled' the child and disturbed hospital routines. The Robertsons filmed very young children experiencing brief separations from their parents (published 1967–73) to show how traumatic this could be for the infants, and this changed public policy. Their film of John (Robertson & Robertson 1953), a placid easy-going child aged 17 months sent to a residential nursery for just 9 days while his mother had a baby, is harrowing. We see how quickly John becomes distressed, then angry. He attempts to comfort himself with a big teddy, before giving up and becoming withdrawn. Although all the nurses are kind, no special nurse is allocated to look after him through this time. When his mother returns, John refuses to look at her, and it takes some time before he can allow himself to be comforted by her and recover. This separation had a long-term impact as he remained a vulnerable child as he grew up.

I have seen the same response in babies with mothers who were severely depressed. Their mothers were not physically absent, but they were emotionally unavailable and sometimes rejecting of their babies. The baby's grief was shown in acute distress and avoidance when the mother withdrew into herself, not sensitive to her baby's cues. Often a baby will look elsewhere for tenderness, turning to the father, the nursery nurse or another reassuring figure who can offer comfort until the mother recovers.

Working with loss and separation in psychotherapy

In psychotherapy with young people, the relationship with the psychotherapist provides an opportunity to work through these past losses. For children who have experienced painful separations, leaving the therapist every week can bring back fears of being abandoned, and these will increase if there is a break anticipated in therapy or before holidays. When we hear children's histories from their parents, or read their files at the beginning of treatment, we can try to imagine what it must have been like for the child at that age, to experience a sudden loss of a family home, the break-up of his parents' marriage or the traumatic illness of a parent or sibling. As we will consider in the chapters on divorce and mental illness, the age of the children when these events occur is crucial in understanding their response, as this will shape the child's capacity to make sense of what is happening. Equally important is whether there is a caring adult to comfort the child and to make clear what is happening. We know that it is harder to mourn those who hurt us and made us angry, so it is likely children who have memories of painfully ambivalent relationships will be the most defended, and also the most distrustful of current relationships.

Unresolved mourning leaves children distressed and angry, less able to engage with life and make new relationships. They build up defences to protect themselves from further pain, but these prevent them from getting close to others. The children's unhappiness may show itself in furious or withdrawn behaviour that leaves their carers bewildered. Often adults caring for a child do not make the connections between the youngster's disturbed behaviour and their past traumatic experiences, and they may blame themselves, feeling the care they are offering is inadequate in some way. They are often afraid to talk to the children about their past unhappy times for fear of upsetting them more, and so a distance can develop between them and the children that becomes hard to bridge. Child psychotherapists can play an important role in important offering support to foster carers or adopters caring for these troubled children, as I describe in a later chapter in the work of a post-adoption team.

Edna O'Shaughnessy's paper 'The absent object' (1964) considers the experience of loss for a young child who does not yet have the capacity to hold on to good memories of the absent loved one. She explains how the absent object (the person who is not there for the child) can become a persecuting figure in the child's mind, as one who left when the child needed help. The young person's anger with the persecuting internal figure can lead to a fear of retaliation and the threat of total abandonment. If children were separated from their parents in traumatic circumstances, the fear of this happening again is heightened, and they remain insecure and fearful of dependency.

In psychotherapy, these feeling of fear and anger will occur in sessions, and they are particularly likely when there are further separations at the ending of sessions and in holiday breaks. This time, the child has the reassuring presence of the therapist to help make sense of the feelings, and recognise them as a response to the acute pain of past losses, re-evoked by the current parting.

It is interesting to observe how these issues surface in therapy. As each therapy session comes to an end, I usually draw the more vulnerable youngster's attention to the time left, a '5 minutes' warning, to ease the anxiety about ending. I often ask children how they would like to finish their play or story for this week, reminding them that they can continue next session. Some children find it hard to tolerate endings, so I will help them put away the play materials, symbolically packing away their feelings for the day. Children often ask to take something home, maybe something as simple as a piece of string, 'a transitional object' to hold on to, until they return next session. I judge with each child what feels right. Do they need something physical to hold on to, or can I encourage them to hold on to the memory of me instead? With teenagers, I might broach the subject of managing the separations in a different way, asking if they can remember our discussions between sessions or do they leave them behind on the doorstep, to avoid feeling the pain of absence, as many do. Recently, I was preparing a young teenager for a holiday break, which I knew would be difficult for her to manage. I gave her a notebook suggesting that she keep a diary in the break to record how she felt. This idea appealed to her and she elaborated on it, deciding to draw a picture each day showing how she felt, her way of keeping our contact alive in my absence.

At first, feelings about loss are often denied by our young patients. When they return, after a holiday, they recount all the exciting things that they have done instead of seeing us. Yet, as the therapeutic relationship deepens, they may become more aware of missing the contact with their therapist between sessions, but this can be infuriating, as dependency on others has been so unsafe in the past. Sometimes their anxiety and fury from the past, stirred up by the current feeling of abandonment by the psychotherapist, is expressed in destructive play or behaviour. This can be difficult to manage, but the repetition of past emotions in the present makes it possible to talk to the young person about how angry they feel now, without having to directly address earlier more traumatic separations. A therapist told me in supervision about Tommy, aged seven, who became furious with her in anticipation of her next holiday break:

> After receiving his Easter holiday calendar, with the dates of the therapist's absence, Tommy became more and more provocative in his play, tipping sand from the sand tray onto the floor, then throwing it at his therapist, watching her reaction to see if she was getting angry. She suggested that he was showing her just how cross and upset he felt about her going away for the Easter week. That was why he was making a mess, which she would have to clear up. He looked up with a slight nod of agreement, and the sand-tipping slowed down. It did not stop completely until she firmly replaced the lid on the sand tray, indicating she would not tolerate any more of this behaviour, but she did understand how upset he felt.

Adolescents may be equally challenging and distressed about being left, but their fury may show in a cynical response to the therapist, or a refusal to engage in therapy. This can be equally hard to tolerate unless the therapist recognises that this is a similar defence against the pain of loss, hiding the underlying distress, and is eventually to talk about this in the sessions.

Determination, understanding and firm boundaries are needed by the therapist to bear the storm of this phase when previously unmanageable feelings resurface. Gradually, young patients will be able to think more about the distressing feelings that have come to the surface and so they do not need to act them out so much. The anger is often replaced by sadness as Monica Lanyado describes:

> When the emotions of sadness and missing start to soak through the layers of defence that have protected the child from the intense pain of loss, this is an important sign of healthy and appropriate mourning processes starting to function within the child, possibly for the first time. Initially these feelings may not seem to be directly connected to the child's major losses. Interestingly, they may be experienced more directly within the new relationship with the therapist who is missed when there are weekend or holiday breaks in therapy or angrily rejected before or after these breaks.
>
> (Lanyado 2018: 56)

The therapist may feel the sadness from the child 'seep' in, but know that the child is not ready yet to talk directly about these feelings. Often, with younger children, we see these feelings of sadness and rejection are first expressed in their play, as in the next phase of Tommy's therapy, the seven-year-old I described earlier:

> Months later in the therapy, Tommy was able to show his sadness when his therapist went away for a week by tipping more and more cups of water onto the figures in the sand tray so they became soaked. The psychotherapist knew the water represented the young boy's tears, the sadness he found difficult to express directly when he had to say goodbye for the week. She simply responded in the moment by helping Tom find towels to mop up the water and dry the dripping figures in his game. Later, when she felt he was ready to listen, she commented that she thought he was worried and sad about missing her over the holidays.

Working with the child's feelings, like this, at a safe distance in the displacement of his play, the child psychotherapist helps him to manage his distress without raising his anxiety by talking about it directly, until he is ready for her to put his feelings into words.

In these moments of sadness, a child like Tommy experiences his psychotherapist as a person who can bear to be sad without feeling overwhelmed and the child can introject (take in) this experience and, over the months of therapy, discover this capacity within himself. Working through this process, the child gradually becomes less anxious and defensive, and this frees energy for other developmental gains, which we so often see later in therapy. The child begins to learn better at school, makes friends and becomes warmer and more relaxed in his relationship with his parents, or carers and siblings.

When is it right to end? Assessing change

Some very deprived children never want to end therapy. They enjoy the experience of a secure relationship with a person who listens closely and helps them understand themselves. Due to their early neglect, these children may never feel they have had enough care, and this can make the prospect of ending psychotherapy a worrying process. Yet, more often, a stage is reached when a young person feels ready to consider ending psychotherapy, and the therapist feels it is right too. So what underlies this response? How does one assess change and what are the signs there has been enough development?

During the assessment and over the months of therapy, a picture emerges about the child's internal world, the sense of self and relationship with family and with friends. We observe how rigid the young person's defences are and the level of anxiety. If the treatment is progressing well, the young person begins to feel freer to express thoughts and feelings in the therapeutic relationship and this growing trust leads to closer, more satisfying relationships with others. As the youngster gains confidence and a sense of self-worth, it becomes easier to hold on to both loving and hateful feelings, to think first rather than just react, and to recognise when to seek help. Ego capacities develop as a child matures emotionally so there is a growing sense of competence. The young person is more able to learn and be creative, and there is more optimism about the future. Sheila, eight years old at referral, whom I heard about in supervision with a therapist, made this type of slow but purposeful development.

> Sheila was a troubled young schoolgirl who had been neglected and traumatised as a small child. Her young, immature mother had a violent relationship with Sheila's father when she was an infant, and she used drugs to blank out her suffering. Now the mother was determined to give Sheila a better future and she brought her weekly for psychotherapy, as well as getting treatment for herself.
>
> Sheila was a slight girl with a perky expression, but she became a bundle of fury when her wishes were frustrated or she felt a failure at school, as she had some specific learning difficulties. Over the months of therapy with a resilient young therapist, Sheila learnt to express her anger and upset in words or play, rather than throw everything about, as she did in the beginning. She felt listened to and understood in her sessions, and this helped her become calmer and more thoughtful. She was able to say how she felt when she was upset and she was more able to accept the help she

needed at school As she became more secure in her relationship with her therapist, she was better able to manage breaks in therapy. She learned that she could hold on to an image of her therapist in her absence (object constancy) and she would greet her warmly on her return. She progressed from attacking her therapist to becoming protective of her, and she even tried to be fair in board games, after relentlessly cheating for months.

Of course, the therapeutic journey for each child is different, but we can see here that, as this child's development progresses, some defences soften, like her need to avoid intimacy, and she became better able to communicate how she felt. The good experience with the psychotherapist is internalised and transferred to other relationships, and she can allow herself the comfort of closer, warmer relationships. The more kindly feelings she feels towards herself and others are mirrored in a more benign inner world.

Planned and unplanned endings

A planned ending in psychotherapy offers the young person an opportunity to develop emotionally by working through feelings about loss and change in a new way, but often endings do not happen in the smooth way that we all wish for. Events in the child's life intervene to prevent a carefully planned conclusion to therapy or the therapist may need to bring therapy to an end early, due to illness or pregnancy. On these occasions, there may still be time to plan a few sessions to say goodbye. The most difficult situation to deal with is a sudden disruption to therapy, when even a brief ending phase cannot happen, due to a foster placement breakdown, or the family prematurely ending treatment. This is quite shocking when it happens, and painful to manage, as both the child and the therapist can feel helpless if the decision was made without their involvement. It is hard then for the psychotherapist to take the child's appropriate anger at the loss of therapy when the therapist feels this loss too. Despite these feelings of frustration and upset, it is still worth trying to negotiate an extra session or two, or agree to visit a child at home if there has been a transfer to a new placement, as I have done. This avoids another sudden disappearance in the child's life which would leave the child with the feeling that you did not care or that you were relieved to end the work.

We are fortunate when we are able to fix a date some time in advance and we can plan for a proper ending. Ideally, after a substantial period of therapy, say one year to eighteen months, we allow a minimum of several weeks to three months before the end date. This gives time for the working through of the final phase, and one short holiday break to anticipate the final separation of ending. In a planned ending to a complex situation, there is time to involve those close to the child, the parents, the school and professionals, to ensure that there is support through this difficult phase, and unexpected interferences with this plan are kept to a minimum.

Every ending has its own course, and it is often surprising what comes up in therapy as the work comes to an end. Sometimes, while exploring their anxieties about finishing treatment, young people reveal concerns that they have kept hidden previously. In the final phase of therapy a young teenage girl I saw revealed disturbing memories and fears she had not discussed before: she talked to me for the first time about her memories of her mother's psychotic episodes when she was younger, and how she felt somehow responsible for them. She was worried that she might become mentally ill like her mother when she grew up. I had suspected she might feel like this, but I had not wanted to raise these issues directly without an indication she was ready to think about it. She was relieved to have these anxieties in the open at last.

This adolescent, like others, was pleased to be ending therapy but fearful that the gains she made in her sessions, her new-found self-confidence and capacity to make friends, would disappear once our relationship ended. It was hard for her to recognise that her growing capacity to manage feelings and make new relationships was due to internal change, a new maturity in her that would continue to develop after leaving therapy. There can be some regression in this ending phase, as old patterns of behaviour emerge once more in response to the anxiety about ending, but these are usually more quickly resolved as they are recognised as belonging to the past. This teenager had been socially quite anxious and she feared making herself ridiculous if she was asked to talk in front of the class. These fears briefly reappeared in the final weeks, as her self-confidence wavered, then disappeared when she recognised that she had actually managed a recent role in a drama sketch quite well.

I have found I can guide this process of 'working through' the ending by identifying the key points in our work together, which I think of as 'a trip down memory lane'. I talk about the gains made in therapy, the positive qualities the young person has developed and internalised in the process of the work. We also think together about the future and anticipate anxieties about ending, the new challenges ahead.

I also have to let go of my relationship with the young person. Even though I might not take to some young people at first, I usually become quite fond of them, as it is not possible to work well in psychotherapy without investing a great deal in this relationship. I work towards the end with mixed feelings: some sadness and anxiety, and relief and pride if considerable progress has been achieved. I usually encourage the young patient to decide how to spend the final session, maybe with a familiar game or activity. It is customary to allow children to take home their drawings, and I usually suggest a child can choose one piece of play material to take with them. Often children choose the least expected things: a small ball, a little animal or some sticky tape. I sometimes offer to make a farewell card for the young person as something tangible to take home after the final session. Despite the fact I am a hopeless artist, which they usually know by this stage, I draw a familiar toy or game inside the card, adding my good wishes for the future as my way of saying farewell.

We can be flexible about arranging one or more follow-up therapy sessions, if this will help the young person or the family feel more confident in facing the future. It can also be reassuring to the psychotherapist to see the young person return after six or twelve weeks, having built on the work done in therapy. I approach these follow-ups in a more informal way than therapy sessions, encouraging the young person to tell me their news since we last met. I find that if there are any concerns that need airing, these naturally come up in these more open discussions.

A change that lasts: the sleeper effect

A good ending in psychotherapy can lead to sense of hope for the future. Resolving feelings of loss and regret about the past gives the young person the emotional space to move on to make new relationships. One of the fascinating aspects of psychotherapy confirmed in recent research (Midgley & Kennedy 2011) is the sleeper effect. Follow-up research has shown that the benefits of therapy become most obvious a year after the psychotherapy has ended. Improvements are sustained or even enhanced in the long term, with adults who had been treated as children or adolescents still feeling the benefits of psychodynamic psychotherapy many years later. This can be explained by the fact that, for the first three months after the ending of therapy, the patient is managing loss and change, but the next stage brings a sense of new confidence as the developments are integrated into the patient's sense of self, so that the capacity to form new better relationships is enhanced. As one girl said to me in a farewell card, 'The therapy helped me with growing up, thanks so much, you helped me keep on the right path …'.

References

Bowlby, J. (1960) Grief and mourning in infancy and early childhood. *Psychoanalytic Study of the Child* 15: 9–52.

Lanyado, M. (2018) Complex traumatic childhood losses: Mourning and acceptance, endings and beginnings. In M. Lanyado (ed) *Transforming Despair to Hope: Reflections on the Psychotherapeutic Process with Severely Neglected and Traumatised Children*, pp. 51–66. London and New York: Routledge.

Midgley, N. & Kennedy, E. (2011) Psychodynamic psychotherapy for children and adolescents: A critical review of the evidence base. *Journal of Child Psychotherapy* 37(3): 232–260.

O'Shaughnessy, E. (1964) The absent object. *Journal of Child Psychotherapy* 1(2): 34–43.

Robertson, J. & Robertson, J. (1953) *Young Children in Brief Separation.* Five films including 'John, 17 months, for 9 days in a residential nursery' (Robertson Films), available from Concord Media, London.

Part 3

Therapeutic work with children and parents in crisis

Behind closed doors

Therapeutic work with children and adolescents living with mentally ill and vulnerable parents

Behind Closed Doors, the title of a conference about young carers looking after mentally ill parents, captures the isolation of young people and their families struggling to care for a mentally ill parent or one who is vulnerable to stress and breakdown due to early trauma and abuse.

The young person's experience of a parent's mental illness is usually not seen. The stigma associated with mental illness, and the shame that is often felt by all involved, means that it is not discussed openly. Help is sought only when the crisis is severe. Vulnerable parents may be not recognised unless their distress becomes acute. Then it may become visible as severe clinical depression or mania, suicide attempts, drug, alcohol dependency or anti-social behaviour. Similarly, their children's distress may not be seen unless the children become disruptive or unable to learn in school. The quiet child is the one likely to be forgotten, whereas the acting-out child gets attention, although the behaviour may be seen as 'attention-seeking' or naughty rather than a response to unmanageable stress at home.

Many young people will not tell teachers and friends what is happening at home, wanting to hide that part of family life. So they feel isolated, different from their peers and not able to talk about their difficult times at home. Yet school can be a real refuge for young people whose life at home is so stressful and full of responsibility.

In this chapter I will discuss the experience of children and adolescents growing up with mentally ill or vulnerable parents and how therapeutic work can help these young people. Then I will consider the support parents need, and the difficulties faced by the professional team attempting to provide a coordinated response to help the family hold their life together.

The child's experience

Imagine Jo, a girl aged about eight years old, standing in the kitchen, facing her mother who has a withdrawn, anxious but distant look on her face. The mother is in a deepening depression and her daughter is angry, fearful, despairing. She is imagining the life ahead for the next few months. Her mother becoming more withdrawn and silent, being taken into hospital against her will, the frightening visits to the acute ward of the shabby old mental hospital. Jo is desperate, wondering how to stop the inevitable slide into another crisis. She feels very alone, responsible. There is no one to help, no one to comfort her and help her manage her panic. Her dad is at work, her older sister is in her room, her younger brother will only cry. She tries telling her mother to see the doctor, to get some more pills. She wants to shout, scream at her mother to take control, look after herself before it's too late. But she knows that shouting will drive her mother further into silence. Her stomach churns as her mother looks at her blankly, appealing almost, asking her 'what shall I do?' This provokes fury and hatred in Jo. She stops feeling she wants to help. Her mother knows she has to get help, so why doesn't she?

This all happens early in the morning. Jo goes to school and when she returns, she finds that her father has come home from work and taken her mother to hospital. Jo realised she had not even said goodbye to her mother. There is a guilty relief that this agony of waiting and uncertainty will soon be over, that her dad and her brother and sister can now relax. Maybe even go out for fish and chips and watch a film. The guilt of this relief follows on, making her feel she is hateful. Did she push her mother out because living with her was so awful? Is there a sense of triumph alongside the guilty relief at her departure? Who could love someone like her who has such a mess of miserable feelings inside. No one; she could not help her mother. The loneliness is the worst.

So began three months of hospital visits. A small family, the father despairing of another episode but carrying on, and the three children silently facing the change of the warm capable mother they knew into an alien forbidding figure, a pale copy of the person she was when she was well.

This story is typical of many children with mentally ill parents. The help this family and others like them would receive is likely to be fragmented, split between adult mental health and child welfare services. As child psychotherapists, our attention is drawn to the child's need for support and understanding and maybe therapeutic intervention. Yet the person seen to be in crisis is the mother, and the professional input is likely to be focused on her, and the children's emotional needs might not be considered. The GP, the psychiatrist and the mental health workers will rapidly organise crisis treatment and care for mother, and hopefully offer support to the father to maintain family life. The children's immediate need will be for their ordinary life to continue; going to school, meeting friends, having an organised home life with regular meals, clean clothes and birthday celebrations. People tend to stay away when they are unsure how to help, or the family retreats and can become very isolated. Children may be too embarrassed to bring home friends from school.

The emotional impact on the children of the strain of the weeks preceding the crisis call, and the difficult months of slow recovery afterwards, may not be considered by the professionals at the time of the parent's acute episode, so help is not offered to them.

The numbers of young people experiencing the stress of living with mentally ill and vulnerable parents is high. *Think Child, Think Parent, Think Family*, the report published by the Social Care Institute for Excellence (2011), gathered the evidence from research. It showed that in a class of 26 primary school-children, six or seven will live with a mother with mental health problems. In the 2001 Census, 50,000 children were caring for a parent with mental health problems. One in five adults will experience mental illness during their lifetime and a quarter of these will be parents. Parenting can have a negative effect on adult mental health, and the parents' mental illness can adversely affect child mental health and development.

The emotional impact on the growing child

Observing small children and talking to adolescents in therapy, whose parents are suffering from mental illness, has taught me a great deal about their experience and the therapeutic work needed. With older children and adolescents, it may take time to unravel the cumulative impact of the parents' emotional disturbance on their development. These young people may cope adequately until some aspect of life becomes too much of a challenge. It may be the emotional upheavals of adolescence, difficulties in friendships, starting secondary school or preparing to move to university. These experiences reveal an underlying insecurity and lack of confidence in the young person that may have remained hidden beneath a competent exterior.

The term mental illness covers widely differing conditions including psychotic disorders like schizophrenia and bi-polar disorder where there is a loss of touch with reality, alcoholism, drug addiction, and borderline personality disorder. All these cause frightening changes to the parents' personality that can be traumatic to their children who cannot understand their parent's disturbed and distressed state. The young people will also sense how frightened the parents are themselves of their shattered mental health. Even small children will often attempt to comfort and care for their parent, sensing that the parent is scared and does not know what to do. In the acute phase of the parent's illness, the children may experience frightening disturbance in their parents, but mental illness can also become chronic misery, which is equally hard to endure. The children may then have to become carers for the parent, rather than being cared for themselves.

The need for emotional security

For the child, this loss of the parent's care and attention, at times possibly equalling neglect, is one of the most distressing aspects of the parent's illness. The parent is there but not emotionally available, and sometimes openly hostile if paranoia sets in. Then the child may be seen as a persecuting figure in the parent's disturbed world. The importance of a responsive warm relationship to a baby was shown vividly in the Still Face experiment by Edward Tronick and colleagues (1975). During periods of illness, the mother's face can become rigid and defensive, and the baby, who cannot tolerate this unresponsiveness, will stop looking and withdraw in despair. In the Still Face study, a well mother looks at her baby with a non-responsive and expressionless face. The researchers describe how, after three minutes of this 'interaction' with his mother, the baby grows wary, makes repeated attempts to get her attention, then pulls away from her with a hopeless facial expression. (These videos can be seen on YouTube.)

As well as being unable to comfort her baby, the ill mother (or father) may not be able to separate her paranoid fears of persecution from her perception of her child, and their relationship will become confused and distorted. Then children receive a very negative picture of themselves and may feel to blame for their parent's unhappiness, not understanding any other cause. Although an older child may know intellectually that this hostile response is because the parent is ill, it will still feel hurtful and rejecting. The impact of this on the children with disturbed parents, whom I have seen in therapy, is that they are often insecure, doubting themselves, and they have a constant fear that things will go wrong. The effect of this negative parenting pattern is evident in an analysis of recent attachment research (Martins & Gaffan 2000) which showed that children of depressed mothers are more likely to have an insecure attachment style of relating, either more avoidant or disorganised, (a response to parents who are frightened/frightening or both), as a result of an early experience of maternal depression. A child needs reliable and loving confirmation from a parental figure to develop self-confidence. When one parent is emotionally disturbed, then this consistent emotional care needs to be provided by another significant protective figure in the child's family life. A concerned partner, grandparent or close relative can offer support and balance this lack of positive relationship during the parent's illness if they can be reliably present in times of need.

Gianna Williams (1998) describes her work with adolescents who have been the recipients of hostile parent projections. She suggests that they either become highly defended to ward off the intrusion of their parents' disturbing feelings or they appear to have little protection against these negative feelings which they internalise as foreign bodies (i.e. something foreign to themselves). She describes the highly defended group as developing 'no entry' defences due to their fear of taking anything in:

> the extreme and pervasive dread of being invaded and intruded upon ... related to early very persecutory experiences of being at the receiving end of projections perceived as inimical.
>
> (Williams 1998: 80)

When she worked with a young woman with this experience who became anorexic, she described a powerful sense of being projected into in the countertransference, which she recognised as an alert that the patient was on the receiving end of massive projections.

Gianna Williams contrasts this with psychically porous young patients whose parents have suffered trauma and who rid themselves of psychic pain, anxiety and anger by projecting out these unbearable feelings. Their children closest to them are often on the receiving end. She cites Bion and says the parents are 'either frightened or frightening or both', and these parents are 'likely to project anxiety rather than contain it' (p. 81). She continues:

> When projections enter a child's psychic space, they can be experienced as inimical foreign bodies. These parents need to divest themselves of their own anxieties, psychic pain and ghosts. It is a failure in the relationship between container and contained which is in my opinion even greater than one described as engendering nameless dread, a failure of containment.
>
> (p. 80)

This reminds me of therapy with a young boy of six whose mother periodically became seriously depressed, and suicidal.

> In his sessions, he seemed to collapse emotionally when his mother became emotionally disturbed, no longer able to build the towers and train tracks that he had created so hopefully in previous sessions. Trying to understand this, I thought that it was the experience that his mother could no longer encourage and support him like usual, that took away his confidence in himself. He identified with her helplessness and felt scared by it.

This identification with the depressed, disturbed aspect of the parent can become a self-destructive influence on the growing child. Williams described working with a boy, Daniel, who like his mother became severely anorexic and subsequently developed bulimia, switching from starving himself to bingeing and vomiting. He said, early in treatment, that he was going to relive every step of his mother's life and that she told him she was sure he was just like her. He was haunted by this idea and he seemed oblivious to his considerable achievements

Williams goes on to wonder whether, in contrast to a feeling of being contained, these internalised projections can have a disorganising impact on the internal world. She asks:

> Could one say that the introduction of a parent overflowing with projections has an obverse function, namely a disorganising impact on the internal world?
>
> (Williams 1998: 95)

She says that a porous patient like Daniel evokes in her in the counter-transference an idea that he would like help to separate the positive and destructive aspects of his relationship with his mother. He is seeking the capacity to keep a feeling of organisation and structure inside himself. It's as if he says:

> Please help me to differentiate foreign bodies from what is nourishing and to internalise a filing system and organising function of my own.
>
> (p. 96)

This describes well my experience of working with a young teenager, Jonathan, who lived alone with his loving but emotionally vulnerable mother who experienced periods of depression.

> Their life had been unsettled, and Jonathan's mother had several partners as she found emotional relationships difficult to sustain. Jonathan was aged 16 when he asked for therapy. He said he was unhappy and found it difficult to concentrate in school and make friends. In psychotherapy, he found it hard to find the words to tell me about himself and his life. He seemed unaccustomed to talking about his feelings. His mother was often absorbed in her own distress, so he lacked the experience of an empathic parent from whom he could learn to understand himself.
>
> Jonathan wanted to fit in with peers, but he felt he was different, his life was unlike theirs. He had lived a see-saw existence, life at home was often in crisis, never stable for very long. These experiences had damaged his pattern of relating to others. He would become anxious or avoidant at times and he was always vigilant. He strived hard to protect his life from this unpredictability, trying to maintain order in his school work, keep up his friendships and an image of respectability, like everyone else. He appeared to have no special interests to give him pleasure, excitement or distraction from the worries at home.

Listening to Jonathan. it appeared that his lack of confidence came partly from this experience of neglect for long periods of his childhood, and also the sense of uncertainty in his life. It intruded on his thinking, which became closed off or chaotic when he was upset, as Gianna Williams suggested. Over many months, therapy provided reliability and a secure relationship in which he tentatively began to explore his feelings, hopes and anxieties. He was gradually able to internalise an internal sense of structure and order from our therapeutic work, that made it possible for him to discover who he was as a person.

Therapeutic work with the child and adolescent: an overview

Jonathan's story shows how a young person, deprived of good parenting at key points of development, can develop a false self. Children may be able to perform well, but underneath they feel emotionally fragile. When life gets difficult, self-confidence can collapse. However, for many young people it may be hard to accept the idea of therapy. It accentuates the feeling of difference, and they may be accustomed to hiding feelings, so the need for help will be hard to acknowledge. The recognition that the parent's illness has had a negative effect on a young person's life may stir up thoughts and feelings that are difficult to handle. There may always have been feelings of anger towards the sick parent, jealousy towards other families who seem to have a more normal life, and sadness at the lack of happy times in child-hood, which have all been pushed away as somehow disloyal.

An important first step in establishing a therapeutic alliance will be recognising the likely conflict about exploring these feelings about a loved but disturbing parent. The feelings towards the therapist could be ambivalent. There is likely to be a wish for support but also cynicism about whether this experience will be of much help. There may be a worry that bringing difficult feelings to the surface will make it harder to manage life at home, particularly if the parent is still mentally ill or vulnerable.

In my experience, the young person first brings current life stresses to therapy, difficulties in making friends or managing at school, before sharing deeper anxieties about living with mental illness in the family. Gradually the impact of the parent's distress and unavailability will reveal itself in the transference and countertransference relationship. The young person's experience of the unpredictability of the parent's mental states is likely to show in an initial compliance and sensitivity to any change in the therapist's emotional state, any suggestion of anger, sadness or anxiety. The expecta-tion is that the therapist, too, will be vulnerable. Over time, what may emerge is the young person's pattern of anxious, insecure and at times hostile relating. There is often a need to control the therapist, as a defence against earlier feelings of powerlessness when the was child was dependent on adults who could not reliably offer care.

In the therapeutic relationship there will be a chance to explore these feelings. The young person can safely express anger with the therapist for smaller 'failures', like failing to remember to replace toys or art materials, for only offering 50 mins for a session, or for always taking holidays at a bad time. These stand in for larger failures in the child's past and provide a chance to explore the feelings of outrage and distress that could not be expressed to the parent who was ill and vulnerable. Often there is a longing for an idealised mother or father to compensate for the disappointments that the child has experienced growing up and, as therapist, you will inevitably be a disappointment by not meeting this ideal. The therapist takes the young patient's fury about this, but may be able, at some point, to suggest these feelings belonged to those times when there was no one available to offer comfort and care. This need for care may have been seen as weak or unacceptable to the young person trying to cope at home, but can now be seen more kindly, as a necessary part of growing up.

The child therapist's countertransference to this sense of deprivation in the child is likely to be a wish to make up for the lost mothering, and maybe anger with the neglectful ill parent in identification with child. These feelings can be a helpful indicator of the child's unexpressed emotions but have to be monitored carefully to ensure they do not to undermine your relationship with the parents. We can also feel angered and frustrated by a highly defended, controlling young patient who is dismissive of therapy. I have found that retaining a curious but interested stance is a way of keeping a sense of balance. Gradually, the young patient will discover it is safe to be angry and depressed, to disagree and be different from the therapist. Feeling more secure will enable the young person to become more emotionally separate within therapy and also in the home environment, where it may become easier to stand back and take a more realistic view of the ill parent's demands and difficulties.

What can also emerge in the young person's therapy is a deep sense of sadness and emptiness. This sadness seems to be a response to the parent's depression in the child's early pre-verbal development. André Green (1986) talks about the negative effect of a child's early identification with a depressed and emotionally unavailable mother in his paper 'The dead mother', and I think this is similar.

In the following pages, I will look in more detail at this therapeutic work, focusing first on small children, then young school-aged children and adolescents.

Therapeutic work with parents and infants and children under five

In her chapter 'Managing post-partum depression in the community' (Urwin 2012: 179), Cathy Urwin wrote movingly about the value of parent–infant psychotherapy with mothers who are vulnerable to mental illness. She describes the recent research on mothering and identity carried out in an inner London borough which showed that, across diverse ethnic groups and social classes, having a baby can have profound effects on a woman's sense of who she is.

She discusses the social and emotional transition involved in becoming a mother and, particularly, what she calls the

> existential loneliness as the mother experiences anomie, no longer being who she was and yet uncertain in her new identity.
>
> (Urwin 2012: 179)

The research shows how these difficulties become greater if the mothers experience other major stresses including unresolved loss, trauma and a lack of family support which contribute to severe postnatal depression.

Urwin (2012: 180) then describes a project aimed at supporting mothers in a largely Bangladeshi community in East London, which sought to prevent admission to mental hospital by creating a well-resourced team in the community with close cooperation between the local adult and child care services involved. She gives an example of her therapeutic work in this project with two mothers and their toddlers, which showed how a combination of both internal and external stress had precipitated the mothers' postnatal breakdown. Both pairs of mothers and toddlers had problems around separation, which became visible when their toddlers could not settle in the nursery. The mothers' relationship with their small children had become fraught. They were depressed and isolated and depended on their children for comfort, a role these young children could not fulfil. The young mothers felt abandoned by their own mothers at a time of need and were unable to understand their toddlers' boisterous and challenging behaviour which was partly a response to their own distress. Instead they interpreted it as rejection and wilful opposition which escalated the conflict between them. Cathy Urwin said that, as a psychotherapist, she had to be conscious of three 'babies' (p. 189) in the therapy sessions needing her care and protection. There was the actual baby, the toddler feeling pushed aside by the new baby's arrival and the mother's baby-self, crying out for love and care when she felt so overwhelmed by the demands of a new baby and frightened of her own precarious mental state.

The value of such well coordinated intervention to support the family and prevent babies being removed from their parents during hospitalisation is emphasised by the researches of Bowlby (2005 [1988]) and James and Joyce Robertson on loss and separation (1971) discussed earlier. The Robertsons' films show the impact of brief separations on young children who were too young to understand why their parents were absent. Recalling the small children's profound sadness at their mothers' absence in their films made me wonder how often this is the experience of young children, whose quiet grief and fear may go unrecognised at home, when their mothers are acutely mentally ill and then hospitalised. This event would be traumatic for a child as the anxiety and the distress would be overwhelming, unless there was a close relative there to give comfort. This early experience can remain hidden and impair the child's sense of secure attachment, particularly if there is a repeated pattern of separation from the parent.

Having a partner or a close relative available to offer comfort and reassurance or provide substitute care is one of the significant factors in protecting children's emotional well-being when a parent is mentally ill. We know that a baby can have a responsive relationship with a well parent, grandparent or another close adult at the same time as responding in an avoidant way to a withdrawn, hostile or highly anxious mother. When a father takes on the role of primary carer for the children for a while, he may find it a challenge, having to be more emotionally in touch with children at a time when they are anxious and needy. I describe below how a brief period of parent–infant psychotherapy helped Sammy's father become more attuned to his child and more understanding of his communication when his wife was ill.

Supporting the well parent: father–infant psychotherapy

Sammy was 20 months old, and his father was his full-time carer while his wife was in hospital recovering from clinical depression. Sammy had become angry and withdrawn in his mother's absence, and his father did not know how to comfort him. In the initial meeting with father and son, I offered Sammy some toys to play with while I talked to his father. In our conversation, it became apparent that he had not explained to his little boy why his mother had gone away. He did not know what to say. With some encouragement from me, Sammy's father found the words to tell him that his mummy was not well, but she would get better with the doctors' help and come home soon. He thought Sammy would not understand but the little boy listened intently while we talked. Sam then moved towards the radiator that was hot, put his hand on it and then pulled it away. His father was curious why was he doing that, as he said Sammy knew he shouldn't. Together, we worked out that Sammy was letting him know that sometimes the feelings he had inside were getting too hot, he was so angry since his mother had gone to hospital, His father looked tearful when I suggested this, and picked Sammy up and held him close on his lap. Sam snuggled in. He needed his Dad's comfort and reassurance that he loved him even when he got cross. This was the first step to starting a play-based conversation between them in therapy sessions that lasted several months. This provided the support both father and son needed through the months of his wife's illness.

Therapeutic work with latency children

In the discussion about latency children (young school-aged) in Chapter 4, I emphasised the importance of a stable life at home for children of this age, so that children can focus on developing skills and relationships at school and in the community. For the child with a mentally ill or vulnerable parent, this outward focus may not be possible if the child is concerned about the parent's emotional state at home. Often there is a reversal of roles, as the child is pre-occupied with the parent's care. Typically, children who are parentified in this way become accustomed to keeping watch over their ill parents, never quite daring to lose themselves in play or activities. These children may come across as older than their age, with the weight of adult responsibility on their shoulders, and this can take away the spontaneity and joy in life. I remember from my work on the Families Unit at the Cassel

Hospital, a seven-year-old girl checking with me about the times of her mother's therapy sessions and ensuring that all her family came to family meetings on time. This was a role she had become accustomed to playing at home where she felt she was the only responsible one.

Children of this age know and recognise their parents' suffering. They will often communicate their experience symbolically through their play and behaviour, rather than in words, and the child psychotherapy provides a setting where the child can share and process these experiences with a supportive adult to give comfort.

The constant worry of a parent's distress and the traumatic experience of a parent's acute admission to hospital can affect the child's emotional state in disturbing ways that may be misunderstood at school or in the community. The young person will often find it hard to concentrate in school and may become restless and disruptive. This may be seen as bad behaviour unless the adults around are aware of the difficulties at home and can offer extra support and understanding to the child. It was a thoughtful teacher who suggested to his mother that Jethro might benefit from psychotherapy:

> I saw Jethro, aged seven, for an assessment. His teacher was very worried as he had begun acting in a bizarre way, flapping his hands and running about the classroom. His mother had a psychotic break-down following her husband's death and the teacher was concerned that her son was mentally ill too.
>
> I first saw Jethro with his mother who was recovering from her illness. He was a young boy of mixed parentage. His mother was English and his father, who had recently died after a brief illness, was Caribbean. His mother desperately wanted to know how to help and protect her son, while she slowly got her health back. She was a well-dressed, likeable woman, a fashion designer. There were grey lines of anxiety on her face, and a frightened look in her eyes. Her son was small and trim. He looked worried at first, but he moved forward with a lively interest when he saw play materials on the table. While he appeared absorbed in building the Lego, I noticed he frequently looked up, keeping a watchful eye on his mother as she talked to me about her concerns.
>
> Jethro had three individual therapy sessions with me in the assessment. He created a story using play figures about living on a farm with lots of animals. One session he described cooking Jamaican patties in the kitchen with his father on this farm. He told me that his shared dream with his father, when he visited him in hospital, was that they would move to a farm in the country and rebuild their family life together, when he recovered. I realised that despite the recent crisis and his worrying behaviour, Jethro had a healthy ego and a secure sense of self, but he

was suffering from the trauma of his mother's state following his father's loss, and he needed care and protection until she recovered.

When I met his mother to conclude the assessment, we agreed that what he needed most was the support of family, not therapy. His mother arranged for him to live with his paternal grandmother nearby, so he could continue at school and see his mother often in the week.

For this boy, cooperation between his mother, the extended family, the school and adult mental health services ensured that both mother and son were supported through her illness, but this is often not the case. The separation of adult and child services mean that children of mentally ill parents are often unnoticed, or the uncoordinated intervention of different professionals can worsen the plight of these families

As Rosemary Loshak comments:

> Where services involved with the family are characterised by [such] fragmentation and lack of coordination, the effects on vulnerable parents may be to increase anxiety, arouse fears of intrusion and loss of control, and ultimately to undermine precarious parenting skills.
>
> (2012: 9)

For a child psychotherapist, it is particularly important with vulnerable families like these to ensure you are linked in with the team working around the family to share the concerns about the child in treatment, and the others in the family,. There are times of intense pressure which can precipitate unhelpful interventions and misunderstandings about the children's needs.

Therapeutic work with adolescents

In adolescence, there is a search for one's own identity. Then questions can begin to crystallise about the experience of growing up with a parent who has suffered from mental illness. Why did this happen to my mother or father? Will I become mentally ill, will my children? Could I have made a difference and stopped my parent getting so ill?

Teenagers often turn to the internet for answers. It provides a wealth of knowledge but it can be misleading, too, especially when teenagers are searching for answers to such emotionally laden crucial questions. Helping young people begin to separate out their own life story from their parent's experience will be a key focus in therapy. The complex close relationship that can develop between a dependent parent and a youngster who grew up supporting that parent can result in a merged, confused relationship between them. Then it is difficult for the adolescent to discover the parameters of the 'self' and 'the other', so necessary for adolescent individuation.

This was the dilemma facing one young teenage girl, Sandra, aged 13, who grew up with a severely depressed mother. She was referred to me by her parents for psychotherapy because she was shy and bullied at school and she had little confidence in herself. It was complicated to unravel but what emerged in her psychotherapy was her identification with her mother. Depression was familiar to Sandra, and she felt miserable often, whereas she felt anger was not acceptable in her family. She feared that if she expressed any opposition, it would tip her vulnerable mother into fury and depression. In the past, her mother had been withdrawn and unavailable for hours. Sandra tended to be passive and compliant. She had no healthy model for being assertive, expressing anger or managing sadness. In therapy, the task was to help her begin to tolerate these feelings and discover what she wanted for herself. This slow process of self-discovery gradually gave her the confidence to manage the teasing and bullying she had experienced at school as a vulnerable adolescent. She began to enjoy better times, both at home and with her friends, as her life had been overshadowed by her unhappiness until now. Crucially, her psychotherapy was supported by my colleague who worked with her parents to help them encourage her moves to become more assertive and independent.

This work with Sandra showed some of the difficulties faced by young people who have grown up with a parent who has suffered a severe mental illness. In her family, much of the attention had been on the ill parent, and she was not accustomed to being the focus. At first, Sandra pushed away her parents when they attempted to help her, implying that they had not recognised her need for support in the past. She was self-conscious, wary of sharing her feelings as she feared this would disturb what she felt was the precarious balance of her life. Psychotherapy was a slow arduous process for us both. She was very watchful of me and could easily misinterpret my cues. She would instantly apologise to me for any small mistake she made in the session. In the transference, I could quickly become like the intrusive or paranoid parental figure she had experienced in her mother's acute phases of illness. It took many months before Sandra became more comfortable in psychotherapy and began to trust me. Then she began to recognise how her dismissive behaviour towards others had prevented her getting the attention and love she so desperately wanted.

Winnicott is eloquent about the negative mirroring process that can begin very early in development when a young infant feels threatened by the mother's disturbed state of mind, and I think this is relevant to young people throughout childhood. He suggests how the baby might feel when his mother is depressed:

> The baby quickly learns to make a forecast: 'Just now it is safe to forget mother's mood and be spontaneous, but any minute the mother's face will become fixed or her mood will dominate, and my personal needs

must then be withdrawn, otherwise my central self may suffer insult'. ... When there is greater pathology and the parent feels very precarious to infant ... the infant is strained to the limit of his capacity to allow for events. With the threat of chaos, the infant will withdraw and not look except to perceive, as a defence.

(1971: 132)

This need to withdraw to protect one's core self, 'not to look except to perceive', undermines the development of the self-reflective capacity that will help the young person learn about themselves as they go through life. A young person may be intellectually and socially capable, but the core of the self may be fragile as it has to be hidden in this way. This is what Winnicott describes as a false self. He suggests that, in the process, a child's spontaneity may disappear and, with that, there is a loss of creativity as the young person develops.

Sometimes a more self-destructive pattern develops and teenagers provoke the crisis that confirms their fears, with negative beliefs that date back to their early experiences of trauma in the family. This was true of Arthur, whose behaviour was worrying his parents and his teachers, as it had deteriorated in the last year. I was asked to see him for a psychotherapy assessment.

Arthur was an intelligent young man of 16 who was haunted by the memories of his father's psychotic episodes when he was a young boy, shouting and frightening him. His father was now stable and more settled in the relationship with his mother, but these memories came to the surface when Arthur was not coping with his studies and feeling depressed. In these moods, he became suspicious of friends, seeing criticism when it wasn't there. His early experience of feeling rejected and unloveable in his relationship with his father had become part of his inner world, reinforced by his angry rebelliousness, which now caused further rejection. His expectation was that this alienation would happen in all other relationships too, so that any teacher, or a friend who seemed dismissive, would be perceived as rejecting rather than preoccupied with their own issues. If his parents let him down at all, it provoked in him a fury that belonged to the past, and these early experiences of deprivation and rejection.

Despite these difficulties, Arthur wanted to understand his recent volatile moods and difficulties with friends and studying, so he was prepared to work with me in therapy. Here we could explore the links between his present struggles and his early trauma, and he began to re-evaluate his very critical view of himself to gain a more balanced hopeful picture. This helped him manage his mood swings better and hold on to a more realistic understanding of his relationships with others.

The search for identity in young adulthood encourages this type of self-exploration and a re-examination of the past. However, the process of emotional separation from the parents can be more difficult for teenagers who are carers for a depressed or vulnerable parent. They may face the conflict between their need to become more independent and find their own identity, and the pull of the parent who may still need their close involvement and care. Alternatively, there may be a loss of confidence at this crucial step of becoming more self-reliant. Early separation anxieties can reappear at this stage of transition, as the growth to independence in earlier years was too rapid for these young people to feel truly secure in themselves. The move to university or college can often precipitate these fears, and therapeutic support through this time of transition can bring new confidence to a teenager who previously felt too anxious to take these steps away from home.

The impact of mental illness on the family

Illness in one member of the family will affect each child and adult in a different way. The report mentioned earlier, *Think Child, Think Parent, Think Family*, highlights the importance of thinking holistically about the family. It stresses the need for community services in adult and child mental health to work closely together, but also emphasises that professionals need to assess in depth the experience of each person in the family to understand the support they need. The report suggests questions that should be asked like: who is doing the parenting in this family? can the family with support become more child-centred? are family services needed to protect children from harm by ensuring other services are available?

My experience as a child psychotherapist working with families which have experienced trauma and mental illness is that this can disturb the family dynamics in such a way that relationships become stuck in unhelpful patterns. These patterns are described in family therapy as a frozen narrative, an evocative phrase that pictures how stuck and circular these interactions can become. Within the same family, one young person may become 'the problem child', carrying the distress and anger for everyone. Another child may be as tightly confined in the role of 'the good child', often carrying the burden of responsibility for the parent's needs. A child psychotherapist working with the parents can help the parents recognise these dynamics and consider what therapeutic approach would be most helpful to meet everyone's needs more effectively. It may be that working with the family as a whole initially, or giving support to the parents, might be more appropriate than starting individual psychotherapy with the child causing concern, which might confirm this unhelpful split. Therapy for the referred child may be an important next step once the family and parental issues have been considered.

Therapeutic work with vulnerable and distressed parents

An important factor in ensuring a good outcome for child psychotherapy is the parents' willingness to recognise the negative patterns that have developed when the family was in crisis. They can see how their child's needs might conflict with their own. This capacity to reflect will become clear in the initial meeting with parents where you can explore the pressures on the children, and how their anxieties may have been overlooked in the daily struggle for survival. If the parents can be supported to change the focus in the family, so that the children are more protected from the impact of their parent's illness, the long-term emotional harm to their development may be reduced.

Working at the Cassel Hospital with parents who suffered from mental illness or personality difficulties, I saw how mental illness and a chaotic home life had severely disrupted families' lives. What was also evident was the potential for change. It was not the parents' history of illness, or even the history of family breakdown, that predicted outcome but the parents' willingness to look at their own parenting and vulnerability, and make a commitment to protecting their children and meeting their needs. The aim of the psychotherapeutic work with the parents was to help them to develop their capacity to self-reflect and this proved to be the best predictor of long-term good outcomes for them as parents and for their children.

In this in-patient setting, parents had their own psychotherapy where they could explore their troubled past and they saw how this had shaped their relationship with their children. They were then able to take back the projections of fear, anger and anxiety that had been disturbing to the children. A mother who had been in a violent relationship with her partner was able to recognise how she overreacted and even precipitated conflict in her relationship with their son, as she sometimes could not separate him from her ex-partner in her troubled thoughts. Another traumatised mother, who had been sexually abused, saw how her anxieties about her daughter's sexuality and safety were intruding on her daughter's life as she became fearful and controlling when her daughter wanted to go out and meet friends or stay away overnight.

This work to help parents recognise the impact of their illness on their children, and to repair and rebuild relationships where they have become disturbed, was an important first step in the rehabilitation of the family. In similar work with vulnerable parents in the community, it is important to be clear about the areas of life where they will need to change. This openness can create an alliance which will ensure that the child therapist has the parents' support once therapeutic work begins and the young person begins to assert himself. Otherwise there is a danger that, as the young person attempts to gain more independence, this progress will be undermined by the parents' anxiety about change.

Perhaps it is most helpful to end this chapter with the voices of the children themselves. Researchers interviewed young people in three inner-city boroughs who were living with mentally ill parents (Bromley et al. 2012). Many of those involved were young carers. They were asked about their life experience and what help they wanted. The young participants talked about the painful struggles of daily living, their anxiety and wish for more knowledge about the facts of their parents' mental illness. Some said they feared that asking for help might lead to them being taken into care by social workers. They also emphasised how important it was to them that the positive aspects of their lives were recognised by professionals and their resilience too. They wanted to feel supported and confident in their commitment to helping their family to manage, and be offered practical help when it was needed (Loshak 2012).

References

Bowlby, J. (2005 [1988]) *A Secure Base: Clinical Applications of Attachment Theory*. London: Routledge.

Bromley, C., Hadleigh, L. & Roe, A. (2012) Living with a parent with mental health needs: What children say. In R. Loshak (ed) *Out of the Mainstream: Helping the Children of Parents with Mental Illness*, pp. 14–30. London: Routledge.

Green, A. (1986) The dead mother. In A. Green (ed) *On Private Madness*, pp. 142–173. London: Hogarth Press. Translated by Katherine Aubertin from 'La mère morte', *Narcissisme de vie, narcissisme de mort*, Paris: Éditions de Minuit, 1983.

Loshak, R. (2012) *Out of the Mainstream: Helping the Children of Parents with Mental Illness*. London: Routledge.

Martins, C. & Gaffan, E.A. (2000) The effects of early maternal depression on patterns of infant–mother attachment: A meta-analytics investigation. *Journal of Child Psychology and Psychiatry* 41(6): 737–746.

Robertson, J. & Robertson, J. (1971) Young children in brief separation: A fresh look. *Psychoanalytic Study of the Child* 26: 264–315.

Social Care Institute for Excellence. (2011) *Guide 30: Think Child, Think Parent, Think Family: A Guide to Parental Mental Health and Child Welfare*. London: SCIE.

Tronick, E., Adamson, L.B., Als, H. & Brazelton, T.B. (1975, April). Infant emotions in normal and perturbated interactions. Paper presented at the Biennial Meeting of the Society for Research in Child Development, Denver, CO.

Urwin, C. (2012) Managing post-partum depression in the community: Who cares for the babies? In R. Loshak (ed.) *Out of the Mainstream: Helping the Children of Parents with Mental Illness*, pp. 178–191. London: Routledge.

Williams, G. (1998) Reflections on some particular dynamics of eating disorders. In R. Anderson & A. Dartington (eds) *Facing It Out: Clinical Perspectives on Adolescent Disturbance*, pp. 79–98. London: Taylor & Francis.

Winnicott, D.W. (1971) Mirror-role of mother and family in child development. In D.W. Winnicott (ed) *Playing and Reality*, pp. 130–138. Harmondsworth: Penguin, 1985.

Chapter 12

Therapeutic work with children whose parents have separated or divorced

Introduction

A stable family supports and protects children. It helps them survive difficult life events, as experiences are shared within the family, bringing a sense of continuity. When parents separate or divorce, this protection is disrupted, and many children experience a period of loss, conflict and uncertainty in their family life. According to the Office of National Statistics (ONS), in 2012 42% of marriages in England and Wales ended in divorce, and of these 48% involved children under 16 (ONS 2014). Most parents strive to manage this separation with a minimum of disruption for the children, and mediation services encourage a non-conflictual approach to divorce, placing the children's needs at the centre of the discussion. A good co-parenting alliance following divorce is a strong predictor of a good outcome for the children (Sobolewski & King 2005). However, it is estimated that around 20–25% of divorced parents remain in a conflicted co-parenting relationship. There are frequent clashes, and they are unable to think about their co-parenting role as distinct from their troubled relationship with their former partner. Their behaviour is angry and children can become tools in their conflict (Hetherington & Kelly 2002).

As child psychotherapists, we see many children and adolescents who have been unable to cope with the distress of their parents' separation. The disruption in their external world can have a shattering effect on their inner world, reshaping the way they see themselves, their parents and their family. In this chapter I will explore how young people respond when their parents' separation is conflictual, and how therapeutic work can help them to recover from the impact of this experience. I will also consider the parents' perspective and the value of therapeutic support to help them shield their children from the distress of divorce.

When I begin therapeutic work with children of divorced and separated parents, I try to involve both parents to help them rebuild their alliance around the children, encouraging them to agree to parent support work. I have learnt the value of this approach from co-working with my family therapy colleague, Caroline Penney. She works hard to get both parents to see her regularly, either together or separately, to think about how they can support their children through this difficult time. This allows me to focus on the needs of the distressed child or adolescent. The parents may have separated many years before. We build up a picture of this time retrospectively from meetings with the parents and from the child's recollections in psychotherapy. We learn how the family has rebuilt itself, the challenges facing step-parents and the stresses of developing new relationships between half siblings.

The emotional impact of marital conflict and divorce on children

Children's understanding of their parents' separation will be shaped by their age and their stage of development. This will influence their perception of events at the time. Children of three or four years are intensely pre-occupied with relationships with their parents, Oedipal fantasies about loving the parent of the opposite sex, and struggle to deal with their anger when frustrated. At this age, children see everything in relation to themselves and they believe they are the centre of the world. This can make them feel responsible for their parents' unhappiness and anger when the parents are in conflict. Their interpretation of the break-up of their parents' relationship will be shaped by this world view, whatever rational explanation parents give.

Children are also very vulnerable to loss and change as they are still so dependent on the family for security and love. When the parents' conflict is extreme, their separation can feel traumatic and overwhelming to their children. This was Sandra's experience. She was three years old when her parents separated. I saw her for therapy aged eleven:

> Sandra was aggrieved and unhappy when she was referred to me for once-weekly psychotherapy by her parents. She had been temporarily excluded from school because of her rudeness in class and her daredevil behaviour. Her parents had been caught up in a prolonged court battle over their divorce for years, and she was intensely loyal to both of them. She felt she was still at the centre of their conflict, when she visited each in their own home. Her resolution of this dilemma was to focus her anger first on the school, which she hated, and also on any of her peers who were 'disrespectful.' But she also attacked her own capacities, refusing to study even those subjects that interested her at school. Her bad behaviour had the function of involving both her parents, forcing them to communicate and even to attend joint meetings with the headmaster.
>
> Sandra accepted the idea of psychotherapy. She was polite to me, but she denigrated anything I said or ignored it. Each week in therapy, she used the figures in the sand tray to create endless stories about a terrorist who was captured by the army, locked up and tortured as a punishment for killing his family. He escaped, but he was always found and returned to captivity. I felt a useless observer watching her play, but Sandra never

missed a session, so I thought they must mean something to her, although I was not sure yet what.

It gradually became clear that Sandra's story was a re-enactment of her inner imaginative world, where she was endlessly punishing herself for destroying her family, I began to talk to her about what I saw in her story; the suffering of the terrorist and the cruelty of his captors who seemed to enjoy sadistically making him suffer. Eventually I felt the time was right to see if she could allow me to link this story with her own. I said she seemed to feel responsible for breaking up her family, and so she felt she should be punished. To my surprise she accepted this idea in quite a straightforward way. She told me that she remembered the day her father left home, and her mother crying. For the first time she allowed herself to be sad and I saw a softer side of her than I had seen before. I had not found it easy to like Sandra but now I began to warm to her.

Sandra's play shows the effect that warring parents can have on their child. She hated and blamed herself for her parents' bitter and protracted separation. She was convinced they had fought over her, and that it was her behaviour that drove them apart and had kept the battle going between them. In her internal world, she lived with this picture of an endlessly warring parental couple. She had lost the idea that once she may have been lovingly conceived and a much-wanted baby, as her parents had lost touch with those early memories too.

My colleague's work with the parents was as important as my individual psychotherapy. Sandra shared her time between the two family homes. My colleague encouraged Sandra's parents to adopt a similar approach, setting firm boundaries to her angry behaviour while also trying to understand what led to her outbursts. She thought about their parenting strategies with them, suggesting they reward her moments of cooperation and ensure that they each set aside some enjoyable individual time for her, separate from the half-siblings who were now part of their families.(see Penney 2017 for further discussion of parenting strategies) Towards the latter part of treatment, the parents agreed to come to one joint meeting with Sandra to talk to her about their separation, to get the facts clear and to explain what really happened. They talked about their unhappiness and anger with each other which had led to the divorce and court battle. They said that they had both continued to love her, and they had not wanted her to suffer. Sandra was touched and relieved to hear their account and to see them being more considerate towards each other and thinking about her together.

Meanwhile, in therapy, I could see that Sandra had begun to forgive herself and her parents for the years of distress. Her play became more humane. There was prison for the offender now, instead of torture and death, and the chance of rehabilitation. I heard from the parents that Sandra had begun to do well at school as she now could allow herself to succeed. The teachers praised her talent in art and history, and her skill in gymnastics. This enjoyment of competitive sports took the place of dangerous escapades they had seen previously. Sandra also began to build a more friendly relationship with her parents' new partners and their children, which meant she felt more relaxed in both homes. By the end of this long period of therapy, the parents had worked through some of the trauma of their separation, and Sandra had found a new and more positive sense of herself and her relationship with others.

Looking back, I can see that it was this parallel process of parent support work alongside the child psychotherapy, and our close cooperation in this work that made change possible. Although we worked separately, I think we were perceived by the parents as a reflective parental couple holding the family system together until the parents were able to reconcile and to communicate between themselves effectively.

The parents' experience of conflict and the implications for the children

Working in psychotherapy with the children of parents who have been involved in such long-standing and bitter court battles over custody and contact, it is clear how the bitterness and feelings of persecution can seep into every aspect of family life. It is easier to understand this from the parents' perspective after reading the recent research by Nick Midgley and colleagues (Target et al. 2017). The research interviews show the high levels of distress experienced by the parents in these court battles. It describes their extreme states of mind, the anger, jealousy, hurt and despair they feel, particularly when the child is visiting the other parent. The intense, almost maddening emotions that parents feel when they are caught in a protracted divorce case seem to undermine their reasoning, as they function well in other aspects of life. Continued child contact with the non-resident parent is strongly recommended post-divorce, but that can be hard to maintain in reality. It is difficult for a couple to separate emotionally, dealing with the loss and anger involved in ending a relationship, while maintaining a rational approach to the children's needs. Children can get lost in the disputes, even though they are the central issue in the legal conflict.

There is also the danger of competitiveness between the parents. Winning or losing the battle for contact time can become a continuation of the conflict in their relationship. The parents described a sense of loss of control, especially for the parent who no longer has the children living with them. These battles can dominate the lives of the parents and the children for many years, making it hard to focus on the child's needs.

Children can feel like they are in the middle of the battle between their parents, trying to make peace. They try to protect both parents and are often prematurely thrust into an adult role.

In the research interviews, some parents describe how they managed the conflict by ensuring that their mutual communication is formal, distant and kept to a minimum. Parents also said they lost confidence in their ability to parent following their separation and conflict with a partner. Parents often wished for some support through this time, but feared that they would have to justify themselves as if they were still in court, if they sought the help of a professional like a psychotherapist.

Recovery from loss: psychotherapy with a young man whose parents had divorced

Peter was aged 10 years when he was referred for psychotherapy by his father because he was unhappy and anxious much of the time, and quite withdrawn. He found it hard to make friends and to concentrate at school. His sister, a year older, was more confident and clever, but rather tough and challenging to the teachers. He was a quiet child whose unhappiness was probably not noticed at school except that he was often tired and his mind seemed far away. His teachers thought he had more intellectual capacity than he showed.

I saw Peter for once-weekly psychotherapy for four years. He lived with his father and father's new partner and saw his mother one evening in the week and at weekends. He was three when his parents separated. There was a quiet hostility between his parents, although they had agreed financial and contact arrangements and kept to these.

> I recall my first meeting with Peter. It was like seeing a child through glass. I felt no emotional contact with him. His face was drawn and his shoulders hunched as he sat down at the table. He had agreed to write a story, which he then illustrated. It was a tale of a lonely rabbit seeking contact with a friendly horse who was on the other side of a mountain. He told me the rabbit could hear the horse neighing but he could not reach him, just as he must have felt I was unreachable to him. As the sessions went on, I often struggled to stay awake as a deep drowsiness came over me. I had experienced this occasionally with other children, so I knew that it was my response to his suppressed painful feelings which he kept at a distance at all costs. Peter had become a compliant and withdrawn young man who avoided any conflict, but this left him feeling so empty and disconnected from himself that I imagine his peers at school found him rather odd and awkward.
>
> Therapy with Peter was a very slow process as he was reluctant to face the painful and conflicting feelings he had kept at bay for many years. Gradually he told me how he yearned for an earlier time, possibly

a fantasy only, when his family were happy together. He tentatively began to make some negative or critical comments about his life at home with his father and stepmother. I would hear how he would get angry about some small disappointment, like his supper being late, and he would then stay silent for many hours. I was relieved. Peter was beginning to allow himself to feel, and to assert himself. His father was understanding and took a tolerant line. Peter became very anxious that one of his parents might get ill. I thought this might be a reaction to the furious thoughts that were now coming to the surface and his fear of being hurtful to his parents in some way. Over the lengthy psychotherapy, Peter came alive and more expressive as he began to recognise the anger and distress about his parents' separation that he had stifled. I no longer felt drowsy in the sessions as his defensive suppression of his feelings lifted. This emotional integration of previously cut-off aspects of himself enabled further ego and social development too. He started to take an interest in life outside home, meeting up with friends and playing football. I noticed too he began to look more like an adolescent, a prospect which he had not been ready for before.

The reconciliation fantasy

I was reminded of Peter's longing for an idealised past with his parents when I read an article by Lohr et al. (1981) exploring the reasons for children's reconciliation fantasies following their parents' separation or divorce. Children deny the fact that their parents' separation is permanent in the hope that they will return together in a loving relationship, not in the conflict that led to the divorce. The authors suggest that denial is a natural response, a primitive defence to protect the child from the too painful emotions of loss and uncertainty when their parents separate, but it prevents children becoming reconciled to the reality. The authors write:

> The reconciliation fantasy can serve the function of enabling the ego to absorb, within its own timetable, the psychic trauma experienced. It may be a normal and adaptive response to painful affects and to the jolt to the cohesive sense of self associated with loss and family disintegration. If it persists over time it may interfere with further ego development and result in impoverishment in future object relationships.
>
> (Lohr et al. 1981: 125)

Children may keep this denial hidden as they 'know' the truth and they do not want their fantasy exposed, so it is not often cited as part of the presenting problem, but it may be revealed in children's fantasy play in therapy.

The authors suggest several situations when children are likely to persist in this reconciliation fantasy. It can occur if their parents live apart but are unable to separate emotionally, or when their parents' new relationships fail, reactivating the child's unfulfilled wish for them to get together. They also suggest that guilt can drive this wish if the children, like Peter and Sandra, are of the age and psychosexual development at the time of the divorce when they see themselves as responsible for the parents' break-up. They quote Wallerstein and Kelly (1976) who found that this sense of responsibility is particularly strong in preschool children who are struggling with Oedipal issues at this time. If one parent's departure leaves the child in the position of the Oedipal victor, triumphant that he or she now has the sole affection of the remaining parent, then feelings of guilt may add to this need for a reconciliation between the parents.

The other important factor, the authors suggest, is the loss of a model for identification for the child growing up, particularly when it is the same sex parent who leaves:

> For many children, the loss is a narcissistic injury, and may be responded to with a lowering of self-esteem and perception of the self as damaged, worthless, and unlovable. ... [This] can be a major factor in the persistence of the fantasy that the trauma did not occur (denial) or that it is reversible, thus warding off the sense of the self as damaged or rejected. ... The reconciliation fantasy keeps important characteristics of the father alive for the child [when he is living separately] so he can continue the process of internalisation.
>
> (Lohr et al. 1981)

The shadow of the absent father

Mothers assume custodial responsibility for children in the overwhelming majority of cases (Braver et al. 1993) and often there is a loss of contact with the father. For boys, this can lead to anxieties about their own future as men, particularly if they have grown up with a negative image of their father or remember his violence if there was domestic abuse. The danger is that the child identifies with this negative paternal image in the absence of an alternative. A boy may repeat the pattern of angry provocative behaviour towards his mother that he associates with the relationship between his parents, and this can be quite frightening for them both. This places the growing lad in tremendous conflict, wanting to protect his mother whom he loves, but also not able to handle his aggression. In the father's absence there is no third person to come between mother and son and help them emotionally separate as he grows up. This can result in an enmeshed tense relationship between them, with the son resisting the presence of any new boyfriend.

In psychotherapy with the child, and in parent support work, the focus needs to be on helping the boy and his mother emotionally separate, freeing each of them to develop their own relationships with others. Often the therapist has to put firm boundaries on the child's tempestuous behaviour in the sessions as there is likely to be a repeat in the transference of his intensely emotional relationship with his mother. At the same time, the youngster needs help to put into words the distress, confusion and anger that often lie behind such outbursts.

> Jack, aged seven, faced these issues. He was a lively intelligent boy brought up by his single mother. He told me he wanted therapy to help with his anger because he too easily ended up fighting with his mother or with boys at school. Jack had only disturbing early memories of his father who left home when he was two years old. In psychotherapy, he struggled to work out what sort of man he would become. He lacked a positive internal paternal model. In his sessions, he continually played out battles between good and evil male fighters, as if striving to come to terms with these different potential aspects of himself.
>
> His mother had a caring partner but Jack found it hard to accept him. Jack remained closely involved with his mother, and he could be over-protective of her and controlling. He was also sensitive to any insult to his self-esteem and he would respond violently if he was challenged at school. Jack's mother was resourceful and determined and encouraged him to attend therapy even when he found it difficult. In the transference relationship with me, Jack alternated between his fury with me for standing my ground faced with his demands and a desperate wish for closeness. Gradually he was able to get in touch with his underlying feelings of guilt about provoking his mother and his wish for a loving father who might help him grow up. He began to be curious about his dad, and wonder what he was really like. He began to mourn for what life might have been like, if 'Mum and Dad had been happy'. The recognition that he wanted and needed a father figure made it possible for him to develop a more positive relationship with mother's new boyfriend, who offered him friendship. Jack began to go on cycling trips with him and they would mend his car together in the garage.

The process of mourning, for children of separated parents, involves working through many losses. They have lost the family they knew, which was central to their life and on which they had depended for their sense of security. Their parents, to whom they would normally turn for support, might also have been less emotionally available to their children when they needed them, as they were themselves going through a grieving process at the time of their separation. All these factors can make creating a new reconstituted family a difficult challenge, if the parents find new partners, maybe with children of their own.

Therapeutic work with step-parents

Therapeutic support can be helpful to step-parents who are trying to establish a relationship with their step-children. It can be a shock to step-parents to discover that despite their best efforts to connect with their partners' children, they are rejected by them. They may feel they are never good enough to match the child's idealised picture of the absent parent. If the children are still pre-occupied with the parent who has left, then the negative feelings about this loss can be projected onto the new step-parent who can become like 'the evil step-parent' of fairy tales in the child's mind. This is painful to accept and can place a great strain on the new couple relationship. It can be a relief to step-parents to recognise that this is a familiar pattern. The children are working through their grief and anger about a loss they could not control, and these are subjective feelings that colour all their responses to their new parent figure. Given time and patience, the children will recover and be able to develop new attachments, and the new parental couple may need reassurance to look after their new relationship through this time.

A young person's reflections on psychotherapy

Sandra, the young girl with divorced parents I discussed earlier, came back to see me for a couple of sessions a few years after she had finished psychother-apy. She wanted to touch base before going to university. I asked her how she saw our therapeutic work now and what had helped. She said she remembered her early fury and that 'she wasn't herself then'. She couldn't see anything straight because she was angry and hurting at the time. She said that, in psychotherapy, she had realised gradually that it wasn't her fault that her parents had split up and that made her feel better about herself. She said she understood her moods better now, and although they still worry her at times, she now feels confident she can get through them. She said she knows now, looking back, that the teachers and school weren't that bad really either. She remarked that she feels older than other girls in her class because she has been through so much family turmoil, and now they turn to her for advice.

Conclusion

There are many potential risks to young people who go through parental separation particularly if it is protracted and there is conflict between the parents. If it is too traumatic, it can feel to the child as if the family is fragmenting, and this interrupts the sense of stability, which Winnicott described as the 'going on being' (Winnicott 1956) that children benefit from most, as they grow up. It can have the impact of jolt to the child's cohesive sense of self, interfering with children's emotional development, as well as their life outside the home, at school and with friends. All involved go through a period of loss and disappointment, and often there is a sense of blame that circulates round the family. Children are sensitive to these spoken and unspoken aspects of family relationships and often misperceive their own role in the break-up, blaming themselves as part of the problem. Child psychotherapists can intervene on many levels to ameliorate the impact of this time of difficulty, through individual therapy with the children on their experience of loss, work with separated parents to help them bridge the divide for their children, and with reconstituted families to help with the process of building new relationships while holding on to a realistic picture of the past.

References

Braver, S., Wolchik, S.A., Sandler, I.N., Sheets, V., Fogas, B. & Bay, R. (1993) A longitudinal study of noncustodial parents: Parents without children. *Journal of Family Psychology* 7(1): 9–23.

Hetherington, E.M. & Kelly, J. (2002) *For Better or Worse*. London: Norton.

Lohr, R.B., Chethik, M., Press, S.E., Solyom, A.E. & Arbor, A. (1981). Impact of divorce on children: Vicissitudes and therapeutic implications of the reconciliation fantasy. *Journal of Child Psychotherapy* 7(2): 123–136.

ONS (Office for National Statistics) (2014) *Divorces in England and Wales: 2012*. Newport: ONS.

Penney, C. (2017). *The Parenting Toolkit: Simple Steps to Happy and Confident Children*. Stroud: Hawthorn Press.

Sobolewski, J.M. & King, V. (2005). The importance of the coparental relationship for nonresident fathers' ties to children. *Journal of Marriage and Family* 67(5): 1196–1212.

Target, M., Hertzmann, L., Midgley, N., Casey, P. & Lassri, D. (2017). Parents' experience of child contact within entrenched conflict families following separation and divorce: A qualitative study. *Journal of Psychoanalytic Psychotherapy* 31(2): 218–246.

Wallerstein, J.S. & Kelly, J.B. (1976). The effects of parental divorce. Experiences of the child in later latency. *American Journal of Orthopsychiatry* 46(2): 256–269.

Winnicott, D.W. (1956). Primary maternal preoccupation. In D.W. Winnicott (ed) *Through Paediatrics to Psychoanalysis*, pp. 300–305. London: Karnac, 1992.

Part 4

Taking child psychotherapy outside the psychotherapy room

New pathways

Applying psychotherapy to other settings

Introduction

Child psychotherapy has broadened its scope as services have moved outside the psychotherapy room into the community where they are more accessible to the children and families who need them most. Child psychotherapists work in GP surgeries, children centres, hospitals and schools, alongside other professionals in specialist teams, as well as offering consultancy and teaching to others working with children and adolescents. These developments allow psychotherapeutic ideas to be integrated with those of other disciplines to achieve a holistic approach to children's needs. This involves adapting our technique to the resources available and the needs of the services.

This process is not without its tensions. Working with children and families in complex situations can place a strain on multi-professional teams, where clinicians have differing approaches and roles in relationship to the child and the family. Unless they are understood, these differences can disrupt the team's thinking about the child. In this chapter, I will look at how child psychotherapists have adapted to a range of settings: in hospitals, schools, in work with refugees, looked-after children and post-adoption services, and in consultation. This interdisciplinary approach has led to child psychotherapists developing new skills and techniques adapted to the children's needs.

Child psychotherapy in hospital

The emotional impact of serious or long-term illness on children's development can get overlooked if the focus is primarily on medical diagnosis and treatment. Research suggests that children with long-term illness are twice as likely to suffer from emotion or conduct disorders (Parry-Langdon 2008). Child psychotherapists working in paediatric services and child and adolescent mental health teams can redress this balance with their expertise in assessing children's emotional and developmental needs. They can offer therapeutic support to children and their families. There are several physical illnesses where it is known that emotional distress can increase the severity of symptoms like eczema, asthma, epilepsy and diabetes. Government guidelines for treatment of diabetes recognise this, stating that young people with diabetes 'are at high risk of anxiety and depression, and it is important that they have early access to mental health professionals when they need it' (National Institute of Clinical Excellence [NICE] 2016).

The work of child psychotherapists in two very different medical settings illustrates their role. The first is in paediatric liaison and the second on a teenage oncology unit.

Paediatric liaison

In paediatric liaison, child psychotherapists are often asked to see children and adolescents with unexplained physical illness to consider if emotional factors within the child and the family are contributing to the child's illness. Paddy Martin, a child psychotherapist illustrates this in his work with a refugee family (2012). He cites Joyce McDougall (1968) who explains psychosomatic illness as a bodily expression of emotional pain that is so unbearable, it is shut off from consciousness and instead experienced as a physical illness.

> Fozia, aged two years, was referred to Paddy Martin, for psychotherapy with an unexplained history of reflux, food refusal and vomiting. She was brought by her depressed mother and her 19-year-old sister, who had taken on most of the parenting. Martin describes how Fozia's inability to take in food and nourishment appeared to represent her family's inability to 'take in' their tragic history, until they had received some understanding and care through their daughter's illness. They had experienced police brutality in their home country, the loss of home and community, and uncertainty about finding a permanent home in the UK. The mother eventually was able to talk about how depressed she had been when Fozia was a baby, and how this had made it difficult for her to give her little girl the love and care she needed. Paddy Martin took on a paternal supportive function for this fatherless family. He ensured they received the practical services they needed, while also helping the family process the distressing events that previously had been too painful to think about. He felt the family trusted him because he had understood their sense of hopelessness and displacement. Eventually they were able to recognise that Fozia's illness was an expression of their grief and anger, feelings which they needed to own for her to recover.

Child psychotherapy in a teenage and young adult oncology department

On a teenage and young adult oncology department in a large London hospital, child psychotherapists consult to the staff and support children and their families from the time of diagnosis of cancer to the end of treatment, and on occasion to the end of the child's life. They are an integral part of the medical and the multidisciplinary teams, observing the impact of illness on children's emotional life and their unconscious world, and how this will differ according to the child's age and stage of development.

Child psychotherapists here have to be adaptable. They do not have a regular room or time for seeing a child or a space to bring along a toy box. Instead, therapy may be having a conversation with a young person at the bedside on a ward, in a treatment room or in the corridor. Jane Elfer (personal communication) describes how a psychoanalytic viewpoint can clarify the thinking when there is high emotion and anxiety in the team. The child psychotherapist's capacity to bear anxiety and not rush to action is valued in the medical setting. They also have to bear the sadness and grief of the very ill teenagers:

> Sitting with a young person who has no hope of cure is painful but important as it allows the young person to feel understood, especially when to share these thoughts and feelings with family members who they love and wish to protect, feels unbearable. They can listen to and understand the feelings whilst at the same time gently encouraging the possibility of a conversation with those they love.
>
> (Jane Elfer, personal communication)

The work is fortunately not always around death but nevertheless loss is an important feature of the work. There are celebrations when a young person finishes cancer treatment and can return to ordinary life, but then there is a difficult adjustment to make as the young person will face 'the loss of who they felt they were' and 'their dreams for the future' may have to change (Elfer, personal communication) Children are seen for therapy during and after treatment, sometimes many years after their medical care is over, when they feel ready to talk about their illness. This may have happened when they were very young and unable to deal with the pain and anxiety caused by the illness. Reflecting on these past experiences in therapy helps the young people to process the trauma, make sense of the past events and integrate these experiences into their life.

Although child psychotherapists are part of the multidisciplinary team, they are not directly involved in the medical care of the children and adolescents. This makes it is easier for them to be alongside families and their sick children to help them cope with the distress that illness brings, and increase their resilience. They can also support the medical team coping with the distress that is involved in this work, as well as be involved in teaching the professionals about the psychological aspects of illness in children and adolescents.

Child psychotherapy in schools

Child psychotherapists in school are in a prime position to intervene when young people are distressed and this is interfering with their learning. Their presence can help teachers understand the emotional needs of young people facing difficult times at home or in school, and of those with neurological difficulties who may struggle in the educational system. These services have now developed widely, in primary and secondary schools, colleges and universities.

Sometimes, the young people with emotional difficulties are those who challenge the teachers in the classroom. As Graham Music (2008) points out, the pressures of school life can lead to 'difficult children' becoming labelled as troublesome, without an understanding of the underlying difficulties that have led to their behaviour.

A major part of our work consists of trying to contain unmanageable affects, such as fear and distrust and hurt, so that it becomes possible to help others see a child as sad rather than bad, hurt as well as angry, distressed rather than malevolent, and in need of support and help as well as exclusion (Music 2008).

School-based therapists can offer individual psychotherapy, therapeutic group work, support for parents and consultation to the educational team. Emil Jackson, a child psychotherapist who has led many school-based groups for teachers, describes how teachers feel freer to discuss the tense and challenging relationships that can develop with students in the safe setting of a work discussion group. These consultations can have a ripple effect. As teachers gain more experience in thinking psychologically about children's needs, they use this understanding to support each other when difficult situations arise.

In supervision with school psychotherapists, I have seen how therapeutic services become an essential part of the school's provision. Initially the request is for brief psychotherapy for students, but the demand for therapy is so high that the child psychotherapists begin to offer regular consultations to the teaching staff alongside. Here they consider the pupils causing concern, intervene early where possible and reduce the number of emergency requests for help.

There are key transition times in the school life, like new admissions or exam times, when extra therapeutic support is often needed by the students. However, young people also seek help for personal issues around sexuality, identity and gender, difficulties in peer group relationships, and conflicts at home. How and when to involve parents can be a dilemma for the child psychotherapist as the school's focus is usually on the child, and parents are not involved unless necessary. This is so different from our usual approach of seeing the child's problems within the context of the family and the child's history, it can be difficult for the child psychotherapist working alone to maintain the ability to think analytically. Having an external supervisor to reflect on the more complex situations can be an essential support for the work.

School life is so busy that the educational team have little time to reflect on individual children's emotional needs. Young people in severe emotional distress cause the most concern, particularly when there is risk, like suicidal behaviour. Staff often turn to the child psychotherapist for help in deciding how best to help the young person, and when to involve the parents and local child care services. Bearing this level of responsibility can be challenging for the lone child psychotherapist, and it helps if there is a group of supportive, allied professionals within the school to share these concerns.

It is interesting to consider how the child psychotherapy service is seen within the school which, like any system, will have its own organisational dynamic. To simplify rather, child psychotherapy may be viewed as a service that is quietly functioning in a corner to mop up the emotional distress and issues of risk that interfere with the learning and achievement of the students. Or it might come to take on a more central role as a vital part of the school's focus on children's emotional well-being. These differing perspectives, often an unconscious part of the school life, may not be recognised by those involved, but they will influence how the child psychotherapist can function within the school culture. It will affect how openly concerns about young people are recognised and discussed between the staff, how often parents are involved, and how much use is made of the local child mental health services and other specialist resources. The child psychotherapists I supervise have found that their work has had a cascade effect. As the school-based psychotherapy service becomes embedded in the school, there is more open recognition within the educational team of the emotional and developmental challenges children can face in their school careers and their need, at times, for psychological help.

Therapeutic education

Young people who have experienced severe early trauma and neglect are often unable to survive in an ordinary school setting. Their complex emotional needs have led to the development of therapeutic educational settings, 'spaces for growth' (Onions & Browner 2012) for these troubled children. I will describe two of these here – the Mulberry Bush School, a residential therapeutic community, and Gloucester House, a day school. Both these schools have developed a therapeutic milieu where the whole setting is dedicated to the children's emotional recovery and learning, and psychoanalytic understanding underlies their approach.

The Mulberry Bush School

The Mulberry Bush School is described by John Diamond, its Chief Executive Director, as:

a therapeutic setting where young people can internalise a lived experience of caring and empathic relationships within a nurturing and containing environment.

(2013)

Barbara Dockar-Drysdale, who later trained as a psychotherapist, founded the school in 1948. Working closely with Winnicott, she developed an assessment model for emotionally disturbed children that looked at the level of integration in the child. The aim of the treatment at the school was to help children become emotionally integrated and recover from their developmental delays. The school would 'fill the gaps' by offering the primary experience they had missed in a symbolic form, as she described in her book *The Provision of Primary Experience* (1990).

Since that time, the school has continued to develop its treatment programme in line with the new understanding of trauma from neurological researchers like Bruce Perry. He explains that when traumatised children are in an emotionally charged situation, they will become anxious and regress to brain-stem fight or flight functioning. Then they behave in primitive ways and act out, and they are less accessible to therapeutic approaches using words or relationships as a basis for change. He says they

> need new experiences that will allow the brain to break false associations or decrease the over-generalisation of trauma related associations.
>
> (Perry 2006: 34)

The Mulberry Bush school offers this 'new experience' in the nurturing and containing environment of the therapeutic milieu. Browner and Onions, child psychotherapists in the school, describe just how challenging this is for the staff. The children, who have long histories of deprivation, neglect and abuse, often refuse affection when they are distressed, and may attack the staff instead. They say:

> The trauma inhabits the children's bodies leaving them with an internal muddle of persecution that lives inside them and follows them around throughout their day-to-day lives, interfering with ordinary interactions and distorting potentially positive experiences ... many spend their days harshly rejecting warmth and care, verbally and physically attacking others at the slightest internal activation of these persecutory feelings.
>
> (Onions & Browner 2012: 146)

Milieu therapy offers the children a nurturing and containing setting where they can recover from this trauma. They are helped to manage these powerful feelings through careful management by the staff with firm boundaries, time for cooling off and involvement in relaxing, enjoyable activities.

The residential care staff, the teachers and therapists work closely together sharing their understanding of the child's emotional struggles and supporting each other with the challenge of caring for such troubled children. The young people spend their day in group settings, in their house or the school. They are often deeply suspicious and fearful of relationships with others, but in these groups they begin to experience cooperation and care which challenges their mistrustful view of the world.

Therapeutic staff work with the children's families to help them with their care on their weekend and holiday visits. The aim is to help restore children to family life, often with dedicated foster carers, and to return to schools back in their community. Treatment often lasts three years but, by the end of this time, the majority are able to return to their homes and to an educational setting which matches their emotional and educational needs.

Child psychotherapy in Gloucester House School

Milieu therapy is also the approach of this small therapeutic day school in London, part of the Children, Young Adults and Families Service of the Tavistock and Portman NHS Foundation Trust. The staff work with up to 21 children aged between 5 and 14 years. The children here have experienced severe trauma or abuse, and some have been in the care system with multiple breakdowns of placement. Kirsty Brant, Fanny Lena and Ruth Glover, three members of the therapeutic team, described to me how the children often come to the school in a hypervigilant state. They can be violent, emotionally defended and unable to think. The feelings that cannot be managed are projected onto those around them, and often the children can be physically violent. In this setting, the therapeutic task is held by the whole team, the therapists, specialist nurses and education staff working closely together. Psychoanalytic thinking helps the staff understand the meaning of the children's behaviour, and their own emotional responses to the children.

> The staff's receptivity to the children's projections of unthinkable and disturbing emotional experiences allows change to happen over time. Thinking together about an individual child from many perspectives allows an in-depth understanding of the child's psychological functioning, inner world and emotional needs.
>
> (Glover and Brant, personal communication)

They recount how children's feelings of despair, rage, isolation and helplessness can at times penetrate into the team and obscure the individual's capacity to think and remain receptive.

One of the key functions of the child psychotherapy team is to support the staff in supervision and team meetings, strengthening the containing function of the therapeutic milieu and their sense of hope. Less experienced members of staff often have to bear intense levels of projections. Glover, the child psychotherapist there, explains how, in supervision, she can help those working closely with the children recognise what the children may be communicating in their behaviour. She gives the example of a support worker in supervision, who says she feels that she is not helping a young girl who targets her with vicious and sustained personal attacks. These make her feel scared, ashamed, bewildered and powerless. This same girl can then go off with another member of staff and get on with her work. The support worker feels she is starting to hate the child and losing her compassion. The supervising child psychotherapist helps the worker recognise the importance of these transference and countertransference feelings to make sense of a child's internal world, and so find a way to connect with the child:

> She is being made to feel something of what this child cannot put into words, cannot even consciously remember of her early experience of extreme abuse as a baby and toddler. The child felt powerless and terrified, not knowing where the next attack would come from, she also watched her mother being beaten and felt worthless and not loveable.
>
> (Ruth Glover, personal communication)

Through this key relationship, the child finds a person who can understand and contain difficult feelings, and also set limits that help her manage the day when they are together in lessons or at lunch.

The child psychotherapists also act as 'case coordinators', linking the different parts of a child's experience across the network, often shedding light on the risk of splits in the system. They see some children for individual psychotherapy but they may also offer a gentle interpretation to a child in the corridor or during lunch, showing they understand a child's urgent need for a response to an impulsive communication. Group therapy has proved to be a valuable intervention for many children. Similarly, therapeutic support is offered to parents and families, adapted to their very different histories and needs.

Individual child psychotherapy differs in this setting where children have a transference relationship to the school as a whole, including the therapist and the consulting room. Children can at times be violent and test the therapist's capacity to maintain internal and external boundaries that are firm but not impenetrable. The transference relationship can become split, and what is meant for the therapist can be taken to the support worker in the corridor, or even to the other children in the class. However, this complexity provides a richness. When the team meet, the therapist is able to contribute to and learn from others working closely with the child. Young people can have an experience of something resembling a 'family' thinking about them in a way that they were often so deprived of in their early years. This can result in remarkable progress.

Therapeutic work with young refugees

Trauma is also a central to therapeutic work with refugees, but here the trauma is more often external as many young refugees come from secure families who have been subject to conflict and war in their own communities and countries. There is a long tradition of specialist services offering therapeutic work for refugees in the UK. The Medical Foundation for the Care of Victims of Torture (now known as Freedom from Torture) was set up in 1985 by an experienced case worker who had worked with Holocaust victims. The Refugee Therapy Centre followed in 1999, and the Baobab Centre was set up in 2008 as a non-residential therapeutic community for young asylum seekers and refugees. These specialist services run alongside community-based support for refugees from social services and CAMHS.

The work of these specialist services gives an insight into how psychotherapy can respond to the traumatic life experiences of many refugees. The Refugee Therapy Centre offers individual, couple, family and group therapy, as well as child and adolescent psychotherapy. Lennox Thomas, a psychotherapist in this service, described how vulnerable refugee families feel when seeking refuge in another country (Thomas 2012). They are often disorientated by their new life, and feel unwelcome, and this makes them more susceptible to psychological and mental health problems. Some people seen at the Refugee Therapy Centre have developed post-traumatic stress syndrome after their arrival in the UK. They may be in states of denial, emotionally frozen or deeply depressed. The children may enact some of the distressing scenes that they have witnessed in the past.

Thomas stressed that the psychotherapist, working with the family as a whole, needs to help parents reclaim their parenting role with their children, recognising that this was once a functioning family. Parents often attempt to hide their difficulties from their children, who may understand English better than their parents but pretend not to know in order to protect their parents. Young people's anger and distress may surface in adolescence when past trauma may be triggered by events in their life here, and they feel enraged about what they and their family have suffered. Managing these powerful feelings can be frightening, and the young people may 'close down' in response to avoid conflict. Therapeutic work with young people is offered individually and in groups where they can share their stories and find mutual support. Many are resilient and survive and want to get on with life. Therapy can support this process helping them build a narrative of their experience so it becomes easier to live with over time.

The Baobab Centre for young survivors in exile

The Baobab Centre for young unaccompanied asylum seekers and refugees was founded by Sheila Melzak, a child and adolescent psychotherapist. Young people separated from their families can get support and practical help here, make friends, and become involved in psychotherapeutic and therapeutic activities. It offers a secure base for young survivors who have lost their homes, their families and their communities at a crucial time in their adolescent development. They may have experienced organised violence, violation, forced recruitment, exploitation, rejection and bereavement in their home communities and on their journeys into exile.

Sheila Melzak (2017) described how play and therapeutic intervention is at the heart of the work of the Baobab Centre. The trauma experienced by the young survivors has disrupted their emotional development, so many function at an emotional level younger than their chronological age. Their development was halted at the age when they were first traumatised, and later fixation points occur with subsequent traumas. The therapeutic interventions offered to each teenager have to address these unmet developmental needs and the fragility of their current state. Melzak said that she has been influenced by the ideas of Anna Freud who believed that play is essential for children, adolescents and adults 'to explore and make sense of difficult experiences, integrating conscious and unconscious experiences' (2017).

The healing power of play for young victims of war and terror has also been recognised by Punamäki (2006) who describes how dreaming and play allow the mind to process disturbing experiences and how children lose this function when they have been terrorised. Her review of research suggests that when traumatised children rediscover their capacity to play, this acts as a form of resilience alongside dreams and community relationships and the sense of belonging.

The therapeutic community at Baobab offers this 'sense of belonging' to the unaccompanied young refugees. They are involved in playful activities such as a music groups, art workshops, a philosophy group and football and climbing activities. Being with other young people who have been through similar experiences to their own reduces their sense of isolation. Young asylum seekers and refugees are offered individual and group psychotherapy. In groups and community meetings, young people who are not ready to talk about their own experiences hear others share their stories and discover how they have coped since. They develop close relationships in this safe setting, and these can become an important source of comfort to them as they settle in this country. Baobab also offers practical help with accessing finance, housing, health care and education, all more difficult to obtain as an asylum seeker. They are given support through the uncertainties of the protracted legal process of the UK Asylum Determination Process in order to have their asylum status recognised including the supportive preparation of specialist clinical reports for appeal hearings in the asylum jurisdiction.

Helping these young people recover from trauma is a complex task. Many feel overwhelmed by their repeated experiences of separation, loss and extreme violence. They may experience hyperarousal and intrusive thoughts, but they can also close off their thinking and contact with others, to avoid repetition of the trauma. Melzak quotes Herman (1997) who describes how this can restrict 'their thinking, their relationships, their fields of exploration, their imagination and their capacity to be creative'.

Playful activity and story-telling are both encouraged to help the young people rediscover their creativity. Some young refugees are unable to talk directly about their experiences in individual and group therapy, but they can participate in exploring their experiences through story-telling. These stories allow the children to explore themes related to their own life, but at a safe emotional distance, like the imaginary play that occurs in child psychotherapy. Melzak (2017) described how traditional story-telling has become a part of their annual therapeutic summer residential retreat. The young people love hearing these tales, which offer an opportunity to discuss many issues important in their lives. Melzak told the story of Snow White and the Seven Dwarfs at a recent retreat. Afterwards, the young people took on different roles in the story, interviewing each other, discussing what it was like to be either the evil Queen or Snow White, lost without her parents, or one of the dwarfs who cared for Snow White as she grew up. The dwarfs, in the version she read, decided to punish the evil Queen with death and the youngsters questioned this. Young people who had been forced in childhood or early adolescence to act against family and community morality identified with the Queen and did not think she should be killed but both punished and understood instead. Indirectly the young people were talking about their life struggles, their sense of loss and morality, but with humour and fun as well as seriousness. Similarly, other activities like music, art, football and climbing help awaken their imaginative world and their capacity to be playful.

To end this section, I will quote a young survivor's view of his experience at Baobab quoted on their website:

> When I am alone it's too much. There is too much stuff going on inside my head. Sometimes I feel like giving up. But when you see people who understand, who are on your side, for the first time, you have courage and hope. It's like when you are fighting a battle and you lose everyone. Then all of a sudden, reinforcements come, you feel that you can win. Baobab gives me the foundations and I can start building from there.
>
> (https://baobabsurvivors.org/content/young-peoples-involvement)

Therapeutic services for looked-after children and adoptive families

> One of the risks of adopting children in care is that they may perpetuate their deprivation by rejecting the loving care offered to them.
>
> (Hopkins 2000)

In 1983, Boston and Szur published *Psychotherapy with Severely Deprived Children*, an account of psychotherapeutic treatment at the Tavistock Clinic with 80 looked-after children, many of whom had been abused and neglected. Their work showed that such emotionally damaged children can be helped to achieve some capacity to love again through a new relationship offered in individual psychotherapy. This can make it possible for the children to accept the care and nurture offered by foster and adoptive parents.

Hopkins explains that the early experience of abuse and neglect shared by many looked-after children will have led to attachment disorders, the children become avoidant of new loving relationships. This was true of a late-adopted nine-year-old boy called Max whom she saw for therapy. His early experiences with a mentally ill mother and marital violence had left him with a terror of close relationships. His fear led to rejecting disruptive behaviour towards his caring adopted parents. This was of the disorganised/disorientated pattern, first described by Mary Main in 1985.

Main's research showed that a child with a frightening parent faces an irresolvable paradox as the child, feeling unsafe, has the impulse to fight, run away or freeze and this conflicts with the urge to seek reassurance from the parent. As a result, the child responds with disorganised and contradictory behaviour. Over time, the child can no longer bear such an impossible, unsafe situation, and will try to overcome this helplessness by defensive strategies which are typical of the disorganised-controlling attachment pattern. These children are very controlling of adults around them, often defiant and oppositional, and they become self-sufficient, turning away from loving attention. Hopkins explains how they have disavowed their need for close loving attachment. In these moments, the child has no wish for caring and reassurance, and it is this defensive dissociation that has to be gradually overcome in individual psychotherapy.

Hopkins' account of individual therapy with Max shows how she had to survive countless attacks, both emotional and physical, as the child brought to therapy the fear, anger and confusion caused by the early traumatic experience of close relationships. In psychotherapy, the child can experience a safe relationship, unlike the earlier abusive ones, and so regain some trust, and begin to seek out this kind of care in the foster or adoptive home. Hopkins points out, in her chapter 'Solving the mystery of monsters' (1986), that this may not mean that the child has faced the memories of the early trauma or acknowledged the failings of the birth parents, as these feelings may be too much to bear. But it will mean that the child's internal world is more benign, and the child will no longer be plagued by the fear of monstrous figures threatening his daily life.

One can imagine how challenging it would be to take on the care of these very troubled children, as many adoptive parents do. The cost of such a commitment is often frequent crises at home and at school, dealing with the child's rejecting behaviour at home towards parents and siblings, and the disruption of family life. In recognition of the severity of the problems faced by adopted parents and their families, the Adoption Support Fund was implemented by the government in 2013 to provide funds which made it possible to set up new initiatives to help adoptive families through these difficult times.

AdCAMHS adoption support service

AdCAMHS, established in 2014 in East Sussex, jointly funded and managed by Child Mental Health and Social Services, set out to address these difficulties.

The complexity of the problems faced by adopted children and their parents often requires a fast, multi-agency response to help the family through a crisis period. Adopters complained this was not usually available and they were left to struggle on alone, or given too little help, too late. AdCAMHS offers a one-stop resource where adoptive parents can get help from social services, education and child mental health. The team organises a coordinated care package suited to each adoptive family with network reviews, consultations with psychologists and psychotherapeutic interventions for the young person or the family. The main contact for the family is usually the post-adoption social worker supported closely by the AdCAMHS clinician.

The service offers a range of interventions. Alongside brief and longer-term individual psychotherapy, there are specialist assessments for children and young people with complex and enduring disorders, often the result of exposure to harmful influences in the womb, or early traumas, or both. These children have complex neurobiological and relationship difficulties which require skilled and experienced intervention to manage the severity of risk involved in the young people's lives. Consultations are available to support adoptive parents, and therapeutic work is offered to the whole family. This ensures that the emotional challenges of caring for adopted children who have been traumatised do not undermine family functioning.

Therapeutic groups for parents and adolescents

Alison Roy, child psychotherapist and clinical lead of the service, describes (Roy et al. 2017) how groups have been set up for adopters. Many parents who attend are in crisis, and gain support from sharing their experience with other adoptive parents, as well as the two facilitators from the team, one of whom is a child psychotherapist. The group runs for 12 sessions with a psycho-educational focus. Parents have the opportunity to discuss their child with the group and learn the theory behind children's developing minds, early relationships and disturbance, and the impact of early neglect and trauma on children's attachment patterns.

There are also therapeutic groups for teenagers and children, a creative response to the pressures these young people face. The groups were requested by East Sussex's adopted young people and have developed over the years in communication with young people and their families. There are 12 sessions of group work, each lasting two hours, which take place in a local theatre. The group ends with a woodland camp outdoor experience. Therapists, social work practitioners and Forest School professionals work in partnership to plan the programme, which is tailor-made for each different group of adopted young people (Roy et al. 2017).

There are regular reflective discussions for all the professionals involved to explore the challenges and complexities of this work and the potential difficulties that can arise in the professional network.

Parents and young people have said how much they appreciated this model. They valued the joined-up approach so that the children did not have to face duplicate assessments and they said they could trust the team who worked well together and were supportive. The model of early intervention prevents crises escalating and potential breakdowns in the care of the adopted children.

Consultation

Consultation to other professionals, either individually or in a team, is an important aspect of child psychotherapeutic work. The consultant, unlike a supervisor, is not responsible for the clinical or managerial aspects of the work, so is able to take the position of the outsider, observing the conscious and unconscious dynamics influencing the work.

In the chapter on teamwork, I described the rigid, self-protective defences that can develop within individuals and institutions as a protection from the emotional demands of the caring role. To avoid this retreat into defensive behaviour and to support the staff with the emotional impact of the work, some residential care homes for children arrange ongoing consultation for the staff. The 'care' staff, as their name implies, are in a parental role for these children and may never feel 'good-enough', as the children transfer their anger and disappointment about their earlier deprivation onto their relationship with their carers. Peter Wilson, a consultant in residential child care, describes the demands on those giving practical everyday care to children:

> It is not uncommon for a child to behave for several days in a co-operative and affectionate way, only to change suddenly and relate to the residential workers quite differently. The child may become sullen, withdrawn or tearful; he or she may become secretive, devious and undermining; or at other times obstinate, defiant and antagonistic.
>
> (Wilson 2009)

This volatile mix of emotion, day after day, can tax even the most resilient adults. The reflective group led by a consultant offers the residential staff a space to talk through these experiences. They can then stand back from these troubling feelings and recognise them as projections from the children's inner world, rather than a personal attack on their competence, as it so often feels.

Similar pressures face community-based social workers and other professionals working with troubled children. Looked-after children often cause the most concern because of the difficulty of finding appropriate substitute family care when they are separated from their own family of origin. Child psychotherapists often work in specialist teams dedicated to their care. A vivid account of this work is given by Margaret Hunter (2001). Responsibility for planning for looked-after children's care is carried by their nominated social workers, working closely with other professionals in the team around the child. This can be very demanding, as these decisions are fraught with anxiety and uncertainty, as I recall from my own experience of planning for looked-after children as a social worker.

Marigemma Rocco-Briggs recognised the stressful dynamics that can build up between the professionals working with looked-after children and undermine their decision-making. She developed a consultation service which she described in her paper '"Who owns my pain?"' (2008). It grew from her experience of working as a child psychotherapist with looked-after children. She discovered that her feelings mirrored those of the children she was working with. She often felt alone, isolated from the network, left with all the child's distress. A high percentage of looked-after children have severe emotional difficulties, yet there was an expectation that, by her therapeutic intervention, she could sort it all out and help the children recover. She saw that the professionals working with these children often found themselves in conflict, rather than functioning as an effective team around the child. To address this difficulty, she arranged network meetings for all those involved, including the foster parents, so they could share their different experiences of the child, and their anxieties and expectations of therapy, and their hopes for the child's future.

Rocco-Briggs considers an important dynamic that causes this conflict is that the team carries the children's anger and distress about their deprivation. This is projected onto the foster parents or other substitute carers, who quickly become the 'bad parents' blamed by the child for any failure of parenting, and then they feel they have failed the child too. These feelings of distress, disappointment and blame can be reflected in the network and need to be recognised:

> In order to provide effective therapeutic work with these children, it is crucial to consider their disturbance as affecting the network around them. Enabling the network to understand and process powerful

feelings around the child enhances its self-reflective function, so crucial for thinking about the child's needs.

(Rocco-Briggs 2008)

She comments that it is the network's capacity to be open about their doubts, the painful aspects of the work and their working relationships with each other which will determine how effectively they function, and whether together they can offer a secure base for the child, caring and planning for the future. Consultation work like this is replicated in many settings where child psychotherapists create reflective networks around children's care or take these ideas to their work in multi-professional teams.

Conclusion

This is just a small selection of many projects around the UK showing how child psychotherapy can be applied in different settings. There are common themes. They highlight the importance of integrated team work and a shared reflective space for those working with troubled children. They show the importance of open relationships within the network, so that intense feelings and differences in the team can be shared, and a focus kept on the child's needs. Child psychotherapists may take on different roles; playing alongside a child, sitting by a sick youngster's bedside or facilitating as part of a group, as well as offering individual psychotherapy, but these roles need not conflict if the therapeutic focus remains clear. In each of these settings, therapists and child care workers have found creative ways to reach out to the traumatised child but they share the idea that it is playful activity and new relationships, either individually or in a 'family group', that often begin the healing process. Our work as child psychotherapists is often to support this process and to offer individual psychotherapy alongside or later, when the time is right.

References

Diamond, J. (2013) The Mulberry Bush School and UK therapeutic community practice for children and young people. *International Journal of Therapeutic Communities* 34(4): 132–140.

Dockar-Drysdale, B. (1990) *The Provision of Primary Experience: Winnicottian Work with Children and Adolescents*. London: Free Association Books.

Herman, J.L. (1997) *Trauma and Recovery: The Aftermath of Violence – from Domestic Abuse to Political Terror*. London: Basic Books.

Hopkins, J. (1986) Solving the mystery of monsters: Steps towards the recovery from trauma. *Journal of Child Psychotherapy* 12(1): 61–71.

Hopkins, J. (2000) Overcoming a child's resistance to late adoption: How one new attachment can facilitate another. *Journal of Child Psychotherapy* 26(3): 335–347.

Hunter, M. (1986) The monster and the ballet dancer. *Journal of Child Psychotherapy* 12(2): 29–39.

Hunter, M. (2001) *Psychotherapy with Young People in Care: Lost and Found.* London: Routledge.

Martin, P. (2012) 'Grief that has no vent in tears, makes other organs weep': Seeking refuge from trauma in the medical setting. *Journal of Child Psychotherapy* 38(1): 3–21.

McDougall, J. (1968) *Theatres of the Mind.* London: Free Association Books.

Melzak, S. (2009) Psychotherapeutic work with children and adolescents seeking refuge from political violence. In M. Lanyado & A. Horne (eds) *The Handbook of Child and Adolescent Psychotherapy: Psychoanalytic Approaches,* 2nd edition, pp. 381–405. London: Routledge.

Melzak, S. (2017) Anna Freud, play and refugees. Paper presented at conference at King's College London.

Music, G. (2008) Delivering therapeutic work in schools. *Journal of Child Psychotherapy* 34(1): 43–61.

National Institute of Clinical Excellence (NICE) (2016) *Guidelines for Type 1 Diabetes,* 4.1–4.8.

Onions, C. & Browner, J. (2012) Spaces for growth: Where milieu therapy and psychotherapy meet. In A. Horne & M. Lanyado (eds) *Winnicott's Children,* pp. 143–156. London: Routledge.

Parry-Langdon, N. (2008) *Three Years On: Survey of the Development and Emotional Well-Being of Children and Young People.* London: Office for National Statistics.

Perry, B. (2006) Applying principles of neurodevelopment to clinical work with maltreated and traumatised children: The neurosequential model of therapeutics. In N. Boyd Webb (ed.) *Working with Traumatised Youth in Child Welfare,* pp. 27–52. New York: Guilford Press.

Punamäki, R.L. (2006) Resiliency in conditions of war and military violence: Preconditions and developmental processes. In M.E. Garralda & M. Flament (eds) *Working with Children and Adolescents: An Evidence-Based Approach to Risk and Resilience,* pp. 129–177. New York, Toronto and Oxford: Jason Aronson.

Rocco-Briggs, M. (2008) 'Who owns my pain?': An aspect of the complexity of working with looked after children. *Journal of Child Psychotherapy* 34(2): 190–206.

Roy, A., Thomas, C. & Simmonds, J. (2017) Adoption support: Integrating social work and therapeutic services – the AdCAMHS model. Coram BAAF briefing paper. London: Coram.

Thomas, L. (2012) Working with trauma and the experience of refugees families. Presentation to child psychotherapy trainees at Independent Psychoanalytic Child and Adolescent Psychotherapy Association, BPF Kilburn, London.

Wilson, P. (2009) Consultation in residential care. In M. Lanyado & A. Horne (eds) *The Handbook of Child and Adolescent Psychotherapy: Psychoanalytic Approaches,* 2nd edition, pp. 276–284. London: Routledge.

Final thoughts

Playing with ideas

The importance of play is a theme threading through this book. Children use play to think about themselves and the world. As psychotherapists, we rely on the imaginative play of ideas that come to mind to understand our patients, whether in therapy or in supervision. When children have been traumatised or abused, play of various kinds and story-telling is used in therapeutic settings as a symbolic way to approach disturbing experiences safely in displacement. The approach to child psychoanalytic psychotherapy outlined in this book has been influenced by my training and my interest in the British Independent tradition in psychotherapy, but I enjoy drawing on ideas from any school that helps illuminate a way forward. I have also learnt much from my colleagues, my supervisors and, of course, from my patients of all ages, many of whom have challenged and inspired my thinking. I hope those reading this book treat the ideas discussed here as stepping stones, leading to the discovery of other ideas in their future therapeutic work with children and adolescents.

Deirdre Dowling

Index